CHICAGO HOME BOOK

"HOME IS A NAME, A WORD, IT IS A STRONG ONE; STRONGER THAN A MAGICIAN EVER SPOKE, OR A SPIRIT EVER ANSWERED TO, IN THE STRONGEST CONJURATION."

Charles Dickens

CHICAGO HOME BOOK

A COMPREHENSIVE HANDS-ON DESIGN SOURCEBOOK TO BUILDING, REMODELING, DECORATING, FURNISHING AND LANDSCAPING A LUXURY HOME IN CHICAGO AND ITS SUBURBS.

Photo courtesy of **Sandra Saltzman Interiors**
Photo by **Tony Berardi**

PUBLISHED BY

THE
ASHLEY
GROUP

Chicago New York Los Angeles
Las Vegas Philadelphia Atlanta Detroit Arizona
South Florida Washington D.C. Colorado
San Francisco North Carolina Dallas/Fort Worth
San Diego Houston Boston Seattle Kansas City
Orange County Ohio Connecticut/Westchester County

Published By
The Ashley Group
1350 E. Touhy Ave.
Des Plaines, IL 60018
847.390.2882 FAX 847.390.2902

Cahners Business Information
A Division of Reed Elsevier Inc

ISBN 1-58862-037-9

CHICAGO HOME BOOK

Publisher *Andrew Rees*
Editor-in-Chief *Dana Felmly*
Managing Editor *Laurence P. Maloney*
Senior Editor *James Scalzitti*
Assistant Editor *Alison M. Ishihara*
Writers *Brad Davis, Catherine Kallas*
Office Manager *Julie O'Donovan*
Account Executives *Lori Dub, Tom Schoen, Bob Williams*
Group Production Director *Susan Lokaj*
Production Directors *Paul Ojeda, Catherine Wajer*
Production Manager *Monika M. Kusmierz*
Ad Service Coordinator *Barry T. Krupowicz*
New Business Manager *Margaret Guzek*
Creative Director *Bill Weaver*
Senior Graphic Designer *Chul H. Kam*
Graphic Designers *Samantha K. Zidek, Maria T. Perez,*
Amie L. Smith, Laura Murfin
Prepress *Cahners Prepress*
Printed in Hong Kong by *Dai Nippon Printing Company*

THE ASHLEY GROUP

Group Publisher *Paul A. Casper*
Director of Publications *N. David Shiba*
Regional Director *Joseph M. Lattimer*
Group Controller *Patricia Lavigne*
Group Administration *Nicole Port, Kimberly Spizzirri, Norma Olson*

CAHNERS BUSINESS INFORMATION

President, Global Construction and Retail Division *David Israel*
Chief Financial Officer *John Poulin*
Executive Vice President *Ronald C. Andriani*
Vice President, Finance *David Lench*

Front Cover *Arlene Semel & Associates Photo by James Yochum Photography*
Back Cover *Charles L. Page, Architect*

Note

The premier edition of **The Chicago Home Book** was created like most other successful products and brands are — out of need. **The Home Book** concept was originally conceived by Paul Casper, currently Group Publisher of The Ashley Group. Paul, a resident of Chicago's North Shore, at one time was planning the renovation of his home. However, he quickly discovered problems locating credible professionals to help his dream become a reality. Well, Paul's dream did become a reality — it just happens to be a different dream now! Instead of Paul simply finishing his new home, he saw the need by consumers nationwide to have a complete home resource guide at their disposal. Thus, he created the distinct **Home Book** to fulfill consumers' needs for reliable and accessible home improvement information.

After three successful years, the Home Book drew the attention of Cahners Business Information. In April 1999, Cahners purchased it, and since then, the **Home Book** network has grown rapidly. In addition to Chicago, **Home Books** are available in Washington D.C., Detroit, South Florida, Colorado, Dallas/Fort Worth, Atlanta, San Diego, Los Angeles, New York, Philadelphia, Arizona, Las Vegas and North Carolina. Within the next year, **Home Books** will be published in Houston, Seattle, Boston and Kansas City, among other cities. Public demand for high-quality home improvement services continues to increase. The Ashley Group recognizes this trend, which is why we exact the same amount of dedication and hard work from ourselves that we expect from our **Home Book** advertisers. We hope our hard work rewards you with the quality craftsmanship that you deserve, turning your dream house into a reality.

Congratulations on purchasing a **Home Book**. Now reward yourself by kicking back and delving through its pages. We hope you enjoy the inspiring ideas within.

Dana Felmly *Editor-in-Chief*

Laurence P. Maloney *Managing Editor*

1

Why
You Should
Use This
Book

Why You'll Want to Use the Chicago Home Book

At times, in this high-speed information-driven culture, we can easily become lost and disoriented. Where we find information, how we find it, and how credible this information is, has become critical to consumers everywhere.

The **Chicago Home Book** recognizes and addresses these concerns, and provides ease of use and comfort to consumers looking to build, renovate or enhance their home. As a consumer, the anxiety of searching for trustworthy, experienced housing professionals can be overwhelming.

Relief is in Sight

The **Chicago Home Book** puts an end to this stress. It offers you, the reader, a comprehensive, hands-on guide to building, remodeling, decorating, furnishing and landscaping a home in Chicago. The book also offers readers convenience and comfort.

Convenience

The *Chicago Home Book* compiles the area's top home service providers with easy-to-read listings by trade. It also dissuades readers' fears of unreliable service providers by featuring many of the finest professionals available, specialists who rank among the top 10 of their respective fields in Chicago. Their outstanding work has netted them many awards in their fields. The other listings are recommendations made by these advertisers.

The goal of the *Chicago Home Book* creators is to provide a high quality product that goes well beyond the scope of mere Yellow Pages. Its focus is to provide consumers with credible, reliable, and experienced professionals, accompanied by photographic examples of their work.

This crucial resource was unavailable to the founders of the *Chicago Home Book* when they were working on their own home improvement projects. This lack of information spurred them on to create the book, and to assist other consumers in finding the proper professionals that suit their specific needs. Now, thanks to the team's entrepreneurial spirit, you have the *Chicago Home Book* at your fingertips, to guide you on your home enhancement journey.

Comfort

Embrace this book, enjoy it and relish it, because at one time it didn't exist; but now, someone has done your homework for you. Instead of running all over town, you'll find in these pages:

• More than 700 listings of professionals, specializing in 40 different trades.

• Instructional information for choosing and working with architects, contractors, landscapers and interior designers.

• More than 1,000 photos inspiring innovative interior and exterior modeling ideas.

• A compilation of the area's top home enhancement service providers with easy-to-read listings by trade.

Excitement...*The Chicago Home Book* can turn your dream into a reality!

Andy Rees, Publisher

The premier resource provider for the luxury home market

Chicago Home Book

About the Front Cover:
Creative interior detail by
Arlene Semel Interior Design

Contents

237

Continued

348

535

204

343

icago Home Book

About the Back Cover:
A warm home created by
Charles L. Page, Architect

Contents

252

117

148

359

350

How To Use

TABLE OF CONTENTS

Start here for an at-a-glance guide to the 12 tabbed categories and numerous subcategories. The book is organized for quick, easy access to the information you want, when you want it. The Table of Contents provides an introduction to the comprehensive selection of information.

DESIGN UPDATE

Read what top home industry professionals thin are the most exciting new styles, future trends and best ideas in their fields as we continue int the millennium. See even more inspiring photo of some of the Chicago area's most beautiful, t to-date luxury homes and landscapes. It's a vis feast, full of great ideas.

TIMELINES

An innovative reference tool, TimeLines gives you an at-a-glance chance to see the step-by-step progression of a home project. The projects include the building of a custom home, the remodeling of a luxury home kitchen and bath, a multi-phase landscaping project, and the interior design of several rooms. The TimeLines appear as eight-page gatefolds with glossy pictures, clearly laid-out timelines and easy-to-read paragraphs.

"HOW-TO" ARTICLES

Each tabbed section begins with a locally researched article on how to achieve the best possible result in your home building, remodeling, decorating or landscape project. These pages help take the fear and trepidation out of the process. You'll receive the kind of information you need to communicate effectively with professionals and to be prepared for the nature of the process. Each article is a step-by-step guide, aiding you in finding the materials you need in the order you'll need them.

This Book

DIVIDER TABS

Use the sturdy tabs to go directly to the section of the book you're interested in. A table of contents for each section's subcategories is printed on the front of each tab. Quick, easy, convenient.

LISTINGS

Culled from current, comprehensive data and qualified through careful local research, the listings are a valuable resource as you assemble the team of experts and top quality suppliers for your home project. We have included references to their ad pages throughout the book.

FEATURES!

From Interior Design Spotlight to New in the Showroom, we've devoted attention to specific areas within the various sections. We've also gone in-depth, with feature articles in the Architects and Home Builders sections.

COST ESTIMATES

If you're wondering what costs you may incur while undertaking a home project, check out our sample cost estimates. From architecture to arts and antiques, we describe a project in each chapter and give a sample cost break down for each.

BEAUTIFUL VISUALS

The most beautiful, inspiring and comprehensive collections of homes and materials of distinction in the greater Chicago area. On these pages, our advertisers present exceptional examples of their finest work. Use these visuals for ideas as well as resources.

INDEXES

This extensive cross reference system allows easy access to the information on the pages of the book. You can check by alphabetical order or individual profession.

The
A
Grou

THE ASHLEY GROUP

The Ashley Group is the largest publisher of visual
quality designing, building and decorating information and
For more on the many products of **The Ashley
Cahners Business Information** (www.cahners.com),
U.S. provider of business information to 16
manufacturing and retail. Cahners' rich content portfolio
Publishers Weekly, Design News and 152 other

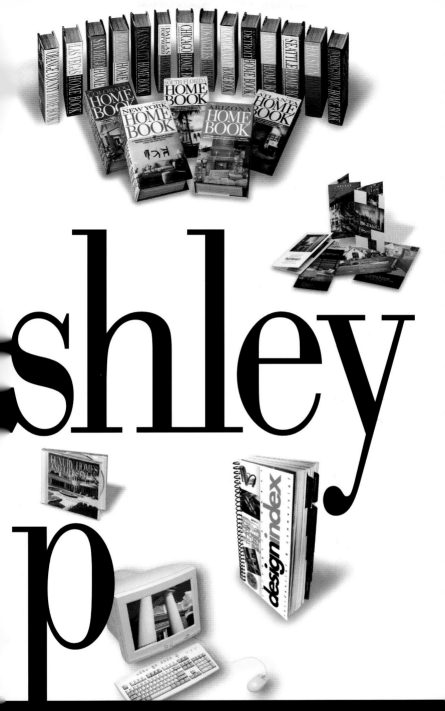

RESOURCE COLLECTION

home resource images, and strives to provide the highest
resources available to upscale consumers and professionals.
Group, visit our website at www.theashleygroup.com.
a member of the Reed Elsevier plc group, is a leading
vertical markets, including entertainment,
encompasses more than 140 Web sites as well as *Variety*,
market-leading business-to-business magazines

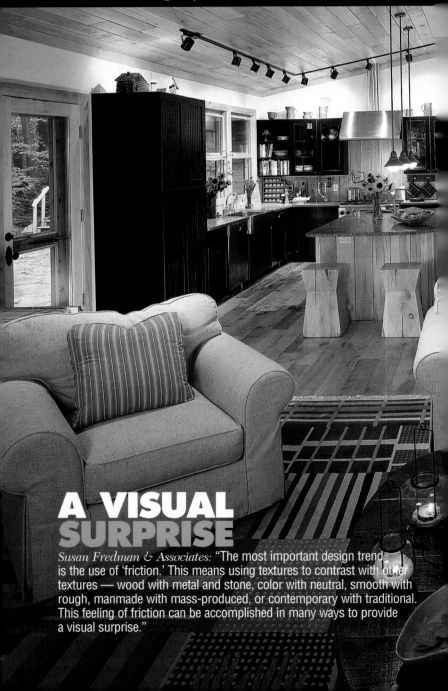

Design

*What are the hot ideas and attitudes that are shaping hom
Read Design Update, where top local professionals*

A VISUAL
SURPRISE

Susan Fredman & Associates: "The most important design trend
is the use of 'friction.' This means using textures to contrast with other
textures — wood with metal and stone, color with neutral, smooth with
rough, manmade with mass-produced, or contemporary with traditional.
This feeling of friction can be accomplished in many ways to provide
a visual surprise."

Update

riors and landscapes in the metropolitan Chicago area?
at's happening now and what's coming in the future.

Photo by **Linda Oyama Bryan**

29

Photo by **William Kildow**

REUSING
NATURAL MATERIALS

A. William Seegers Architects: "Active spaces have become more popular with the reuse of natural materials such as wood, stone and steel in a simplified way, enhancing today's lifestyle."

WIRING FOR THE FUTURE

Keyth Security Systems:
"When it comes to structured wiring and home network systems, there is one reality: traditional wiring of the past can't even support today's technologies. Homes are advancing toward 'future-proof' wiring. Not only does advanced wiring give access to the latest in telecommunications, security, computing and home entertainment, it also makes homes ready for tomorrow's technologies."

DISPLAYING
INDIVIDUALITY

Mary Rubino Interiors:
"Asian influences and the spa look are two current trends in bathrooms today. Homeowners like to express their individuality. They want to see their designer use different colors and accessories to create entirely different atmospheres.

Photo by **Robert Maue**

BEGINNINGS
TO MEET ENDS

Full Circle Architects: "Home and hearth take on
new significance as an individualized sanctuary from
the outside world. We recognize that a dwelling is
more than a passive reflection of values, economics
and aesthetics. It is an active tool that also shapes
personal experiences. Designs are increasingly
addressing deep personal needs, so 'Living Spaces'
can be created to responsively meet those needs."

A PERSONAL
VISION

Sandra Saltzman Interiors: "Today, a distinctive contemporary design scheme encompasses a refined environment and continues with a modern aesthetic without sacrificing warmth. The personal vision of the homeowner should always be foremost."

PERSONAL STYLE

Chicago Kitchen & Bath: "Versatility. Clarity. Spirit. Kitchens allow consumers to reflect their personal style. Longevity and timeless inspiration can be achieved through innovative materials — the final expression must feel flawless."

Design Update

35

36

POOL
ESSENTIALS

Barrington Pools: "In-floor cleaning systems are extremely popular as a pool essential. By distribution to zones in the pool floor, heated water is used most effectively to clean and efficiently heat the pool. Stonework of all kinds plays an important role in today's final pool presentation. In particular, field-stone is used for water features, waterfalls, ponds and adjoining fountains. The idea is to create a relaxing atmosphere where one's backyard exhibits a return to the natural look."

NATURAL STONE'S
TIMELESS BEAUTY

Krugel Cobbles: "The simplicity and timeless beauty of natural stone and antiqued pavers have made a resurgence in the hardscape industry. Materials such as bluestone, granite, flagstone and tumbled concrete pavers give the appearance of having been a part of the original environment, rather than being something recently added. These materials, installed with expert craftsmanship, create a classical elegance for homeowners."

CREATING THEIR OWN LOOKS

von Weise Associates: "Whether a renovation or ground-up construction, enlightened clients are beginning to move beyond a simple mimetic approach to recreating the past in order to 'fit in' in their surroundings. The trend toward nostalgia during the past few years is starting to abate. Now clients are asking for a house or addition that visually reflects their own unique needs. Europeans have done this for decades, often with spectacular results."

ELEGANCE AND VERSATILITY

Bang & Olufsen: "Today, customers want high-quality picture and digital surround sound. They want a complete cinema experience that blends with their décor. Price is no longer the determining factor, rather the concern is how the system fits with one's own lifestyle. Compromise is not in the vocabulary of these customers. Home theater has the versatility to deliver the impact of a cinema experience for event viewing, or compact elegance for daily viewing."

SIMPLE YET FUNCTIONAL

Youngman & Company, Inc.: "In this increasingly complex world, many people seek simplicity and functionality in a design. This goal can be achieved through material selection and straightforward architectural expression. Often, this also benefits the project's bottom line."

COMBINING
DIFFERENT FUNCTIONS

Elinor Gordon Design: "With space at a premium and more people working out of their homes, individuals want to combine different functions in one room—for example, a home office and workout area. Thus, the need of the client is driving the design. With the change of lifestyles, clients want the rooms to be livable and comfortable. Plants, for example, make the room seem more alive, and they don't require a lot of attention.

Photo by **Jesse Walker**

ERGONOMIC
BENEFITS

EXOTIC WOODS IN DEMAND

Apex Wood Floors:

"We are seeing greater demand for exotic and non-traditional woods such as Brazilian cherry, mahogany, African hardwoods and even bamboo flooring. Also popular are custom finishes such as handscraped floors that provide a luxurious yet casual Old World look and feel to the room. Custom inlays and borders are also experiencing a vibrant resurgence. They are used to enhance and highlight such areas as entries, galleries and dining rooms."

Dream Kitchens: "As the world of technology continues to expand, consumers continue to look for more effective ways to work at home, at school or at the office. One product recently introduced into the residential market allows users to recess their computer and monitor beneath the work surface through a tempered, tinted glass. The ergonomic benefits include less eye and back strain. This system can be used in any area of the house, including the kitchen."

PLEASANT SURROUNDINGS

Off the Bolt:

"Textiles continue to be one of the most sensual aspects of interior design. People like to feel secure, comfortable and warm in their homes. That's why they like to consider the softness of a chenille, the elegance and patina of a fine silk, the richness of mohair or the smoothness of velvet."

BEYOND
THE BASICS

J & B Builders: "Design services must go beyond basic design. One must work closely with homeowners to develop a blend of aesthetic beauty and functionality to reflect their individual requirements."

ENHANCING THE DESIGN

Gregory Maire Architect, Ltd.:
"Clients involved in extensive renovation today are showing a keen interest in original design details. Owners appreciate the uniqueness of their property and want to enhance what's already there. Contemporary or traditional elements such as the spatial flow, the impact of daylight or the presence (or absence) of trim become defining elements of the redesign. Beneath all the later additions, the framing of a fine home defines its beauty."

COMFORT
IN SECURITY

Windward Builders: "Natural materials, woods
for flooring and cabinetry, use of stone and granite.
These are the things that today's home-oriented
people are using to make their homes more comfortable, secure, and representative of their individual
taste, personality, and lifestyle."

A TRADITIONAL
CHARACTER

Roberts Architects, Ltd.: "Homeowners want their new or remodeled homes to have a traditional character incorporating interesting materials, proportion, sensitive detailing, and appropriate scale. This complete architectural composition has floor plans and design elements tailored for the family's lifestyle. Most clients prefer one dependable company to provide complete design and construction services. Desired is a blend of architectural design, quality craftsmanship, cost control, professional management, and fun."

CUSTOM MILLWORK

Lange Custom Woodworking: "Custom architectural millwork is becoming a standard for individuals whose home is an extension of who they are. Sometimes it's the traditional look of raised panel walls with carved capitals and heavily detailed moldings. At other times it's the more contemporary look of white maple or French white ash and metal accents. Another trend is using existing antique architectural elements to create pieces of furniture that blend perfectly with the existing atmosphere of the space."

CAPTURING DESIGNS
FROM THE PAST

Visbeen Associates, Inc.: "Clients consistently desire to capture the authenticity of classic architectural design from the past. Whether it is an English manor home, shingle style, French country or European cottage, there is a desire to recreate the feeling of eras gone by. But there is also the desire to provide for the demands of a modern lifestyle."

JOYFUL DISCOVERY

Bryan Associates: "Homeowners are taking the time to let the joyful process of discovery that is good design define what their home wants to be. Home theaters, Internet connections, gourmet kitchens, exercise room workshops, and master bedroom suites are all part of trend toward people staying in. Now, more than ever, plans must be tailored to owners' individual needs."

SIMPLIFICATION AND ORDER

Sarah Van Assche Interiors: "Although the immense spectrum of style preferences will always endure, there has been an increased demand for simplification and order in the home. In many ways, this is evidenced in the recent popularity of Asian furnishings and accessories, which are essentially simple."

53

54

CUSTOM STAIRCASES

Creative Stairs and Woodworking, Inc.:
"The recent trend for custom staircases is metal balusters, railings and newels with a variety of woods, giving the home a warm, European look. The finished staircase blends in perfectly with its surroundings, while adding the right touch of elegance."

56

ART
IN GLASS

Chardonnay Designs: "More and more people are turning to art glass to give personal expression to their living and working spaces. One-of-a-kind designs use the windows to set the tone of a room. Colors and textures pick up light and shadow, enhancing an ever-changing art piece. New techniques in designer glass use lead as an artistic, rather than a structural, element. This creates a lighter look with much more design freedom to meet today's level of sophistication."

METALLIC GLAZING

Hester Decorating: "Subtle nuances in color and texture can dramatically impact the feeling in a room. One of the hottest trends in faux finishes is achieved through a metallic glaze effect, which is a pearl or metallic look used to highlight a certain area in a room. Available in any color imaginable, the possibilities are limitless. This particular living room has a metallic glaze texture on the ceiling that gives the appearance of an anodized pewter finish."

59

BRINGING CABINETS
INTO THE LIGHT

Cohen & Hacker Architects: "In custom homes, built-in cabinetry and other storage solutions that are part of the architecture have become very important. For example, traditional houses with contemporary, open floor plans are connecting spaces by creating cabinetry with glass doors on both sides. This brings in natural light and doesn't obstruct scenic views."

FUNCTION, NOT SIZE

Keystone Builders, Inc.: "Infill building is often the only option in urban areas. The size of the home is limited to the size of the lot. In this new approach, houses are created with function in mind, nooks and common shared spaces, built-ins, and proper orientation of the house on the lot to incorporate natural surroundings. Family needs — not sheer square footage are the main objectives. Needs of the family and how they function in the house dictate the design and layout. Thus, the family receives a more interesting, functional and personal home."

EXOTIC WOODS FOR STAIRS

Lake Shore Stair:
"Red oak is still the most commonly used wood for stairs. But more clients are asking for maple, walnut, cherry and mahogany. There is a desire for iron balusters. Used with wood newel posts and top rails, they can create a look that can be either contemporary or traditional. Even though the styles are always changing, the traditional wood stair with a painted and stained combination seems to still be the favorite."

DEVELOPING INNOVATIVE KITCHENS

SeBern Homes, Inc.: "Homeowners want to develop efficient and innovative kitchens that are perfect for gourmet cooking and entertaining. Sometimes this means featuring not one but two islands. Granite countertops, custom-finished cherry cabinetry and the finest stainless steel appliances are popular."

Photo by **Jeff Guerrant**

THE IMPACT OF COLOR

K+B+Arts, Inc.:
"Colors have a strong
visual impact on the essential
elements that define the bathroom area. Super functional,
high-quality furniture and
glass basins, available in
various colors, emphasize
the idea of lightness. A blend
of practicality and beauty
define new visual spaces."

BE TRUE TO YOUR VIEW

Frank J. Klepitsch, AIA: "It takes a skilled architectural designer to preserve homes with historic architectural and aesthetic significance. The goal is to integrate new home construction into the surrounding neighborhood and include the landscape. Borrow from the past in detail and design, yet also design space that coordinates with today's life. Pay meticulous attention to detail, so the new home blends seamlessly with the old and enhances the streetscape-not overpowers it."

ART
AT NIGHT

Lightscape: "I look at outdoor lighting as a work of art. It paints a picture in the landscape, beautifies the property, and blends daytime enjoyment into night-time ambiance."

REMOTE CONTROL

Audio Consultants: **"Audio/video systems and home theater systems are becoming more complex and versatile, and as a result, more difficult to operate. Special remote controls, however, can make even the most complicated multi-room systems operational at the touch of a button."**

WINDOWS FOR YOUR SOUL

H & R Custom Designs: **"In our ever-changing society, traveling has taken second place to spending time at home with family and friends. Refresh the house while providing comfort and beauty with a new design. Creative window treatments and draperies are a beautiful way to set the mood and freshen the ambiance of your home."**

COLOR TREATMENT

SCE Unlimited, Inc.: One of the biggest changes in the closet industry is the ability for homeowners to match their trim and furniture with color and design. White, beige and off-white are replaced more by maple, cherry, dark mahogany and walnut. Customers can actually order from hundreds of different shades of colors."

LET THE
COLOR FLOW

Olafsen Design Group: "We find that a number of homeowners are requesting spaces that flow one into the other, while each space maintains a distinct character for its different functions. Media rooms, for example, can be a comfortable nucleus from which other areas emanate. Subtle color schemes, both ethereal and welcoming, can work to unite an ensemble of rooms, thereby connecting the spaces of the home visually."

Photo by **Tony Berardi**

TRENDY IS OUT.
CLASSIC IS IN!

Geudtner & Melichar Architects: "Typically, homes are an owner's biggest investment, in addition to being a safe haven from our hectic world and lifestyle. Therefore, customers seek architectural designs that will last for years and endure the different stages of their lives. People may periodically change their interior dÈcor with whimsy, but they crave architectural permanence."

Photo by **George Lambros**

HOMES
AS HAVENS

Gray & Walter Assoc.: "Life has become far more complicated, and homeowners want more amenities in their homes. They want more entertainment space, perhaps a home theater in the basement, and extensive workout rooms. They want high-tech gizmos they can 'hide' in their home offices. They're concerned about safety and privacy and want their homes to be an absolute haven for them. In sum, they're 'cocooning' to a degree and are using their homes more than they used to."

CONNECTING TO THE EARTH

Senses Gift Gallery: "Many people today like to bring the elements of nature into their homes or work environments. They know that their home dÈcor will enhance how they feel about their space. So they find it important to bring such items as crystals and candles to their home offices or have them at home to connect to Mother Earth."

STONE FOR STRENGTH AND CHARACTER

70

Stonecrafters: "As custom buyers look for that 'special something' to add to the beauty and value of their homes, they are turning to marble and granite, slates, soapstone, limestone, English Kirkstone, and travertine, all of which can be finished in a variety of ways."

FIRST IMPRESSIONS

Adams Stair Work & Carpentry, Inc. "First impressions count, and the entryway is typically the first area experienced. Whether building a dream home or restoring a relic from the past, attention to details is needed."

COMPUTER-AIDED
DESIGN

Page One Interiors: "Designers today can use different state-of-the-art elements to draw up a room for a client's house. For example, computer-aided design helps a designer draw a room for a house with all the details and electrical integration before the house is bid."

CREATING MOVEMENT IN HOMES

Rovituso Strange Architects:
"Today's living has dictated a different attitude toward the use of space. Confined and isolated rooms are no longer appealing. Openness and continuance from one room to another is preferred. Layering of walls and ceilings provide a sense of integration from one room to another. People enjoy seeing the movement throughout their homes."

73

GARDENS
EXPRESS FEELINGS

Milieu Design, Inc.: "Homeowners want their gardens to be an expression of their feelings. They want to create a space which supports a feeling of peace and comfort and compassion for those passing through."

74

Photo by: Pfoertner Photography

NEW TRENDS
IN CLOSET FINISHES

Closet Works: "During the past several years, customers have become more knowledgeable about the construction materials that are available for closet systems. And just as laminate had replaced wire as the preferred material, veneer is now gaining prominence in closet systems. Real wood finishes have been demanded by consumers, and the industry has responded with a variety of wood species and available finishes."

STONE'S
UNIQUE CHARACTERISTICS

Unique Marble & Granite Corp.: "The elegance of natural stone has become popular in both new home construction and remodeling projects. Natural stone, such as granite, marble, limestone and travertine, are used as a hard surface material for countertops, floors, fireplace surrounds, tables and so forth. Stone has many unique characteristics in style and color, which can complement any decor. Granite is a popular choice in kitchen countertop applications due to its durability and easy maintenance."

THE ELEGANT
SHOWCASE

Kreiss Enterprises, Inc.: "An international mix of custom handmade furniture, one-of-a-kind accessories, and luxurious fabrics and bed linens can give a room - or an entire house - a unique look of elegance and casual comfort. Like fine tailored clothing, a well-detailed room creates an elegant showcase for the people who live in it."

AN OUTDOOR FAMILY ROOM

Fenceworks: "Customization has become the number one consideration in outdoor design, followed by quality of fabrication and installation. Customers want fences that are built on the site and contoured to the topography. They also want their playground and basketball equipment to blend well with their surroundings, resulting in a yard that functions as an outdoor 'family room.'"

80

CONTEMPORARY STORAGE SYSTEMS

California Closets: "With the increased demand for storage, people are looking for contemporary storage systems that reflect their personal styles and complement the designs of their homes. Storage systems can be designed for walk-in closets, freestanding wardrobes, entertainment units, bookcases and open shelving. Most feature a full range of accessories in brushed aluminum, solid wood, acrylic and frosted glass, with optional light boxes and illuminated hanging rods."

WOOD FLOORS REMAIN POPULAR

Erickson Decorating Products: "Chicagoans want wood floors, and they like variety. Brazilian cherry and Australian cypress are being sold right next to maple and oak samples. Homeowners also enjoy environmentally safe choices. For example, some newly sawn flooring has been cut from existing beams that were pulled out of old mills and factories. The majority of people like to keep their floors light and prefer a crystal-clear finish. But some prefer an aged look and choose to finish the floor as dark and rich as possible."

NATURE'S VARIATIONS

Terrazzo & Marble: "When choosing countertops, granite is a common choice because of easy cleanup, maintenance, durability and wear resistance. However, it's important to consider the effect of granite movement or veining on the overall kitchen design. For simple cabinetry designs, a lot of veining is ideal; for other design elements, we recommend a more subtle granite. It is also important for the homeowner to realize that granite and/or marble is a natural stone...no two stones will look the same."

VARIATIONS ON A THEME

Kemper Cazzetta: "Homeowners have a strong and continued desire to create variations on the English cottage, Cotswold and Irish country styles of residential architecture. Although the interiors reflect these styles, the plans and uses are consistent with *this* century. It has become challenging to continue to express character and style with integrated and sophisticated kitchens, entertainment and high-tech systems."

TRANQUILITY AND
HARMONY

Ullman Fill Architects: "The recent trend toward minimalism in life as well as architecture seeks certain truths, tranquility and harmony. I don't think it is, out of necessity, confined to modern architecture. A composition that carefully reflects and stirs the individual spirit is a nice thing to come home to."

Photo by C.J. Walker

NATURAL WOOL
AGES GRACEFULLY

Lewis Carpet One: "Wool carpets and rugs are becoming increasingly more popular. People with a sense of style-and a sense of value-choose wool because wool simply looks beautiful longer. Natural wool ages gracefully, continually renewing itself and developing a rich patina as years pass."

86

'SMART HOUSE'
DESIGNS

Design Build by Pasquesi, Inc.: "Today's client
demands 'green' architecture along with the modern
trends of 'smart house' design and cost effective-
ness. Another trend is dividing the large-scale house
into several 'micro' living areas. The incorporation
of the living/family room with the kitchen/dine-in
area is an example of this logical integration. This
area becomes the living core of the home, allowing
mom and dad to prepare meals while the children
do homework, snack or surf the Internet while
under careful supervision."

SLEEK CABINETRY

Karlson Kitchens: Kitchen necessities include cabinetry, and homeowners increasingly desire contemporary cabinetry that is sleek and sophisticated. Lighted shelving can highlight treasured art objects."

89

A ROOM FOR ALL SEASONS

Armcor Design & Build: "A glass sunroom creates views of the outdoors, sun and sky to bring a new dimension of space, light and warmth to what might otherwise be an ordinary room. New glass manufacturing technologies, designed to keep summer heat out and winter heat in, make sunrooms practical even in our harsh winter climate."

ROOMS
THEY CAN USE

Styczynski Walker & Associates: "Instead of designing their homes to meet the demands of the resale market, many of our recent clients are striving to fulfill the needs and desires of their families. Clients are not concerned with having a formal living or dining room that they may seldom use. Instead, they are with creating a home that supports their lifestyles with nontraditional rooms. One example: a formal English pub with a wine cellar, four master suites, multiple laundries, and driving ranges."

CLASSIC
QUALITY

Arlene Semel & Associates: "We believe that good design is not about trend, but rather about classic timeless quality. We think wonderful objects, placed comfortably in a well-conceived background, creates livable, beautiful space."

EXPRESSION IN LANDSCAPING

Heynssens + Grassman: "These days, landscape designers are more involved in the lives of their clients as partners in establishing the tone and flavor of the outdoor living rooms. With each collaboration, homeowners give their own artistic expression to the landscape...be it intimate or grand, fanciful or simple, sculpted or unrestrained."

AT PLAY AT HOME
Burack & Co.: "Today's busy families are finding a new way to pursue their active lifestyles. Indoor basketball and racquetball courts, game rooms, entertainment centers, and home theaters allow them to play and be together without having to leave their homes."

SEAMLESS DESIGN

Hackley/Lang & Associates, Inc.: "The challenge in designing additions and renovations is to create a 'seamless design,' where the new construction is indistinguishable from the existing structure. When designing entirely new construction, the architect must work within the existing traditional fabric and context of the surrounding community for the home to blend seamlessly into the neighborhood."

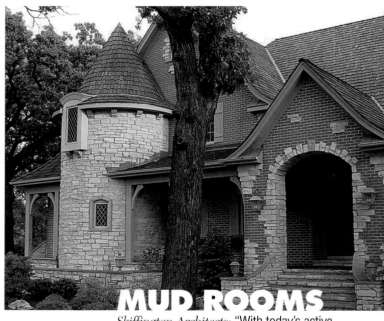

MUD ROOMS

Skiffington Architects: "With today's active lifestyles, we've seen a trend toward well-organized custom mud rooms connecting to the garage. The mud room has become the main entrance for the busy family and needs to have custom cubbies for boots, soccer shoes, backpacks and umbrellas, as well as a bench with storage underneath."

WARMTH & STYLING

Lemont Kitchen & Bath: "The warmth and elegance of glazed finishes continues to be a driving force in the style of cabinetry. Clients are choosing furniture styling in more natural hues for the island, with carvings and corbels to complement the glaze finish of the perimeter cabinetry. While granite is a constant style maker, we see clients turning to limestone for its neutral color and gentle veining. Traditional styling continues to be a large influence in the selection of the kitchen and bath overall style."

Photo by **Stocker Photography**

TODAY'S CUSTOM
HOME MARKET

Stonegate Builders, Inc.: "This is a very exciting time for both clients and homebuilders. Individualism, flexibility and comfort are of the utmost importance in today's custom home market. From home theaters and home offices to indoor driving ranges and basketball courts, today's homes are being equipped to satisfy everyone's needs and passions."

AMBIANCE MEETS
TECHNOLOGY

Thomas Homes: "More buyers are looking for the graciousness and ambiance of the great, stately old homes of the past. However, today's educated and sophisticated buyer expects the ease and technology of today. Homeowners want their builders to blend architectural elegance and beauty with an efficient, easy home to live in."

CAREFUL, CREATIVE DESIGN

FWC Architects: "Homeowners today are more appreciative of the profound effect realized by careful and creative design of their home environment. More than ever, the home is a personal sanctuary that must be healthy and comfortable, as well as inspiring. Our job is to create a clear expression of our clients' goals while maintaining design continuity and providing enduring beauty and utility."

99

CLEAN AND SIMPLE

No Place Like: "In today's world, we want our homes to be comfortable safe havens. Making every space in our environments not only functional, but also soothing becomes the key trend for the home. The clean and simple statements found in modern designs offer important ways to create warmth and individuality, without sacrificing the strength and stability of timeless design."

REVISITED
VALUES

Nuhaus: "A warmer, gentler look is back. It is found in the expression of revisited values. It's everything we want our homes/kitchens to say: cozy, warm, family, safe. A refuge from the hectic pace and world in which we live. It can be seen in the stains on the natural woods, the traditional details being brought back, and the softer, quieter fabrics being used."

102

STYLISH KITCHENS

Morgante Wilson Architects: "The use of simple lines, solid surfaces and efficient but creative kitchen cabinetry is essential when designing a small gallery kitchen. A kitchen cabinet composition of open shelves glass and solid panel cabinets creates a screen which allow light and flowing space while providing efficient storage and display areas."

DESIGNS
FROM THE PAST

Alberts Associates: "Customers often want their new homes to contain elements of antiquity and be timeless in nature. The most-common request is a warm welcoming facade, embellished with the appropriate architectural detail inherent to the specific style. The residence must appear as if it were there for 100 years or more. Interior appointments must reflect the appropriate details for the style of the exterior. To achieve these results, builders are now spending untold hours investigating historically accurate details."

IT'S WHAT'S
INSIDE THAT COUNTS

JMD Builder, Inc.: "What does it mean to build a custom, luxury home? Luxury is something that is not a necessity but provides added comfort or pleasure. Only homeowners themselves can determine what luxury means to them."

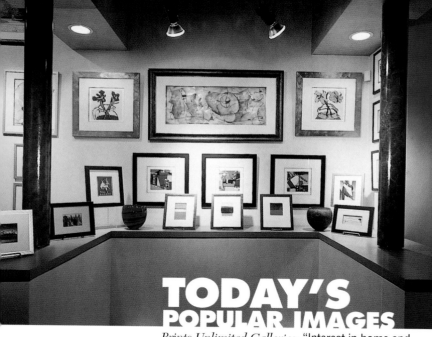

TODAY'S POPULAR IMAGES

Prints Unlimited Galleries: "Interest in home and office décor is bigger than ever these days, as can be seen by the many magazines and television shows that follow current trends. Popular images today include black-and-white Chicago vintage and current photos, vintage posters, florals and 20th century abstract museum prints."

ENDURING HANDCRAFTED FIXTURES

Tower Lighting: "Homeowners are interested in the simple beauty of hand-finished, one-of-a-kind craftsmanship combined with classic lines. They gravitate to the Old World, European handcrafted fixtures that never go out of style. They recognize that proper lighting design not only sets the mood of the space but also creates an artistic focal point."

Photo by **Charvat Photography**

FURNITURE EVERYWHERE

Woodworking Unlimited: "The look of furniture is appearing in every room that has cabinetry. Sculpted legs, variation of depths and heights, and mixes of colors are popular. Rather than the old look of a central theme throughout the home, variations of styles from room to room is becoming quite common."

Photo by **Michael A. Marcotte**

INTEGRATING THE MASTER BATHROOM

Florian Architects: "The contemporary master bathroom has become a refuge and a flexible extension of the character and use of the living room. This reflects a change in lifestyle and taste. The opulent, isolated bathroom look of the 1990s has given way +to the desire to integrate the comfort and activities more typically associated with a library, living room or family room."

Photo by **Mike Kaskel**

SEAMLESS DESIGN

Hackley/Lang & Associates, Inc.: **"The challenge in designing additions and renovations is to create a 'seamless design,' where the new construction is indistinguishable from the existing structure. When designing entirely new construction, the architect must work within the existing traditional fabric and context of the surrounding community for the home to blend seamlessly into the neighborhood."**

105

DESIGNING FOR COMFORT

Sandell Cabinets, Inc.: "Today's homes are designed with comfort in mind. People want to relax after a hard day's work. In their perfect setting, they can read or share time with their family."

INSPIRED DESIGNS

Paul Berger and Associates: "Whether housed in a contemporary or historical structure, today's lifestyles require practical solutions to ever-evolving technology. Beautiful and comfortable living spaces address these issues through the application of careful planning and custom solutions. Design inspiration is the result when unique requirements of the individual homeowner are combined with innovative architectural concepts."

Chicago Home

Your Guide to Your Dream Home

Tired of being lost? Feel that you don't know where you're going without a map? Can't find useful information regarding home improvement? The *Chiago Home Book* website, www.chicagohomebook.com, provides you with a full color atlas of information to map out the home of your dreams.

Book.com

YOU WANT IT, WE'LL PROVIDE IT

The **Chicago Home Book** website covers a full range of resources for building, remodeling, decorating, furnishing and landscaping projects. The site also provides you with a number of unique, functional features designed to help you locate all the necessary information regarding the design or enhancement of your luxury home. Just log on at www.chicagohomebook.com and we'll do the rest.

YOUR RESEARCH SOURCE

The site enables users to search for professionals by specific category: architects, interior designers, kitchen and bath, and many more. Users can also search by keyword — company name and/or profession — right off the home page.

THE PERFECT PAIR

The **Chicago Home Book** website, www.chicagohomebook.com, is best used when complemented by a copy of the **Chicago Home Book.** The website picks up where the book leaves off, allowing consumers to further research their home improvement needs in depth. The two work in unison to provide consumers up-to-date and timely information regarding their most prized investment — their home.

WE'RE ONLY A FEW CLICKS AWAY

If you are planning to design or renovate your home, please don't hesitate to consult your local source to top design/build professionals, www.chicagohomebook.com. Allow us to be your road map, and we will gladly lead you to your final destination. Thank you from everyone at the **Chicago Home Book,** and we all hope to see you online!

There is only one premier resource provider for the luxury design and home enhancement market — the **Chicago Home Book!**

Finally...
Chicago's Own
Home & Design
Sourcebook

The **Chicago Home Book** is your final destination when searching for home remodeling, building and decorating resources. This comprehensive, hands-on sourcebook to building, remodeling, decorating, furnishing and landscaping a luxury home is required reading for the serious and discriminating homeowner. With more than 700 full-color, beautiful pages, the **Chicago Home Book** is the most complete and well-organized reference to the home industry.

This hardcover volume covers all aspects of the process, includes listings of hundreds of industry professionals, and is accompanied by informative and valuable editorial discussing the most recent trends.

Ordering your copy of the **Chicago Home Book** now can ensure that you have the blueprints to your dream home, in your hand, today.

O R D E R   F O R M

INTERIOR DESIGNERS

BUILDERS & REMODELERS

KITCHEN & BATH

BEAUTIFULLY DESIGNED EDITORIAL PAGES

FLOORING

ARCHITECTS

LANDSCAPERS

NEW IN THE SHOWROOM FEATURE

Just a Sampling
of the Spectacular
pages in your
Home Book

You can call any professional in this book TOLL FREE!

Contact professionals in the **Chicago Home Book** directly by dialing (toll free) 800-645-1848 and our Customer Service Representative will be happy to connect you to the professional who will help you build your dream home.

Sample Listing

KREISS COLLECTION   **(312) 527-0907**
  415 North Lasalle Street, Chicago
  See Ad on Page 619   *800 Extension: 1166*

CHICAGO
HOME
BOOK

800-645-1848

ARCHITECTS

Charles L. Page Architect
100 Evergreen Lane Winnetka, IL 60093
8 4 7 . 4 4 1 . 7 8 6 0

Charles Page, North Shore Architect and Builder, is responsible for building some of the Chicago area's most impressive homes.

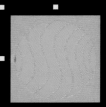

STYCZYNSKI WALKER & ASSOCIATES
architects

535 Plainfield Rd. Suite B • Willowbrook, Illinois 60527
Tel: 630.789.2513 • Fax: 630.789.2515
WEBSITE: WWW.SWA-ARCHITECTS.COM

The First Step

An architect is the first step in realizing your vision
for your new or remodeled home. This professional is
not only skilled in the technical areas of space planning,
engineering and drafting, but also happens to be an
expert in materials, finishes, energy efficiency, even
landscaping. An architect takes the time to find out
how you live, what your needs are, and how you'd like
to see your dreams come to fruition, all the while keeping
your budget in mind. He or she can assemble seemingly
disparate elements into a design that combines your
needs with your desires, with grace, beauty and efficiency.
We have the privilege of featuring the finest of these
creative, technically proficient problem solvers to help
you bring your ultimate home to life.

Photo courtesy of **Visbeen Associates, Inc.**

BRINGING IDEAS TO LIFE

Whether you're building your dream home in the city, a second vacation home, or remodeling your home in the suburbs, it takes a team to design and build a high quality residential project. A team of an architect, builder, interior designer, kitchen and bath designer, and landscape architect/designer should be assembled very early in the process. When these five professionals have the opportunity to collaborate before ground is broken, you'll reap the rewards for years to come. Their blend of experience and ideas can give you insights into the fabulous possibilities of your home and site you never considered. Their association will surely save you time, money and eventually frustration.

THE ARCHITECT — MAKING THE DREAM REAL

Licensed architects provide three basic, easily defined tasks. First, they design, taking into account budget, site, owner's needs and existing house style. Second, they produce the necessary technical drawings and specifications to accomplish the desires of their clients, and explain to a contractor in adequate detail what work needs to be done. Lastly, architects participate in the construction process. This straightforward mission requires more than education.

It requires listening. The best architects have gained their status by giving their clients exactly what they want — even when those clients have difficulty articulating what that is. How? By creatively interpreting word pictures into real pictures. By eliciting the spirit of the project and following that spirit responsibly as they develop an unparalleled design.

It requires experience. Significant architects, such as those included in your Home Book, maintain a reputation for superiority because their buildings are stunningly conceived, properly designed and technically sound. If a unique, steeply pitched roof was custom-designed for you by a licensed architect with an established reputation, you can be confident that it is buildable.

Suggestions by an experienced architect can add value and interest to your new home or remodeling project. He or she may suggest you wire your home for the technology of the future, frame up an attic for future use as a second floor, or build your countertops at varying levels to accommodate people of different heights.

This area is blessed with many talented

WHAT'S YOUR LIFESTYLE?

• Who lives in the house now?
• Who will live there in the future?
• Who visits and for how long?
• Do you like traditional, contemporary or eclectic design?
• Why are you moving or remodeling?
• What aspects of your current home need to be improved upon?
• Do you like functional, minimalist design, or embellishments and lots of style?
• Do you entertain formally or informally?
• How much time will you spend in the master bedroom? Is it spent reading, watching TV, working or exercising?
• What are the primary functions of the kitchen?
• Do you need a home office?
• Do you like lots of open space or little nooks and crannies?
• What kind of storage do you need?

118

architects. It's not uncommon for any number of them to be working on a luxury vacation retreat in another country or a unique second home in another state. Their vision and devotion to design set a standard of excellence for dynamic and uncompromising quality.

WORKING WITH AN ARCHITECT

The best relationships are characterized by close collaborative communication. The architect is the person you're relying on to take your ideas, elevate them to the highest level, and bring them to life in a custom design that's never been built before. So take your time in selecting the architect. It's not unusual for clients to spend two or three months interviewing prospective architects.

In preparation for the interview process, spend time fine-tuning your ideas. Put together an Idea Notebook (See the sidebar 'Compile an Idea Notebook'). Make a wish list that includes every absolute requirement and every fantasy you've ever wanted in a home. Visit builder's models to discover what 3,000 sq. ft. looks like in comparison to 6,000 sq. ft., how volume ceilings impact you or what loft living feels like. Look at established and new neighborhoods to get ideas about the relationship between landscaping and homes, and what level of landscaping you want.

GOOD COMMUNICATION SETS THE TONE

The first meeting is the time to communicate all of your desires for your new home or remodeling project, from the abstract to the concrete. You're creating something new, so be creative in imprinting your spirit and personality on the project. Be bold in expressing your ideas, even if they are not fully developed or seem unrealistic. Share your Idea Notebook and allow the architect to keep it as plans are being developed. Be prepared to talk about your lifestyle, because the architect will be trying to soak up as much information about you and your wishes as possible.

• Be frank about your budget. Although some clients are unrestricted by budgetary concerns, most must put some control on costs, and good architects expect and respect this. Great ideas can be achieved on a budget, and the architect will tell you what can be achieved for your budget.

• However, sticking to your budget requires tremendous self-discipline. If there's a luxury you really want, (a second laundry room, a built-in aquarium) it's probably just as practical to build it into your design from the outset, instead of paying for it in a change order once building has begun.

COMPILE AN IDEA NOTEBOOK

It's hard to put an idea into words, but so easy to show with a picture. Fill a good-sized notebook with plain white paper, tuck a roll of clear tape and a pair of scissors into the front flap, and you've got an Idea Notebook. Fill it with pictures, snapshots of homes you like, sketches of your own, little bits of paper that show a color you love, notes to yourself on your priorities and wishes. Circle the parts of the pictures and make spontaneous notes: "Love the finish on the cabinets," "Great rug," "Don't want windows this big." Show this to your architect, and other team members. Not only will it help keep ideas in the front of your mind, but will spark the creativity and increase understanding of the entire team.

119

ONE PERSON'S PROJECT ESTIMATE

Adding More Living Space

It's fun to imagine, but what might it actually cost to undertake a project described in this chapter? The example below describes a typical project and gives a general estimate of the costs involved.

Project Description
The addition of a 15 x 20 sq. ft. family room and the rehabilitation of the kitchen and powder room.

Architects' fees can be calculated in different ways. One way is to apply a percentage to all items that the architect designs, specifies and coordinates during construction. The following estimate is based on a percentage fee basis.

Family Room Addition
Traditionally detailed family room addition (300 sq. ft./$300 sq. ft.) $90,000
Exterior: brick and stone, classical frieze board, copper gutters and downspouts, cedar shingles or slate roofing.
Interior: 5/8-inch drywall with poplar base and crown moldings, herringbone clear oak flooring.
Entertainment cabinetry.. $10,000
Cherry rail-and-stile construction

Kitchen Rehab
Cabinetry, custom high-end $45,000
Appliances (built-in refrigerator, commercial grade equipment) $18,000
Stone countertops and backsplash.. $10,000
Plumbing, including fixtures $8,000
Electrical, including fixtures $6,000
Demolition and minimal construction $15,000
HVAC (heating, ventilating and air conditioning) $2,000

Powder Room Rehab
Cabinetry, custom high end $2,500
Stone countertops and tilework.. $5,000
Demolition and construction... $3,000
Plumbing, including fixtures $7,000
Electrical, including fixtures $3,000

Sub Total **$224,500**
Contingency (10.00%)...**$22,450**
Architectural fees (15.00%)...................................**$33,675**

Total: **$280,625**

Note: Small additions cost more, on a square foot basis, than a large addition or a new house due to economies of scale.

120

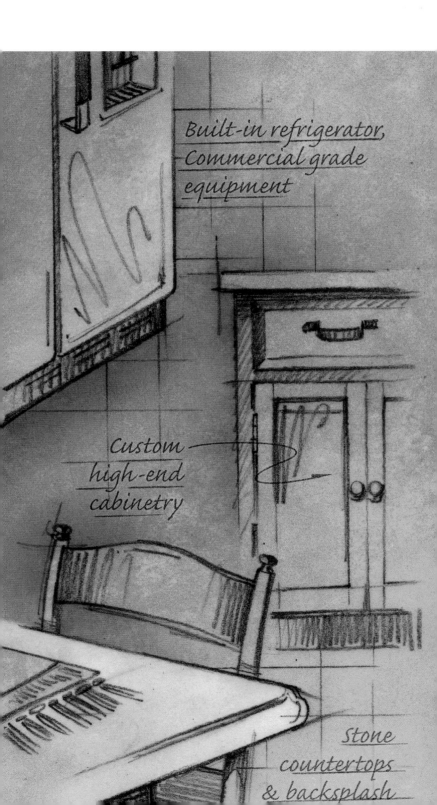

Built-in refrigerator,
Commercial grade
equipment

Custom
high-end
cabinetry

Stone
countertops
& backsplash

BUILT TO LAST

Some custom home clients in the Chicago area are abandoning the quest for the big house in favor of designing a home of high quality, integrity and harmonious balance. When the emphasis is on using top quality materials and custom design to create a comfortable home, the result is truly built to last.

TOO BIG, TOO SMALL, JUST RIGHT?

If you're designing rooms with dimensions different from what you're used to, get out the tape measure. If you're downsizing, can you fit the furniture into this space? Is the new, larger size big enough - or too big? Ask your architect, builder, or interior designer if there's a similar project you can visit to get a good feel for size.

• Ask lots of questions. Architects of luxury homes in the area are committed to providing their clients with information up front about the design process, the building process and their fees. These architects respect the sophistication and intelligence of their clientele, but do not necessarily expect them to have a high level of design experience or architectural expertise. Educating you is on their agenda.
• What is the breadth of services? Although this information is in your contract, it's important to know the level of services a firm will provide. There is no set standard and you need to be sure if an architect will provide the kind of services you want - from basic "no-frills" through "full service."
• Find out who you will be working with. Will you be working with one person or a team? Who will execute your drawings?
• Ask for references. Speak to past and current clients who built projects similar to yours. Ask for references from contractors with whom the architect works.
• Does the architect carry liability insurance?
• Ask to see examples of the architect's work - finished homes, job sites, and architectural plans. Does the work look and feel like what you want?
• Find out how many projects the architect has in progress. Will you get the attention you deserve?
• Decide if you like the architect. For successful collaboration, there must be a good personal connection. As you both suggest, reject, and refine ideas, a shared sense of humor and good communication will be what makes the process workable and enjoyable. Ask yourself, "Do I trust this person to deliver my dream and take care of business in the process?" If the answer is anything less than a strong and sure, "yes!," keep looking.

UNDERSTANDING ARCHITECTS' FEES AND CONTRACTS

Fees and fee structures vary greatly among architects, and comparing them can be confusing, even for the experienced client. Architects, like licensed professionals in other fields, are prohibited from setting fees as a group and agreeing on rates. They arrive at their fees based on:

(A) an hourly rate
(B) lump sum total
(C) percentage of construction cost
(D) dollars per square foot
(E) size of the job
(F) a combination of the above

The final quoted fee will include a set of services that may vary greatly from architect to architect. From a "no frills" to a "full service" bid, services are vastly different. For example, a no frills agreement budgets the architect's fee at two to seven percent of the construction cost; a full service contract budgets the architect's fee at 12 to 18 percent. Some firms include contractor's selection, bid procurement, field inspections, interior cabinetry, plumbing and lighting design, and punch list. Others don't.

One concrete basis for comparison is the architectural drawings. There can be a vast difference in the number of pages of drawings, the layers of drawings and the detail level of the specifications. Some include extra sketchbooks with drawings of all the construction details and in-depth written specs which call out every doorknob and fixture. Some offer impressive three-dimensional scale models to help you better visualize the end result, and computerized virtual walk throughs.

The benefit of a more detailed set of drawings is a more accurate, cost-effective construction bid. The more details noted in the drawings and text, the fewer contingencies a contractor will have to speculate on. The drawings are the sum total of what your contract with a builder is based upon. If a detail isn't included in the drawings, then it's not part of the project and you'll be billed extra for it.

Services should be clearly outlined in your contract. Many local architects use a standard American Institute of Architects (AIA) contract, in a long or short form. Some use a letter of agreement.

Have your attorney read the contract. Be clear that the level of service you desire is what the architect is prepared to deliver.

THE DESIGN PHASE

The architect will be in communication with you as your project progresses through the phases of schematic design, design development, preparation of construction documents, bidding and negotiating with a contractor, and contract administration (monitoring the construction). If any of these services will not be supplied, you should find out at your initial meeting.

The creativity belongs in the first phases. This is when you move walls, add windows, change your mind about the two-person whirlpool tub in favor of a shower surround, and see how far your budget will take you.

The time involved in the design process varies depending on the size of the project, your individual availability, and coordinating schedules.

WHY YOU SHOULD WORK WITH A TOP ARCHITECT

1. They are expert problem solvers. A talented architect can create solutions to your design problems, and solve the problems that stand in the way of achieving your dream.
2. They have creative ideas. You may see a two-story addition strictly in terms of its function - a great room with a master suite upstairs. An architect immediately applies a creative eye to the possibilities.
3. They provide a priceless product and service. A popular misconception about architects is that their fees make their services an extravagance. In reality, an architect's fee represents a small percentage of the overall building cost.

123

Architects

124

A good architect will encourage you to take as much time as you want in the first phases. It's not always easy to temper the euphoria that comes with starting to build a dream home, but the longer you live with the drawings, the happier you'll be. Spread the plans on a table and take an extra week or month to look at them.

Think practically. Consider what you don't like about your current home. If noise from the dishwasher bothers you at night, tell your architect you want a quiet bedroom, and a quiet dishwasher. Think about the nature of your future needs. Architects note that their clients are beginning to ask for "barrier-free" and ergonomic designs for more comfortable living as they age or as their parents move in with them.

BUILDING BEGINS: BIDDING AND NEGOTIATION

If your contract includes it, your architect will bid your project to contractors he or she considers appropriate for your project, and any contractor you wish to consider. You may want to include a contractor to provide a "control" bid. If you wish to hire a specific contractor, you needn't go through the bidding process, unless you're simply curious about the range of responses you may receive. After the architect has analyzed the bids and the field is narrowed, you will want to meet the contractors to see if you're compatible, if you're able to communicate clearly, and if you sense a genuine interest in your project. These meetings can take place as a contractor walks through a home to be remodeled, or on a tour of a previously built project if you're building a new home.

If your plans come in over budget, the architect is responsible for bringing the costs down, except, of course, if the excess is caused by some item the architect had previously cautioned you would be prohibitive.

Not all people select an architect first. It's not uncommon for the builder to help in the selection of an architect, or for a builder to offer "design/build" services with architects on staff, just as an architectural firm may have interior designers on staff. ■

ALBERTS ASSOCIATES, INC. ....**(847) 634-2343**
4180 Route 83, Ste. 204, Long Grove
Fax: (847) 634-9477
See Ad on Page: 186
800 Extension: 1005
Principal/Owner: Ken Alberts
Website: www.albertsassociates.com e-mail: info@albertsassociates.com
Additional Information: A full service architectural firm specializing in custom residences, historic renovation and design/build.

BALSAMO, OLSON & LEWIS LTD. ....**(630) 629-9800**
One S. 376 Summit Avenue, Oakbrook Terrace
Fax: (630) 629-9809
See Ad on Page: 190, 191
800 Extension: 1020
Principal/Owner: Brad Lewis, Partner

BECKER ARCHITECTS, LTD. ....**(847) 433-6600**
595 Elm Place, Ste 225, Highland Park
Fax: (847) 433-6787
See Ad on Page: 136, 137
800 Extension: 1026
Principal/Owner: Richard Becker, AIA
Website: www.beckerarchitects.com e-mail: rb@beckerarchitects.com

PAUL BERGER & ASSOCIATES ....**(312) 664-0640**
1255 North State Pkwy, Chicago
Fax: (312) 664-0698
See Ad on Page: 192, 193
800 Extension: 1233
Principal/Owner: Paul B. Berger
e-mail: info@pbadesign.com
Additional Information: A diverse group of Architects and Interior Designers specializing in custom spaces for Commercial and distinctive Residential use.

BRININSTOOL + LYNCH, LTD. ....**(312) 640-0505**
230 West Superior St, 3rd FL, Chicago
Fax: (312) 640-0217
See Ad on Page: 146, 147
800 Extension: 1029
Principal/Owner: David Brininstool/Brad Lynch
Website: www.Brininstool-Lynch.com e-mail: BL@Brininstool-Lynch.com

125

BRYAN ASSOCIATES, INC. – ARCHITECTS ....**(630) 920-0777**
522 Chestnut Street, Suite 2B, Hinsdale
Fax: (630) 920-0778
See Ad on Page: 206
800 Extension: 1032
Principal/Owner: Daniel W. Bryan
e-mail: BryanRKTEC@msn.com
Additional Information: Established in 1986, Bryan Associates offers client-centered, thoughtful and creative expertise in architectural design of new custom homes and historically accurate residential renovations and remodelings.

❝People may periodically change their interior décor with whimsy, but they crave architectural permanence.❞

— Geudtner & Melichar Architects

continued on page **145**

Erik Johnson & Associates
ARCHITECTURE/INTERIOR DESIGN

154 West Hubbard Suite 306 Chicago, Illinois 6061
tel.312.644.2202

DESIGN

The following design books represent the premier works of selected designers, luxury homebuilders and architects.

This book is divided into 10 chapters, starting with design guidelines in regards to color, personality and collections. In these chapters, interior designer Perla Lichi presents beautiful, four-color photographs of the design commissions she has undertaken for clients accompanied by informative editorial on the investment value of professional interior design.

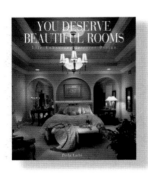

YOU DESERVE BEAUTIFUL ROOMS
120 pages, 9.75" x 14"
Home Design, Architecture
1-58862-016-6 $39.95   Hardcover

Orren Pickell is renowned as one of the nation's finest builders of custom homes. In this collection of more than 80 beautiful four-color photos and drawings, Pickell shows off some of his finest creations to give homeowners unique ideas on building a new home or adding to an existing one.

LUXURY HOMES & LIFESTYLES
120 pages, 9.75" x 14"
Architecture, Home Design
0-9642057-4-2 $39.95   Hardcover

Designer Susan Fredman has spent 25 years creating interiors, which, in one way or another, have been inspired by nature. In this book, she takes readers through rooms which reflect elements of our surroundings as they are displayed throughout the year.

AT HOME WITH NATURE
136 pages, 11.25" x 11.25"
Home Design, Architecture
1-58862-043-3 $39.95   Hardcover

The Ashley Group is proud to present these spec

CALL TO ORDER

BOOKS

Michigan-based architect Dominick Tringali uses the skill and knowledge that has brought him over 20 industry awards to share strategies on building the ultimate dream house. By combining unique concepts with innovative techniques and materials, Dominick's portfolio displays an array of homes noted for their timeless appeal. This $45 million collection of elite, custom homes contains the residences of notable CEOs, lawyers, doctors and sports celebrities including Chuck O'Brien, Joe Dumars, Tom Wilson, Larry Wisne and Michael Andretti's estate in Pennsylvania.

**RESIDENTIAL
ARCHITECTURE:
LIVING PLACES**
May 2002.
128 pages.
9" x 12"
Art & Architecture
1-58862-088-3
$39.95   Hardcover

Across the nation, homeowners often enlist the services of landscapers. Within this group lies an elite sector which specializes in breaking the mold on traditional landscaping. In this book, you will find truly groundbreaking approaches to the treatment of outdoor space.

**PORTFOLIO SERIES:
GARDEN DESIGN**
June 2002.
150 pages.
10" x 10"
**Gardening,
Home Design**
1-58862-087-5
$29.95   Hardcover

es on luxury home style, design and architecture

888.458.1750

STUART COHEN & JULIE HACKER ARCHITECTS
Custom Residential Architecture 847 328 2500

Architecture: Cohen & Hacker. Contractor: Burack & Co.
Interior Furnishings: Handman & Assoc.
Landscape Architect: Douglas Hoerr. Photos: Jon Miller, Hedrich Blessing.

STUART COHEN & JULIE HACKER ARCHITECTS
Custom Residential Architecture 847 328 2500

Architecture: Cohen & Hacker. Kitchen Design: Cohen & Hacker.
Contractor: Windsor Builders. Cabinetry: Exclusive Woodworking.
Photos: Jon Miller, Hedrich Blessing.

Becker Architects Limited

595 Elm Place, Suite 225	Tel 847.433.6600
Highland Park, Illinois 60035	Fax 847.433.6787
www.beckerarchitects.com	

Konstant ☐ Architecture ☐ Planning
847-967-6115

Photo: Jon Miller: Hedrich Blessing

MORGANTE • WILSON ARCHITECTS, LTD.

3813 NORTH RAVENSWOOD CHICAGO, IL 60613

TEL: 773.528.1001   WWW.MORGANTEWILSON.COM

Photo: Jon Miller: Hedrich Blessing

MORGANTE • WILSON ARCHITECTS, LTD.
3813 NORTH RAVENSWOOD CHICAGO, IL 60613
TEL: 773.528.1001   WWW.MORGANTEWILSON.COM

Photo: Jon Miller: Hedrich Blessing

Photo: Jon Miller: Hedrich Blessing

Photo: Leslie Schwartz Photography

MORGANTE • WILSON ARCHITECTS, LTD.

3813 NORTH RAVENSWOOD CHICAGO, IL 60613
TEL: 773.528.1001   WWW.MORGANTEWILSON.COM

Photo: @ DavidGlomb

Photo: @ DavidGlomb

MORGANTE • WILSON ARCHITECTS, LTD.
3813 NORTH RAVENSWOOD CHICAGO, IL 60613
TEL: 773.528.1001   WWW.MORGANTEWILSON.COM

Finally...
Chicago's Own
Home & Design
Sourcebook

The **Chicago Home Book** is your final destination when searching for home remodeling, building and decorating resources. This comprehensive, hands-on sourcebook to building, remodeling, decorating, furnishing, and landscaping a luxury home is required reading for the serious and discriminating homeowner. With more than 700 full-color, beautiful pages, the **Chicago Home Book** is the most complete and well-organized reference to the home industry. This hardcover volume covers all aspects of the process, includes listings of hundreds of industry professionals, and is accompanied by informative and valuable editorial discussing the most recent trends. Ordering your copy of the **Chicago Home Book** now can ensure that you have the blueprints to your dream home, in your hand, today.

Order your copy now!

CHICAGO
HOME
BOOK

Published by
The Ashley Group
1350 E. Touhy Ave. Des Plaines, IL 60018
847-390-2882 fax 847-390-2902
www.chicagohomebook.com

continued from page **125**

NICHOLAS CLARK ARCHITECTS ....**(312) 243-7799**
2045 W. Grand Avenue, Chicago
See Ad on Page: 211
Principal/Owner: Ann Clark
Fax: (312) 243-7836
800 Extension: 1210

STUART COHEN & JULIE HACKER ARCHITECTS ....**(847) 328-2500**
1322 Sherman Avenue, Evanston
See Ad on Page: 130-135
Principal/Owner: Stuart Cohen, AIA
Fax: (847) 328-2922
800 Extension: 1291

CORDOGAN, CLARK & ASSOCIATES, INC. ....**(312) 943-7300**
716 N. Wells, Chicago
See Ad on Page: 165
Principal/Owner: John Cordogan/John Clark
Website: www.cordoganclark.com e-mail: info@CordoganClark.com
Fax: (312) 943-4771
800 Extension: 1060

CULLIGAN ABRAHAM ARCHITECTS ....**(630) 655-9417**
211 W. Burlington Ave, Clarendon Hills
See Ad on Page: 152, 153
Principal/Owner: Michael Culligan/Michael Abraham
e-mail: caarch@msn.com
Fax: (630) 655-9421
800 Extension: 1063

ECKENHOFF SAUNDERS ARCHITECTS ....**(312) 786-1204**
700 S. Clinton, Chicago
See Ad on Page: 172
Principal/Owner: Walt Eckenhoff
Website: www.esadesign.com e-mail: esainc@esa-inc.com
Fax: (312) 786-1838
800 Extension: 1079

CHARLES FILL ARCHITECTS, LLC ....**(773) 548-5980**
1021 E. 48th St., Chicago
See Ad on Page: 189
Principal/Owner: Charles W. Fill
Fax: (312) 944-0541
800 Extension: 1045

145

"Architecture is the will of an epoch translated into space.**"**

— *Ludwig Mies van der Rohe*

continued on page **158**

BRININSTOOL + LYNCH, LTD.

w/ Leslie Jones, Inc. @ J. Padgett

w/ Leslie Jones, Inc. @ J. Padgett

w/ Tom Stringer, Inc.

w/ Leslie Jones, Inc. @ J. Padgett

RUGO/RAFFENSPERGER LTD.

Architects

RUGO
RAFF

20 West Hubbard

Chicago, Illinois 60610

TEL: 312.464.0222

FAX: 312.464.0225

w/ Tom Stringer, Inc.

Geudtner & Melichar Architects

Photo Credit: HNK Photography

THE PRACTICE
OF FINE ARCHITECTURE

Architecture ▢ Interior Design

711 N. McKinley Road, Lake Forest, IL 60045 • (847) 295-2440

211 West Burlington, Suite #4, Clarendon Hills, Il. 60514
Phone: 630 655 9417 Fax: 630 655 9421

SWANSON + DONAHUE

A R C H I T E C T S

Architecture • Land Planning • Construction

810 S. Waukegan Road, Suite 210 • Lake Forest, IL 60045
(847) 234-6655 • Fax (847) 234-6635

37 Sherwood Terrace Suite 122 • Lake Bluff, IL 60044
(847) 615-8055 • Fax (847) 615-8851

You are about to embark on a journey unlike anything you have known before. This relatively short trip will lead you through page after page of exquisite home building. Swanson + Donahue Architects is renowned as a premier design/build firm uncontested in quality and innovation. Swanson + Donahue Architects is the merger of two design oriented architectural firms. R.M. Swanson & Associates founded by Richard M. Swanson, in 1983 and Donahue Design Inc, founded by Thomas F. Donahue, A.I.A. in 1993. Together, Swanson + Donahue Architects have cultivated a rich reputation and history of award winning design, a testament to the quality and sheer brilliance of their homes.

The beauty of each home is immediately evident, but closer inspection provides a better appreciation for the work put into each home. Swanson + Donahue Architects put their name in the details, relentless in their pursuit to make each element of a home a stand alone work of art. Custom home building requires a precise dedication and critical nature. Unwilling to settle for less than perfect, Swanson + Donahue Architects put every ounce of energy into ensuring the reality is somehow better than the dream.

Each home speaks for itself. Inspired by the dreams of their clients, Swanson + Donahue Architects have proven they do what so many builders claim to do: they listen. When building custom homes, it is imperative that the needs and wants of the client are clearly understood. Swanson + Donahue Architects is proud to have consistently built the most challenging of designs successfully. Listening and understanding have played vital roles in the success of Swanson + Donahue Architects.

SWANSON + DONAHUE
ARCHITECTS

Architecture • Land Planning • Construction

810 S. Waukegan Road, Suite 210 • Lake Forest, IL 60045
(847) 234-6655 • Fax (847) 234-6635

37 Sherwood Terrace Suite 122 • Lake Bluff, IL 60044
(847) 615-8055 • Fax (847) 615-8851

SWANSON + DONAHUE
ARCHITECTS

Architecture • Land Planning • Construction

810 S. Waukegan Road, Suite 210 • Lake Forest, IL 60045
(847) 234-6655 • Fax (847) 234-6635

37 Sherwood Terrace Suite 122 • Lake Bluff, IL 60044
(847) 615-8055 • Fax (847) 615-8851

continued from page **145**

FLORIAN ARCHITECTS ....**(312) 670-2220**
432 North Clark, Ste. 200, Chicago   Fax: (312) 670-2221
See Ad on Page: 195   *800 Extension: 1098*
Principal/Owner: Paul Florian
e-mail: info@florianarchitects.com

FULL CIRCLE ARCHITECTS ....**(847) 831-0884**
1510 Old Deerfield Road #209, Highland Park   Fax: (847) 831-0286
See Ad on Page: 201   *800 Extension: 1103*

FWC ARCHITECTS, INC. ....**(847) 498-1900**
3100 Dundee Rd., Ste. 116, Northbrook   Fax: (847) 480-1806
See Ad on Page: 205   *800 Extension: 1104*
Principal/Owner: Arthur Cottrell/James Chambers
Website: www.fwcarchitects.com   e-mail: info@fwcarchitects.com

GEUDTNER & MELICHAR ARCHITECTS ....**(847) 295-2440**
711 N. McKinley Road, Lake Forest   Fax: (847) 295-2451
See Ad on Page: 150, 151   *800 Extension: 1109*
Principal/Owner: Diana Melichar

GIBSON/DARR ARCHITECTURE & CONSULTING ....**(312) 467-9790**
116 W. Illinois St. 4th FL, Chicago   Fax: (312) 467-9792
See Ad on Page: 166   *800 Extension: 1111*
Principal/Owner: John Gibson & Carl Darr
e-mail: GDarchs@aol.com
Additional Information: Fine custom homes & interiors.

GROUP A ARCHITECTS ....**(847) 952-1100**
415 W. Golf Road, Suite 6, Arlington Heights   Fax: (847) 952-1158
See Ad on Page: 164, 258, 259   *800 Extension: 1118*
Principal/Owner: Rob Kirk

158

HACKLEY/LANG & ASSOCIATES, INC. ....**(847) 853-8258**
440 Green Bay Road, Kenilworth   Fax: (847) 853-8351
See Ad on Page: 187   *800 Extension: 1123*
Principal/Owner: Chip Hackley & Bill Lang
Website: www.hackley-lang-architects.com   e-mail: hackley_lang@hotmail.com

"Every great architect is —
necessarily — a great poet."

— *Frank Lloyd Wright*

continued on page **167**

architecture interiors **ideas**

ARCHITECTURE

DESIGN BUILD

INTERIOR DESIGN

53 West Jackson, Suite 530

Chicago, Illinois 60604

312.922.7126

847.778.1285

FAX 847 235 1674

FRANK J. KLEPITSCH, AIA
A R C H I T E C T

LARSON ASSOCIATES

Architecture • Interior Design

542 SOUTH DEARBORN   CHICAGO, IL 60605

312-786-2255   FAX: 312-786-2290

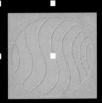

STYCZYNSKI WALKER & ASSOCIATES
architects

535 Plainfield Rd. Suite B • Willowbrook, Illinois 60527
Tel: 630.789.2513 • Fax: 630.789.2515
Website: www.swa-architects.com

ARCHITECTS

GROUP

415 W. Golf Road Suite 6
Arlington Heights, Illinois 60005

Phone: 847.952.1100
Fax: 847.952.1158
Web: www.group-a-architects.com

CORDOGAN, CLARK & ASSOCIATES INC.

ARCHITECTURE ▪ INTERIORS

312.943.7300 CHICAGO ▪ AURORA 630.896.4678

Does your weekend home take you to another place?

Does your kitchen pass the guest test?

GIBSON/DARR

Architecture + Consulting

TEL: 312.467.9790
EMAIL: GDarchs@aol.com

fine custom homes & interiors

continued from page **158**

ERIK JOHNSON & ASSOCIATES ....**(312) 644-2202**
154 W. Hubbard, Suite 306, Chicago — Fax: (312) 645-5883
See Ad on Page: 126 — *800 Extension: 1085*
Principal/Owner: Erik Johnson

KEMPER CAZZETTA, LTD....**(847) 382-8322**
209 E. Franklin Street, Barrington — Fax: (847) 382-4852
See Ad on Page: 168, 169 — *800 Extension: 1159*
Principal/Owner: John Cazzetta

KEMPER CAZZETTA, LTD....**(847) 256-2584**
412 Green Bay Road, Kenilworth
See Ad on Page: 168, 169 — *800 Extension: 1154*
Principal/Owner: John Cazzetta

FRANK J. KLEPITSCH, AIA...**(312) 922-7126**
53 West Jackson, Suite 530, Chicago — Fax: (312) 922-3799
See Ad on Page: 160, 161 — *800 Extension: 1099*
Principal/Owner: Frank Klepitsch

KONSTANT . ARCHITECTURE . PLANNING.....................**(847) 967-6115**
5300 Golf Road, Skokie — Fax: (847) 967-0111
See Ad on Page: 138, 139 — *800 Extension: 1165*
Principal/Owner: Paul Konstant

LA DESIGN ....**(847) 615-0707**
1088 W. Everett Rd., Lake Forest — Fax: (847) 615-9678
See Ad on Page: 208, 209 — *800 Extension: 1169*
Principal/Owner: Randolph F. Liebelt
e-mail: RLiebeltArch@aol.com
Additional Information: We offer: Design/Build Services, Smart Homes, Period Architecture and "Green" Architecture.

167

> **"**The dialogue between client and architect is about as intimate as any conversation you can have, because when you're talking about building a house, you're talking about dreams.**"**
>
> — *Robert A.M. Stern*

continued on page **188**

KEMPER CAZZETTA

ARCHITECTURE • LANDSCAPE ARCHITECTURE
PLANNING • INTERIOR DESIGN

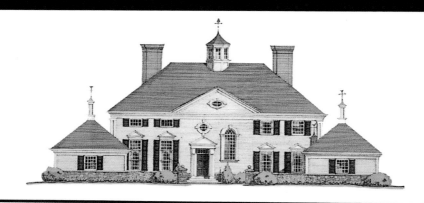

"Dedicated to creating personal spaces which display tradition, detail and creativity."

KEMPER CAZZETTA

ARCHITECTURE • LANDSCAPE ARCHITECTURE
PLANNING • INTERIOR DESIGN

209 E. Franklin Street • Barrington, IL 60010 • (847) 256-2584
412 Green Bay Road • Kenilworth, IL 60043 • (847) 256-2584

"A full-service design firm specializing in residential architecture from gentleman's estates to country cottages."

PHOTO BY CRAIG DUNCAN, HEDRICH BLESSING PHOTOGRAPHY

TRADITIONAL

maire

GREGORY MAIRE ARCHITECT LTD
ARCHITECTURE AND DESIGN

2643 POPLAR AVENUE
EVANSTON, ILLINOIS 60201

TELEPHONE 847 492 1776
FACSIMILE 847 492 1736

WWW.MAIRE.COM

CONTEMPORARY

GREGORY MAIRE COMBINES EXCITING
IDEAS AND LUXURIOUS MATERIALS
TO CREATE A PERSONAL SETTING OF
GREAT STYLE.

Only
If You
Want the Very
Best...

The
Ashley
Group

Sharing
THE DREAM

So you've decided to build your dream home, envisioning your perfect home on the perfect site. You've got your budget worked out. You've got the financing. But there are so many questions. What home style do you like? Will the Smith's home layout work in yours? Though most clients have an idea of what they want, what they end up with is often much different than what they envisioned. A good architect will be able to weed out the details between form and function while leaving the homeowners a sense that it truly is their ideal home.

When an architect has intimate knowledge of the homeowners' living habits—how and where they eat together, for example—exciting designs can begin to develop.

Archi

Photo courtesy of **Brininstool + Lynch, Ltd.**

tects

Modern building materials, such as double- and triple-glazed glass, enable architects to create rooms that weren't possible generations ago.

Photo courtesy of **Larson Associates**
Photo by **Jessie Walker**

176

Gathering information from the client is accomplished in a variety of ways. Architects routinely question their clients. How many bedrooms do you want and how do you want them arranged in relation to the home? Do you want the master suite on the first floor? Will you have visitors or do you entertain often? An open line of communication between the architect and the homeowner is essential to a well-planned design.

Archi

GETTING TO KNOW THE HOMEOWNERS

Most people have done a lot of homework before contacting an architect. "By the time a client comes to us they're pretty well educated," claims Mike Abraham, Culligan Abraham Hinsdale. "They know what they like and what they dislike."

Getting specifics of the clients' style is essential. "We drive around with them and take them through houses to identify the types of things they like," said Abraham. "We ask for photos of houses that they've appreciated through the years and ask them to make a list of what they like and what they don't like on a room-by-room basis."

Using information about the building site also helps distinguish the design. "We go out to the site and go to where the rooms might locate themselves," added Abraham. "There might be views they want to capture—the way the sun rises or sets on the site might also play a part."

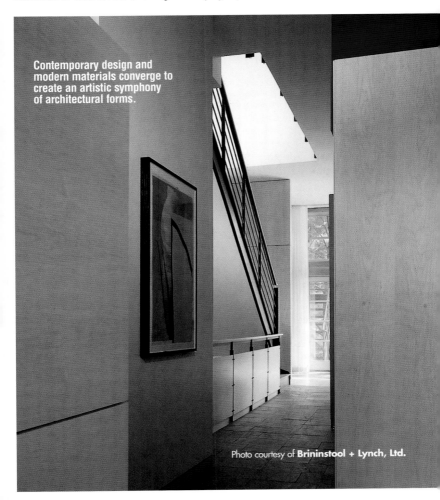

Contemporary design and modern materials converge to create an artistic symphony of architectural forms.

Photo courtesy of **Brininstool + Lynch, Ltd.**

tects

HOW DOES THE FAMILY LIVE?

Getting to the heart of how the family lives gives architects specific information from which to work. They need intimate knowledge about how their clients live. Gathering clues from their daily lives, their hobbies, how they entertain, and family activities can lead architects to determine the best design for their clients.

Rooms that flow into one another and let the light in, typify today's luxury homes.

Photo courtesy of **Larson Associates**
Photo by Jesse Walker

Archi

Today's kitchens must function not only as food preparation areas, but as the hub of family activity.

Photo courtesy of **Brininstool + Lynch, Ltd.**
Photo by Tricia Shay Photography

179

Brad Lynch of Brininstool + Lynch Ltd., Chicago, agrees. "We ask our clients to think about how they like to use space and what they like to do in it," he said. "We ask about their lifestyles. Is one person reading a book in bed while the other is watching television? It's important to think realistically about how you use a home everyday."

Using photos from magazines, books or from other homes is also part of the process. "We can tell certain things from what they show us. It helps us understand what types of things they appreciate," he added.

tects

The abundant use of wood within the home can create a warm and cozy atmosphere.

180

Photo courtesy of **Brininstool + Lynch, Ltd.**
Photo by **Jessie Walker**

WHERE DOES THE FAMILY LIVE?

Paul Konstant, Konstant Architecture Planning, Skokie, finds a home visit the most important way to learn about the family. "We visit them in their home to see how they currently live. It can tell a lot about a client," he said. In fact, over several visits and interviews with his clients, he collects a myriad of personal information.

"There is a whole process of getting to know them. We learn the way they live their lives, how the family interacts, how the household is run," added Konstant. "We get to learn how they do things, right down to the details of where they store their toothbrush. These are all things that we observe and add to the process of design."

Archi

IT'S A QUESTION OF STYLE

He also learns their likes and dislikes. Konstant utilizes magazines and books to determine his clients' style. He asks questions. "The language people use and descriptions of things they like help communicate what they need in a home. I think we do a good job interpreting our clients' wishes."

"The better educated a client is, the better the project will be," said George Larson, Larson Associates, Chicago. Larson, author of *Chicago Architecture and Design*, said making a client aware of the state of modern architecture today is key.

Once an architect knows how a family lives, designing the space to accommodate a unique lifestyle becomes much easier.

Photo courtesy of **Larson Associates**
Photo by **Jessie Walker**

tects

"My goal is to have my client understand what a house of the 21st century is like," he claimed. "They often do not truly understand where we are in the industry today." This includes using modern technology and building materials that are currently available. "For example," he said, "we can use glass today because it's double and triple glazed—this wasn't always a viable option."

Archi

Even with the intense exchange of information between architect and client, there are still surprises. "Although they are 95 percent clear about what you've shown them on paper, there is no way your client will be able to visualize it until it's being done," said Abraham. "Someone might tell me they were surprised that the ceiling would be so high or the windows would line up a certain way—that's the fun part. ∎

Visiting the existing home of a client is a way that architects get a feel for the homeowners' way of living.

Photo courtesy of **Brininstool & Lynch, Ltd.**
Photo by **Jamie Padgett**

tects

Location,
Location,
Location!

W̶hat better LOCATION for
your advertisement than the
CHICAGO HOME BOOK!

Just as our readers realize how important
location is when choosing a home,
we realize that it's just as important to you
when allocating your advertising dollars.
That's why we have successfully positioned
the CHICAGO HOME BOOK to reach
the high-end consumers you want as clients.

**Call 847-390-2882 to find out about our
unique marketing programs and
advertising opportunities.**

Published by
The Ashley Group
1350 E. Touhy Ave. Des Plaines, IL 60018
847-390-2882 fax 847-390-2902
www.chicagohomebook.com

SKIFFINGTON ARCHITECTS LTD.

Private Residence - Wynstone Subdivision

Private Residence - South Barrington

Design/Build
Custom Residential Architecture
New Homes & Additions

David Patrick Skiffington, A.I.A.
250 North Trail   Hawthorn Woods, IL 60047

847.438.3714

ALBERTS ASSOCIATES, INC.

architects

Long Grove Executive House, 4180 Route 83/Suite 204, Long Grove, IL 60047

PHONE: 847.634.2343

web site: www.albertsassociates.com

HACKLEY / LANG & ASSOCIATES, INC
ARCHITECTURE AND DESIGN
440 GREEN BAY ROAD · KENILWORTH, ILLINOIS
PHONE 847.853.8258 847.853.8351 FAX
WWW.HACKLEY-LANG-ARCHITECTS.COM

continued from page **167**

LARSON ASSOCIATES ....**(312) 786-2255**
542 S. Dearborn, Chicago   Fax: (312) 786-2290
See Ad on Page: 162, 300, 301, 334   *800 Extension: 1175*
Principal/Owner: George Larson

GREGORY MAIRE ARCHITECT LTD. ....**(847) 492-1776**
2635 Poplar Avenue, Evanston   Fax: (847) 492-1736
See Ad on Page: 170, 171   *800 Extension: 1117*
Principal/Owner: Gregory Maire
Website: www.maire.com   e-mail: gregory@maire.com
Additional Information: We are a 5 person practice specializing in up-scale residential and institutional work nation-wide.

MORGANTE WILSON ARCHITECTS ....**(773) 528-1001**
3813 N. Ravenswood, Chicago   Fax: (773) 528-6946
See Ad on Page: 140-143   *800 Extension: 1206*
Principal/Owner: Fred Wilson & Elissa Morgante
Website: www.morgantewilson.com
Additional Information: Morgante Wilson Architects is a comprehensive design office committed to the individual expression of each client's needs and vision.

NICHOLAS CLARK ARCHITECTS ....**(312) 243-7799**
2045 W. Grand Avenue, Chicago   Fax: (312) 243-7836
See Ad on Page: 211   *800 Extension: 1210*
Principal/Owner: Ann Clark

CHARLES L. PAGE ARCHITECT ....**(847) 441-7860**
100 Evergreen Lane, Winnetka   Fax: (847) 441-7862
See Ad on Page: 114, 115, 288, 289   *800 Extension: 1047*
Principal/Owner: Charles Page

ORREN PICKELL DESIGNERS & BUILDERS ....**(847) 914-9629**
2201 Waukegan Road, Suite W-285, Bannockburn   Fax: (847) 914-9781
See Ad on Page: 263- 270, 294, 295, 487   *800 Extension: 1222*
Principal/Owner: Orren Pickell
Website: www.pickellbuilders.com
Additional Information: Named by Custom Home Magazine as the Nation's "2001 Custom Builder of the Year". Winner of Over 100 Key Awards for Excellence.

188

❝God is in the details.❞

— Ludwig Mies van der Rohe

continued on page **198**

CHARLES   FILL   ARCHITECTS   LLC

1021 East 48th Street   Chicago, Illinois 60615

T 773 548 5980   F 312 944 0541

C J Walker Photography   Karen Cabral Furnishings   Wujcik Construction

BALSAMO, OLSON & LEWIS LTD.
One South 378 Summit Ave., Suite 1F
Oakbrook Terrace, Illinois 60181
630.629.9800
www.balsamoolsonlewis.com

Paul Berger & Associates

1255 N. State Suite 1 South • Chicago, Illinois 60611
312.664.0640 Fax: 312.664.0698
info@pbadesign.com

Photography by Rich Sistos©

"WE SHAPE OUR BUILDINGS; THEREAFTER THEY SHAPE US." -WINSTON CHURCHILL

POULTON GROUP

DAVID J. POULTON, AIA
268 MARKET SQUARE
LAKE FOREST, IL 60045

1 ▪ 847 ▪ 615 ▪ 1178
1 ▪ FAX ▪ 615 ▪ 1177

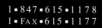

ARCHITECTURE ▪ CONSTRUCTION ▪ HISTORIC PRESERVATION ▪ RENOVATION ▪ INTERIOR DESIGN

BUILDINGS INTERIORS STORES EXHIBITS PRODUCTS PLANNING

FLORIAN ARCHITECTS

32 NORTH CLARK STREET SUITE 200 CHICAGO ILLINOIS 60610
TELEPHONE 312 670 2220 FACSIMILE 2221
EMAIL INFO@FLORIANARCHITECTS.COM
WEBSITE FLORIANARCHITECTS.COM

FEATURED IN: HOUSE AND GARDEN
ARCHITECTURAL DIGEST   METROPOLITAN HOME
CHICAGO MAGAZINE   NEW YORK TIMES
CHICAGO TRIBUNE   TOWN AND COUNTRY

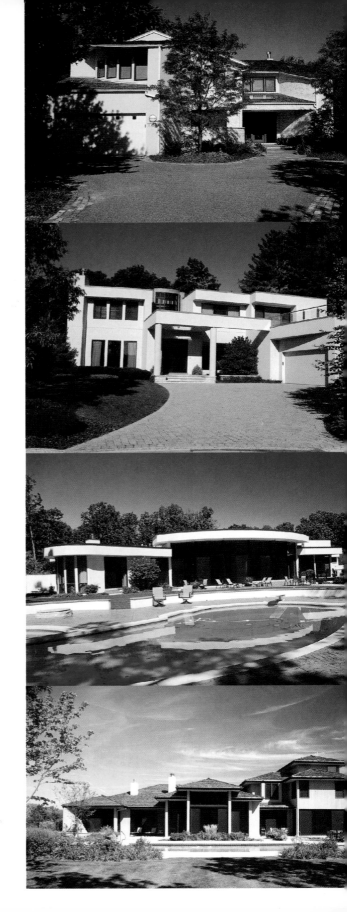

STUART D.
SHAYMAN
ASSOCIATES
ARCHITECTS

1780 Ash Street
Northfield, IL 60093
847.441.7555
FAX 847.441.7588

ROVITUSO STRANGE
ARCHITECTS
INC.

544 W. 58TH PLACE, HINSDALE, IL 60521
PH (630) 455-1780, FAX (630) 455-1709, E-MAIL:RSArchInc@aol.com

Architects

continued from page **188**

THE POULTON GROUP ....**(847) 615-1178**
268 Market Square, Lake Forest   Fax: (847) 615-1177
See Ad on Page: 194, 229   *800 Extension: 1322*
Principal/Owner: David J. Poulton, AIA
Additional Information: A small, exclusive high-end residential design/build firm providing new construction, renovation, preservation and
interior design services.

ROBERTS ARCHITECTS LTD. ....**(847) 251-7193**
2610 Old Glenview Road, Wilmette   Fax: (847) 251-7234
See Ad on Page: 202   *800 Extension: 1253*
Principal/Owner: David Roberts
Website: robertsarchitectsltd.com e-mail: robertsarch@ameritech.net

ROVITUSO STRANGE ARCHITECTS INC. ....**(630) 455-1708**
544 W. 58th Place, Hinsdale   Fax: (630) 455-1709
See Ad on Page: 197   *800 Extension: 1259*
Principal/Owner: Frances E. Rovituso-Strange, AIA
e-mail: RSArchInc@aol.com

RUGO/RAFF LTD. ARCHITECTS ....**(312) 464-0222**
20 W. Hubbard Street, Chicago
See Ad on Page: 148, 149   *800 Extension: 1263*
Principal/Owner: Steven Rugo
e-mail: Steve@RugoRaff.com

DAVID A. SCHAEFER ARCHITECTS PC ....**(630) 928-0122**
2603 W. 22nd Street, Suite 17, Oak Brook   Fax: (630) 928-0181
See Ad on Page: 212   *800 Extension: 1070*
Principal/Owner: David Schaefer
Website: www.das-architects.com e-mail: dasarch2603@aol.com

SCRAFANO ARCHITECTS ....**(312) 944-4828**
750 N. Franklin, Ste. 203, Chicago   Fax: (312) 988-7409
See Ad on Page: 200, 201   *800 Extension: 1270*
Principal/Owner: Elissa Scrafano
e-mail: scrafano@earthlink.net
Additional Information: Scarfano Architects creates innovative and unique solutions to architecture, interiors and design projects of any scale or problem.

198

"Organic buildings are the strength and lightness of the spiders' spinning."

— *Frank Lloyd Wright*

continued on page **207**

A. **WILLIAM SEEGERS** ARCHITECTS

117 NORTH JEFFERSON STREET   SUITE 305
CHICAGO, ILLINOIS 60661   312 454 0099

unnison Townhouses
William Seegers Architects

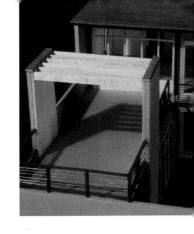

Architecture
Interiors
Design

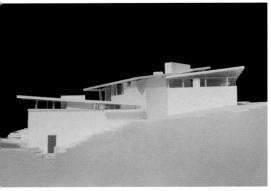

Photography by: Paul Bednarski

Photography by: Paul Bednarski

scrafano architects

29600 Northwestern Hwy.
Suite 101
Southfield, MI 48034
e-mail scrafano@earthlink.net

T 248 613 3112

F 248 827 3377

750 N. Franklin
Suite 203
Chicago, IL 60610
e.mail scrafano@earthlink.net

T 312 944 4828

F 312 988 7409

Hedrich Blessing Photographers©

ROBERTS ARCHITECTS LTD

(847) 251-7193   robertsarchitectsltd.com
2610 Old Glenview Road   Wilmette, Illinois 60091

THE ROBERTS CONSTRUCTION GROUP INC

J.A. WILSON & ASSOCIATES ARCHITECTS
230 W. HURON CHICAGO IL 60610 • PHONE: (312) 337-4689

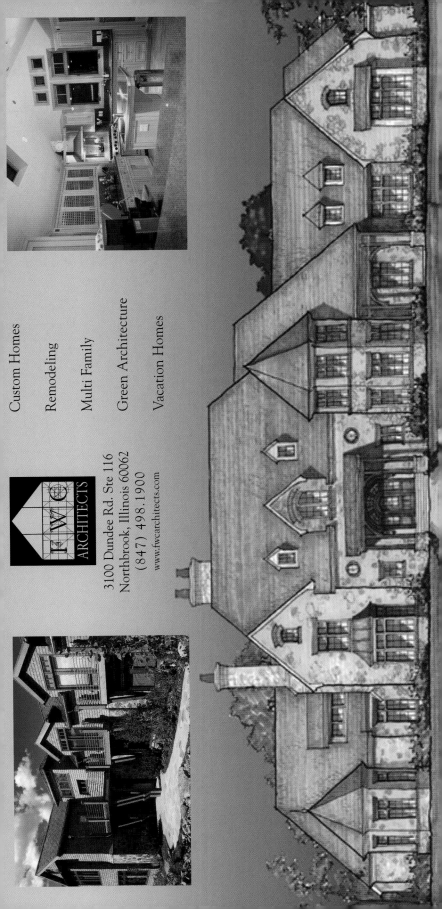

Custom Homes

Remodeling

Multi Family

Green Architecture

Vacation Homes

FWC
ARCHITECTS
3100 Dundee Rd. Ste 116
Northbrook, Illinois 60062
(847) 498.1900
www.fwcarchitects.com

BRYAN
ASSOCIATES
ARCHITECTS

522 Chestnut Street Suite 2B
Hinsdale, IL 60521
PH 630-920-0777 FX 920-0778
BryanRKTEC@msn.com

continued from page **198**

A. WILLIAM SEEGERS ARCHITECTS ....**(312) 454-0099**
117 N. Jefferson Street, Chicago
See Ad on Page: 199
Fax: (312) 454-1456
800 Extension: 1000
Principal/Owner: A. William Seegers
e-mail: AWSeegers@aol.com
Additional Information: Provide high quality, personalized services for all projects of varying size and range.

STUART D. SHAYMAN ARCHITECTS ....**(847) 441-7555**
1780 Ash Street, Northfield
See Ad on Page: 196
Fax: (847) 441-7588
800 Extension: 1292
Principal/Owner: Stuart Shayman
e-mail: sdsarch@aol.com

SKIFFINGTON ARCHITECTS, LTD. ....**(847) 438-3714**
250 North Trail, Hawthorn Woods
See Ad on Page: 185
Fax: (847) 438-3714
800 Extension: 1278
Principal/Owner: David Patrick Skiffington, AIA
Website: www.skiffingtonarchitects.com e-mail: dskiff@quixnet.net

STYCZYNSKI WALKER & ASSOCIATES ....**(630) 789-2513**
535 Plainfield Road, Suite B, Willowbrook
See Ad on Page: 116, 163
Fax: (630) 789-2515
800 Extension: 1293
Principal/Owner: A. William Styczynski
Website: www.swa-architects.com e-mail: info@swa-architects.com
Additional Information: We help you define your own sense of home.

SWANSON + DONAHUE ARCHITECTS ....**(847) 234-6655**
37 Sherwood Terrace, Suite 122, Lake Bluff
See Ad on Page: 154-157
Fax: (847) 234-6635
800 Extension: 1300
Principal/Owner: Richard M. Swanson, AIA & Thomas F. Donahue, AIA
Website: rmswanson.com e-mail: swandonarch@aol.com

207

SWANSON + DONAHUE ARCHITECTS ....**(847) 615-8055**
810 S. Waukegan Road, Lake Forest
See Ad on Page: 154-157
Fax: (847) 615-2808
800 Extension: 1302
Principal/Owner: Richard M. Swanson, AIA & Thomas F. Donahue, AIA
Website: rmswanson.com e-mail: swandonarch@aol.com

"If you are out to describe the truth, leave elegance to the tailor."

— *Albert Einstein*

continued on page **212**

LA DESIGN
1088 W. Everett Road
Lake Forest, IL
847.615.0707

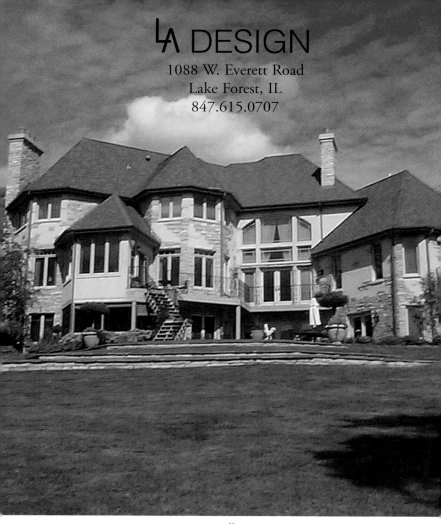

"Una Bella Vista"
To the Lake

The Dream House

Second Story Master Suite Addition

Second Story Addition

Three Story Addition Rear View

Architecture  Interior Design

1510 Old Deerfield Road, Suite 201
Highland Park, Illinois
(847) 831-0884 Fax (847) 831-1055

NICHOLAS CLARK ARCHITECTS
LTD.

2045 W. Grand Ave.
Chicago, IL 60612
312.243.7799
Fax 243.7836
nicholasclarkarch.com

continued from page 207

VISBEEN ASSOCIATES INC. ....**(616) 285-9901**
4139 Embassy Dr. S.E., Grand Rapids   Fax: (616) 285-9963
See Ad on Page: 203   *800 Extension: 1339*
Principal/Owner: Wayne E. Visbeen, AIA, IIDA
e-mail: visbeenaia@aol.com
Additional Information: Visbeen Associates Inc. specializes in architecture, offering
full design services from concept to finished project, including interior design.

VON WEISE ASSOCIATES ....**(312) 341-1155**
417 South Dearborn, Suite 800, Chicago   Fax: (312) 341-1177
See Ad on Page: 159   *800 Extension: 1340*
Principal/Owner: Charles Von Weise
Website: www.vwachicago.com   e-mail: dialogue@vwachicago.com
Additional Information: Von Weise Associates is a ten person design studio committed to excellence in design

J.A. WILSON & ASSOCIATES ARCHITECTS ....**(312) 337-4688**
230 West Huron, Chicago   Fax: (312) 337-4689
See Ad on Page: 204   *800 Extension: 1140*
Principal/Owner: John A. Wilson
e-mail: jawilsonarchitects@earthlink.net
Additional Information: Custom residential architects with a feel for detail, aesthetics
and comfort.

YOUNGMAN & COMPANY, INC. ....**(312) 263-2670**
188 W. Randolph, #3100, Chicago   Fax: (312) 263-0976
See Ad on Page: 127   *800 Extension: 1356*
Principal/Owner: H. Michael Youngman, AIA
Website: www.yciarch.com   e-mail: youngman@yciarch.com

212

DAVID A. SCHAEFER
ARCHITECTS PC
2603 W 22nd Street, Suite 17
Oak Brook, Illinois 60523
T: 630.928.0122   F: 630.928.0181
www.das-architects.com

Finally...
Chicago's Own
Home & Design
Sourcebook

The **Chicago Home Book** is your final destination when searching for home remodeling, building and decorating resources. This comprehensive, hands-on sourcebook to building, remodeling, decorating, furnishing, and landscaping a luxury home is required reading for the serious and discriminating homeowner. With more than 700 full-color, beautiful pages, the **Chicago Home Book** is the most complete and well-organized reference to the home industry. This hardcover volume covers all aspects of the process, includes listings of hundreds of industry professionals, and is accompanied by informative and valuable editorial discussing the most recent trends. Ordering your copy of the **Chicago Home Book** now can ensure that you have the blueprints to your dream home, in your hand, today.

Order your copy now!

CHICAGO
HOME
BOOK

Published by
The Ashley Group
1350 E. Touhy Ave. Des Plaines, IL 60018
844-390-2882 fax 847-390-2902
www.chicagohomebook.com

The Ashley Group Luxury Home Resource Collection

The **Ashley Group (www.theashleygroup.com)** is pleased to offer as your final destination when searching for home improvement and luxury resources the following **Home Books** in your local market. Available Now: *Chicago, Washington D.C., South Florida, Los Angeles, Dallas/Fort Worth, Detroit, Colorado, New York, Atlanta, Arizona, Philadelphia, San Diego, North Carolina, and Las Vegas.* These comprehensive, hands-on guides to building, remodeling, decorating, furnishing, and landscaping a luxury home, is required reading for the serious and selective homeowner. With over 700 full-color, beautiful pages, the **Home Book** series in each market covers all aspects of the building and remodeling process, including listings of hundreds of local industry professionals, accompanied by informative and valuable editorial discussing the most recent trends.
Order your copies today and make your dreams come true!

Order your copies today and make your dream come true!

THE ASHLEY GROUP LUXURY HOME RESOURCE COLLECTION

Yes! Please send me the following Home Books! At $39.95 for each, plus $3.00 Shipping & Handling and Tax per book.

☐ Dallas/Fort Worth Home Book *Premier Ed.* ____ # of Copies	☐ Detroit Home Book *Premier Ed.* ____ # of Copies
☐ New York Home Book *Premier Ed.* ____ # of Copies	☐ Colorado Home Book *Premier Ed.* ____ # of Copies
☐ Chicago Home Book *5th Ed.* ____ # of Copies	☐ Los Angeles Home Book *Premier Ed.* ____ # of Copies
☐ Washington DC Home Book *Premier Ed.* ____ # of Copies	☐ South Florida Home Book *Premier Ed.* ____ # of Copies
☐ North Carolina Home Book *Premier Ed.* ____ # of Copies	☐ Las Vegas Home Book *Premier Ed.* ____ # of Copies
☐ San Diego Home Book *Premier Ed.* ____ # of Copies	☐ Philadelphia Home Book *Premier Ed.* ____ # of Copies
☐ Arizona Home Book *Premier Ed.* ____ # of Copies	☐ Atlanta Home Book *Premier Ed.* ____ # of Copies

I ordered (# Of Books) _____ X $42.95 = $ _____ Total

Credit Card: _____ Exp. Date: _____

Name: _____ Phone: _____

_____

Address _____ Email: _____

_____

City: _____ State: _____ Zip Code: _____

Send order to: Attn: Book Sales–Marketing, The Ashley Group–Cahners, 1350 E. Touhy Ave., Suite 1E, Des Plaines, Illinois 60018
Or Call Toll Free at: 1-888-458-1750 • Or E-mail ashleybooksales@cahners.com • Visit us on-line at www.theashleygroup.com

---

All orders must be accompanied by check, money order or credit card # for full amount.

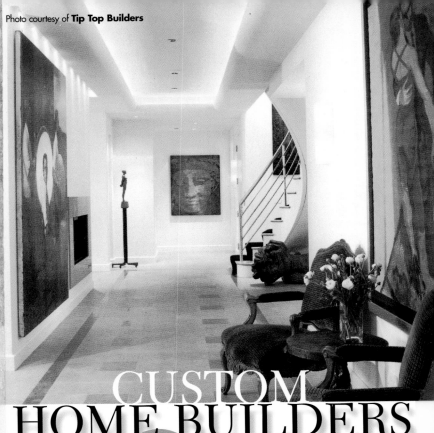

CUSTOM HOME BUILDERS

& REMODELERS

JMD
BUILDERS, INC.

444 Lake Cook Rd. Suite 10
Deerfield Illinois 60015
847.945.9670

From the Ground Up

 One of the key players in every homebuilding and remodeling success story is the builder. Architects envision possibilities, but builders create new realities. While design/build teams of architects and builders are becoming increasingly popular, the home in which you will be living will be the direct result of your contractor's efforts and expertise. So much of your satisfaction in the final outcome depends upon the selection of the right builder. It is essential to choose a company or individual with whom you have a good rapport, who has excellent references as well as experience with your type of project. While the planning phase of a new home or remodeling project may be exciting, creating the finished product is hard work. Seek out a builder whose attention to quality detail, willingness to listen to your concerns, and in-depth knowledge of the trades assures you a smoother road on the way to your new home.

Photo courtesy of **Charles L. Page Architect**

SETTING THE STANDARD FOR QUALITY

THE TEAR-DOWN TREND

Land for new residential construction is getting harder to find, and "tear-down" renovations are becoming more common. If you are considering a "tear-down" property, be sure you work with a builder and architect who are sensitive to the character of the neighborhood, and will help you build a home that fits in.

HOME
BUILDER
SOURCES

220

The Home Builders Association of Greater Chicago
1919 S. Highland Ave., Building A, Suite 225
Lombard, IL 60148
Phone:
630.627.7575
www.hbagc.com

Northern Illinois Home Builders Association
29 W. 140 Butterfield Rd., Suite 101
Warrenville, IL 60555
Phone:
630.393.4490
www.nihba.com

National Association of the Remodeling Industry (NARI)
Phone:
847.298.9200
www.nari.org

A strong commitment to providing top quality materials and craftsmanship is the most important contribution a builder can make to your professional team. Working in concert with your architect, interior designer, kitchen and bath designer and landscape architect, a custom home builder will take the designs, and your dreams, and make them happen. Selecting a builder who shares your dedication to building only the best is how you build quality into your new home. This kind of quality is as tangible as it is intangible. You can see it in the materials used - not necessarily the most expensive, but always the best for the situation. More interestingly, you can feel it. There's an unmistakable sense of integrity in a well-built home, of a dream fulfilled.

IS IT A(ARCHITECT) BEFORE B(BUILDER) OR B BEFORE A?

A nswering this question can seem like the "chicken or the egg" riddle: Do you hire the builder first, the architect first, or choose a design/build firm, where both functions are under the same roof?

If you work first with an architect, his or her firm will recommend builders they know have a track record in building homes of the same caliber you desire. Most likely, your architect contract will include bidding and negotiation services with these builders, and you may expect help in analyzing bids and making your selection. Your architect contract also may include construction administration, in which the architect makes site visits to observe construction, review the builder's applications for payment, and help make sure the home is built according to the plans.

Perhaps you've seen previous work or know satisfied clients of a custom home builder, and wish to work with him. In this scenario, the builder will recommend architects who are experienced in successfully designing homes and/or additions similar to what you want. The builder will support you, and the architect will cost-control information through realistic cost figures, before products are integrated into the house.

If you like the idea of working with one firm for both the architectural design and building, consider a design/build firm. Design/build firms offer an arrangement that can improve time management and efficient communication, simply by virtue of having both professional functions under the same roof. There is also added flexibility as the project develops. If you decide you want to add a feature, the design/build firm handles the design process and communicates the changes internally to the builder. When you interview a design/builder firm, it's important to ascertain that the firm has a strong architectural background, with experienced custom home architects on staff.

All scenarios work and no one way is always better than the other. Make your choice by finding professionals you trust and with whom you feel comfortable. Look for vision and integrity and let the creative process begin.

FINDING THE RIGHT BUILDER

The selection of a builder or remodeler is a major decision, and should be approached in a thoughtful, unhurried manner. Allow plenty of time to interview and research at least two candidates before making your choice. Hours invested at this point can save months of time later on.

At the initial interview, the most important information you'll get is not from brochures, portfolios, or a sales pitch, but from your own intuition. Ask yourself: Can we trust this person to execute plans for our dream home, likely the biggest expenditure of our lifetime? Is there a natural two-way communication, mutual respect, and creative energy? Does he have the vision to make our home unique and important? Is his sense of the project similar to ours? Will we have any fun together? Can we work together for at least a year?

If you answer "Yes!" you've found the most valuable asset — the right chemistry.

TAKE TIME TO CHECK REFERENCES

The most distinguished builders in the area expect, even want, you to check their references. More luxury home clients are taking the time to do this research as the move toward quality work-manship continues to grow.

Talk to clients. Get a list of clients spanning the last three to five years, some of whom are owners of projects similar to yours. Call them and go visit their homes or building sites. Satisfied customers are only too happy to show you around and praise the builder who did the work. If you can, speak with a past client not on the builder's referral list. Finding one unhappy customer is not cause for concern, but if you unearth a number of them, cross that builder off your list.

Visit a construction site. Clients who get the best results appreciate the importance of the sub-contractors.

TEN GOOD QUESTIONS TO ASK A BUILDER'S PAST CLIENTS

1. Are you happy with your home?
2. Was the house built on schedule?
3. Did the builder respect the budget and give an honest appraisal of costs early on?
4. Did the builder bring creativity to your project?
5. Were you well informed so you properly under-stood each phase of the project?
6. Was the builder accessible and on-site?
7. Does the builder provide good service now that the project is complete?
8. How much help did you get from the builder in choosing the products in your home?
9. Is the house well built?
10. Would you hire the builder again?

221

Creating a Country-Style Home

It's fun to imagine, but what might it actually cost to undertake a project described in this chapter? The example below describes a typical project and gives a general estimate of the costs involved.

Project Description

Construction of a 10,000 sq. ft., country-style home with brick and stone veneer and a slate roof.

Rough Lumber and Exterior Trim	Exterior	$15,000
	Rough framing	$95,000
Carpentry	Caulking	$2,000
	Rough framing	$90,000
	Interior trim	$12,000
Steel and Ornamental Iron	Ornamental iron	$5,000
	Structural steel	$7,500
Windows	Skylight	$1,500
	Windows and doors	$75,000
Exterior Doors	Front door	$12,000
	Service door	$2,500
Roof	Slate	$140,000
Plumbing	Fixtures	$25,000
	Labor	$25,000
Heating	HVAC forced air	$45,000
	Radiant heat	$12,500
Electrical	Electrical	$50,000
	Security system	$5,000
Masonry Veneer		$215,000
Insulation		$10,000
Drywall		$38,000
Wood Floors		$30,000
Tile	Ceramic tile	$30,000
	Hearth and surround	$10,500
Cabinets and Vanities		$125,000
Interior Trim	Mantel	$10,900
	Wine rack	$3,000
	Closets	$8,000
Shower Doors and Tub Enclosure		$9,000
Gutters and Downspouts		$13,000
Garage Doors and Opener		$4,800

Total: $1,147,200

Note: This estimate covers the basic construction costs of the project. Other costs include insurance and legal fees, survey and site plans, grading, light fixtures and appliance installation, and clean up of the site.

Rough cut
siding

Stone
veneer

Slate
roof

IT TAKES HOW LONG?

Some typical construction time frames:

Total Kitchen Remodel:
From total demolition to installation of new cabinets, flooring, appliances, electrical, etc.
SIX - EIGHT WEEKS

A 1,400 Sq. Ft. Addition:
New first floor Great Room & powder room, extension of the existing kitchen; master suite upstairs.
FOUR - SIX MONTHS

Total Home Remodel:
An 1,800 sq. ft. Colonial expanded to 4,000 sq. ft. All spaces redefined, added third floor, three new baths, new high-end kitchen, deck.
SIX-NINE MONTHS

These estimates depend on factors such as the size of the crew working on your project, the timeliness of decisions and delivery of materials.

Their commitment to quality is at the heart of the job. Do the subcontractors appear to be professional? Are they taking their time in doing their work? Is the site clean and neat?

Contact subcontractors with whom the builder has worked. If they vouch for the builder's integrity and ability, you'll know the firm has earned a good professional reputation. Meeting subcontractors also provides a good measure for the quality of workmanship you'll receive.

Visit the builder's office. Is it well-staffed and organized? Does this person offer the technology for virtual walk-throughs? Do you feel welcome there?

Find out how long the builder has been in business. Experienced custom builders have strong relationships with top quality subcontractors and architects, a comprehensive knowledge of products and materials, and skills to provide the best service before, during and after construction.

Ask how many homes are currently being built and how your project will be serviced. Some builders work on several homes at once; some limit their total to 10 or 12 a year.

LAYING A FOUNDATION FOR SUCCESS

Two documents, the contract and the timeline, define your building experience. The contract lays down the requirements of the relationship and the timeline delineates the order in which the work is done. While the contract is negotiated once at the beginning of the relationship, the timeline continues to be updated and revised as the project develops.

THE CONTRACT

The American Institute of Architects (AIA) provides a standard neutral contract which is widely used in the area, but some firms write their own contracts. As with any contract, get legal advice, read carefully, and assume nothing. If landscaping is not mentioned, then landscaping will not be provided. Pay careful attention to:

• Payment schedules. When and how does the builder get paid? How much is the deposit (depends on the total cost of the project but $10,000 to $25,000 is not uncommon) and will it be applied against the first phase of the work? Do you have the right to withhold any payment until your punch list is completed? Will you write checks to the builder (if so, insist on sworn waivers) or only to the title company? Remodeling contracts typically use a payment schedule broken into thirds - one-third up front, one-third half-way through the project, and one-third at completion. You may withhold a negotiated percentage of the contract price until you're satisfied that the terms of the contract have been met and the work has been inspected. This should be stipulated in the contract. Ten percent is the average amount to be held back, but is negotiable based on the overall size of the project.

Builders and remodeling specialists who attract a quality-minded, high-end custom home client are contacted by institutions offering attractive construction or bridge and end loan packages. Ask your contractor for referrals if you want to do some comparative shopping.

• The total cost - breakdown of labor and materials expenses.
• Change order procedures. Change orders on the average add seven to 10 percent to the cost of a custom home. Be clear on how these orders are charged and the impact they eventually will have on the timetable.
• The basic work description. This should be extremely detailed, including everything from installing phone jacks to the final cleaning of your home. A comprehensive list of specified materials should be given, if it hasn't already been provided by your architect.
• Allowances. Are they realistic? This is one place where discrepancies will be evident. Is Contractor A estimating $75,000 for cabinets while Contractor B is stating $150,000?
• Warranty. A one-year warranty, effective the date you move in, is standard in this area.

THE TIMELINE

This changeable document will give you a good indication if and when things will go wrong. Go to the site often enough to keep track of the progress according to the timeline. Do what you need to do to keep the project on schedule. One of the main causes of delays and problems is late decision-making by the homeowner. If you wait until three weeks prior to cabinet installation to order your cabinets, you can count on holding up the entire process by at least a month. (You'll also limit your options to cabinets that can be delivered quickly.)

THE SECOND TIME'S A CHARM

Renovating a home offers the unique excitement of reinventing an old space to serve a new, enhanced purpose. It's an evolutionary process, charged with creative thinking and bold ideas. If you enjoy a stimulating environment of problem solving

SOURCE FOR HISTORIC PROPERTIES

Landmarks Preservation Council of Illinois
53 W. Jackson Blvd., #752
Chicago, IL 60604
Phone: 312.922.1742

The National Trust for Historic Preservation
1785 Massachusetts Avenue, N.W.
Washington, D.C. 20036
Phone: 202.588.6000

Having a home listed on the National Register doesn't restrict homeowners from demolishing or making changes (local restrictions do that), but offers possible financial assistance and tax credits for renovations, and limited protection against federal 'takings.' The organization sponsors programs, publishes newsletters and books, and advocates preservation.

Local foundations and historical societies are established in most of the Chicago area communities that have older homes.

and decision making, and you're prepared to dedicate the needed time and resources, remodeling will result in a home which lives up to all of your expect-ations. You'll be living in the neighborhood you love, in a home that fits your needs.

A WORD ABOUT FINANCING OF REMODELING PROJECTS

Payment schedules in remodeling contracts typically require a deposit or a first payment at the start of the project, with subsequent payments due monthly or in conjunction with the progress of the work.

It is within your rights to withhold a negotiated percentage of the contract price until you're satisfied that the terms of the contract have been met and the work has been inspected. This should be stipulated in the written contract. Ten percent is the average amount to be held back, but is negotiated based on the overall size of the project.

Remodeling specialists who attract a quality-minded clientele are kept abreast of the most attractive remodeling loans on the market by lenders who specialize in these products. Ask your remodeler for referrals to these financial institutions.

UPDATING THE CLASSICS

Many homeowners at the beginning of the new century are attracted to the historic architecture in older neighborhoods. Maturity and classicism are factors that persuade homeowners to make an investment in an old home and restore, renovate or preserve it, depending on what level of involvement interests them and the significance of the house. Renovations include additions and updating or replacing systems in the house. Restorations involve restoring the building to the specifications original to the house. Preservation efforts preserve what's there.

Like any remodeling project, it's an emotional and personal experience, only more so. Staying within the confines of a certain period or style is difficult and time consuming. That's why it's crucial to find an experienced architect and builder who share a reverence for tradition and craftsmanship. At your interview, determine if his or her portfolio shows competence in this specialty. It's vital to find a professional who understands historic projects and knows experienced and qualified contractors and/or subcontractors who will do the work for you. Ask if he or she knows experienced contractors who work in historic districts and have relationships with knowledgeable, experienced craftsmen. If you want

---

A LUXURY
ADDITION
OF AN
HISTORIC
HOME

Arts and Crafts-Prairie Home, circa 1915.

• **All windows, trim, casings and other details to match the original brick.**
• **Full, finished basement, with bar and workout area.**
• **First level family room, dining room and new kitchen.**
• **Upper level master suite and office. Stone terrace and garden.**

Total Project Cost: $500,000, including arch-itectural fees.

exterior features, like period gardens or terraces, ask if they will be included in the overall plan. Make sure he or she has sources for you to find period furnishings, sconce shades or chimney pots.

There are many construction and design issues particular to old homes. The historic renovation and preservation experts featured in the following pages bring experience, creativity and responsibility to each project.

RESPECT YOUR ELDERS

Before you fall in love with an old house, get a professional opinion. Find out how much is salvageable before you make the investment. Can the wood be restored? Have the casings been painted too many times? Is the plaster wavy and buckled? Can the house support ductwork for central air conditioning or additional light sources?

Notable remodelers are often contacted for their expert advice prior to a real estate purchase, and realtors maintain relationships with qualified remodelers for this purpose. They also keep remodelers informed of special properties suitable for custom renovations as they become available.

PRIVACY? WHAT'S THAT?

Remodelers overwhelmingly agree their clients are happier if they move to a temporary residence during all, or the most intensive part, of the renovation. The sight of the roof and walls being torn out, the constant banging and buzzing of tools, and the invasion of privacy quickly take their toll on children and adults who are trying to carry on family life in a house full of dust. Homeowners who are well-rested from living in clean, well-lighted temporary quarters enjoy better relationships with each other, their remodeler and subcontractors.

Common hideaways are rental homes, suite-type hotels, the unoccupied home of a relative, or a long vacation trip. ∎

CREATE A RECORD

You have a team of highly qualified professionals building your home, but the ultimate responsibility is on your shoulders. So keep track of the project. Organize a binder to keep all of your samples, change orders and documents together. Make copies for yourself of all communication with your suppliers and contractor.

Contractors

APEX WOOD FLOORS ....**(630) 963-9322**
1326 Ogden Avenue, Downers Grove　　　　　Fax: (630) 963-9320
See Ad on Page: 580, 581　　　　　　　　　*800 Extension: 1009*
Principal/Owner: John Lessick
Website: www.apexwoodfloors.com e-mail: info@apexwoodfloors.com
Additional Information: In business for 20 years- no subcontractors- quality assurance- custom borders and inlays- showroom.

BRYAN ASSOCIATES, INC. – ARCHITECTS ....**(630) 920-0777**
522 Chestnut Street, Suite 2B, Hinsdale　　　Fax: (630) 920-0778
See Ad on Page: 206　　　　　　　　　　　*800 Extension: 1030*
Principal/Owner: Daniel W. Bryan
e-mail: BryanRKTEC@msn.com
Additional Information: Established in 1986, Bryan Associates offers client-centered, thoughtful and creative expertise in architectural design of new custom homes and historically accurate residential renovations and remodelings.

BURACK & COMPANY ....**(847) 266-3500**
1741 Green Bay Road, Highland Park　　　　Fax: (847) 266-3707
See Ad on Page: 278, 279　　　　　　　　　*800 Extension: 1037*
Principal/Owner: Robert Burack

DISTINCTIVE CUSTOM HOMES, INC. ....**(847) 295-4500**
611 Rockland Road, Ste. 2, Lake Bluff
See Ad on Page: 274, 275　　　　　　　　　*800 Extension: 1074*

GLEN ELLYN HOMES ....**(630) 469-1070**
489 Taft Avenue, Glen Ellyn　　　　　　　　Fax: (630) 469-1356
See Ad on Page: 256, 257　　　　　　　　　*800 Extension: 1112*
Principal/Owner: Douglas Walksler/Thomas Gale
e-mail: gehomes@aol.com
Additional Information: Custom homes and premium properties in Chicago's Western suburbs.

GROUP A ARCHITECTS BUILDERS ....**(847) 952-1100**
415 W. Golf Road, Ste 6, Arlington Heights　　Fax: (847) 952-1158
See Ad on Page: 164, 258, 259　　　　　　　*800 Extension: 1119*
Principal/Owner: Rob Kirk

J & B BUILDERS, INC. ....**(630) 587-9900**
2000 W. Main Street, Unit H, St. Charles　　　Fax: (630) 587-8566
See Ad on Page: 276, 277　　　　　　　　　*800 Extension: 1138*

228

"A house is a home when it shelters the body and comforts the soul."

— *Phillip Moffitt*

continued on page 280

STONEGATE BUILDERS, INC.
"Building For Your Future"

1480 Old Deerfield Road, Suite 20
Highland Park, IL 60035
T 847.579.1525 F 847.579.1252

STONEGATE BUILDERS, INC.
"Building For Your Future"

www.stonegatebuilders.com

201 E. Dundee Rd
Palatine, IL 60067
(847) 359-3591
(847) 359-5123

SEVVONCO

We are an award winning certified HEALTH HOUSE builder.

Swag drapes, plush furniture and classic accessories such as a grand piano add to the ambiance of this room.

Photo courtesy of **Sevvonco Builders**
Photo by **Dennis Jordan**

HomeB

Detailing
THE DREAM

People come to home building contractors every day with their ideas for perfect homes. And every day these contractors build other peoples' dreams — everything from kitchenettes in master bedrooms to soundproof media rooms to home pedicure spas. But when it comes to building their homes, what do builders like?

uilders

Deep, rich colors lend to the masculine charm of this interior.

Photo courtesy of **Orren Pickell Builders**
Photo by **Linda Oyama Bryan**

The Joy of Entertaining

Rob Kirk, Kirk Partners, prefers lots of light in a natural setting. "I like contemporary homes with large glass walls and high ceilings. I also enjoy natural light with pleasant views of the landscape," said Kirk.

Entertaining is central to Kirk's home life. "The focal point of my home would be the family kitchen area, with an adjacent great room. A large dining room would also be a must," he said. "Since I often have friends and relatives over, an indoor and outdoor gathering area would be very useful too.

But the main concern for Kirk would be the maintenance. "I want a house that's really low maintenance. I don't want to spend my weekends working on the house," Kirk said.

Location is Key

Location plays a major role for builder Mike Wujcik, Wujcik Construction Group Inc. "Ideally, location is key in any new home today. That's why you see so many home additions," he claims. "Finding a superb location and setting allows builders plenty of room to build the structure while giving consideration to the landscaping."

The interior of Wujcik's dream home would be spacious and flowing. "A wide open space plan that flows lets everyone in the family enjoy their home – houses are meant to be lived in," he said. Included in his plan would be organizational areas for hobbies, spaces for the kids to play, off-season storage and rooms for out-of-town guests.

HomeB

A specialized media area also tops Wujcik's list. "Today there's a real trend in high-tech audio visual elements, plasma TVs, specialized remotes and lighting systems integrated into the HVAC," he said. "I would put in a highly sophisticated audio-visual system with integrated lighting to provide different scenes and settings for family and guests."

With young sons, outside means playtime for Wujcik and his family. Besides an in-ground pool, the yard also has areas for gardening, sporting activities and entertaining. "It gives us a place to practice the boys' favorite sports."

Refreshing and inviting, this pool and hot tub beckon its owners to swim under the skylights.

Photo courtesy of **Sevvonco Builders**
Photo by **Dennis Jordan**

uilders

A Home with a View

I just finished renovating my home of 17 years," says Orren Pickell, Orren Pickell Designers & Builders Inc. First thing on Pickell's "must have list" is a great site. His current home sits on a five-acre wooded lot with two ponds. Earlier this year he added a gazebo with a bridge overlooking the pond. "It looks great from the pond and it looks great from the house," said Pickell.

A family workshop with a great view invites family members in from the garage. "This is where my family enters the house, so it serves as our organizational drop-off space with all the features it takes to organize our lives. There's a place for our coats, shoes, anything we've brought in from our car," claimed Pickell.

Pickell's children are almost all gone, but he anticipates they'll be back for visits with his future grandchildren. "We basically built it with four general living areas so our families could live there," he said. "This will be the gathering spot where my kids and grandkids want to come for holidays and special family events."

Additionally, when he renovated the house he lost storage space in the eight-car garage. To make up for the lost space, Pickell added a two-car garage in the back of the house. "Anyone would think the structure is a guest cottage, so it serves two functions to me," he said. "It is an element that adds beauty to the garden as well as added storage space."

This whimsical indoor playground appeals to both adults and teens.

Photo courtesy of **Orren Pickell Builders**
Photo by **Linda Oyama Bryan**

HomeB

Plants and integrated lighting and electronics create a warm and healthy scene.

Architecture with a Bit of English Influence

John Stalowy, Stonegate Builders, enjoys using natural elements. "I like the old English style of architecture. I'd want to have a lot of natural materials: New England slate, hand-molded brick and honed limestone would be included," said Stalowy. Additionally, he would build it for generations to come. "I want to build a home to hand down to my children, an ancestral home, which has been the rule of thumb for centuries in England."

Curb appeal is also important to Stalowy. "Having a grand entrance, great curb appeal and very inviting landscaping and landscape lighting would be essential," he claimed. With his love of old-style architecture, his landscaping would have a formal feel, with ornamental embellishments such as fountains and statuary.

Stalowy's legacy feels grand in scale, with high ceilings and a dramatic entry hall. "Probably the most compelling thing for me would be a wonderful staircase," he said. Using ornately carved woods would add to the grandeur. "If it's really exemplary, it sets the tone for the entire home."

His personal hobbies play a large role in his dream home. Stalowy enjoys cooking and entertaining. "Having a good working kitchen is essential," he said. "This area is a gathering place for family and friends and would be a focal point in my home." He would incorporate state-of-the-art features and technology into classically designed cabinetry and natural stone countertops.

"My passion is fine art photography," claimed Stalowy. "In my dream home, I would probably have a little house in the back where my wife and I could enjoy our passions. I would use it to craft and display my art." Currently, he has his own personal gallery in his office where his works and those of colleagues line the walls.

uilders

The Millennium Home is Electronically Integrated

"My dream home would be a healthy home," claimed Scott Sevon, Sevvonco Inc. The American Lung Association has identified and specified exacting measures to ensure healthy indoor air quality. "We are the first certified 'Health-Home' builder in the state of Illinois."

Building a healthy home requires the use of "green" products, as well as exacting standards for construction and mechanical systems. Some of the elements of the healthy home include foundation waterproofing and moisture control; duct sealing and advanced insulation techniques; energy efficient, high performance windows; high efficiency air filtration and ventilation; and humidity control. "These homes are sealed to keep potential pollutants out while keeping it mildew and mold free, allowing our family to breathe comfortably," said Sevon. "This also increases the energy efficiency of the home 30 to 40 percent by keeping hot air out in the summer and cold air out in the winter."

Photo courtesy of Orren Pickell Builders
Photo by Linda Oyama Bryan

HomeB

Sevon's dream home would feel safe and secure. Cameras installed throughout the home and yard would be an extra measure to ensure peace of mind while at home or away. "When we are away, we would be able to use the World Wide Web to view our home," claimed Sevon.

An electronically integrated home is a must. "All mechanical systems would be monitored and accessible by computer. The system would be energy-efficient, require less maintenance, and last longer," he said. When in "vacation mode" all non-essential systems would be shut down, conserving electricity and natural resources." Appliances and plumbing fixtures would also be monitored. The plumbing system's computerized leak protection could find a leak and shut off the water, preventing any damage. And all of these systems would have emergency battery backup.

Though builders' opinions differ in respect to a dream home, Chicago-area builders are experts in finding what works for each home they build. Gleaning their insight can help prospective homebuyers perfect their own dream homes. ■

Chicago-area builders such as Orren Pickell are often welcomed home by the dream houses they have built for themselves...

241

uilders

Only If You Want the Very Best...

The
Ashley
Group

1350 E. Touhy Avenue, Des Plaines, Illinois 60018
888.458.1750   Fax 847.390.2902

www.theashleygroup.com • www.homebook.com

Building
Your
Dream
Home

This timetable is included to support you in transforming your dream into reality. The sections of this book include specific categories to help you find the best quality craftsmanship available. This timeline will help you to understand the process from start to finish. How long might it take for you from designing the house to making it your own home? It could take from one year to a year and a half. Eighteen months is not unusual for a completely custom-built home. It can take four to six months to receive design approval and city permits alone. So be patient and plan ahead. Often delays occur because of a lack of communication. Take the initiative to keep in touch with all parties necessary. We hope this timeline will help give you an indication of how that dream home of yours will become a reality!

Breaking Ground

What a joy to see that construction of your new home is underway!

Foundation Work

This will include footings and dampproofing. The cement will need a few days to solidify.

MONTH 5

Framing Begins

Rough framing of the house begins. At the end of this phase the structure will be in place, and you'll be able to see the rooms as they're going to look. This phase will take two to three months.

MONTH 6

Roofing Begins

Since the time you broke ground until the time you get to this stage, probably four months have lapsed. With the exterior framing of the house completed, the contractor can start working on the interior (mechanical elements).

MONTH 9

Inspecting the Progress

At various times throughout the process, there will be building/municipal inspections to make sure the house meets all city codes and zoning issues. Often, a builder will insist on a six-month, follow-up courtesy inspection.

• **Choosing a contractor**: The builder is usually considered the general contractor for the job. The general contractor will line up the subcontractors and enter into an agreement with the vendors. The general contractor will be solely responsible for construction methods, techniques, schedules and procedures. The key is that teams need to be in place.

• **Seasonal costs**: The builder will keep in mind that different times of the year require different costs. The cost of lumber, for example, traditionally goes up in late spring to mid-summer. Good builders might also be able to figure when there will be occasional shortages in such items as drywall and brick. They might also know when to buy certain items in bulk to decrease your overall costs.

Building a Custom House

Interview and Select an Interior Designer

A skilled designer will collaborate with the architect on matters such as windows and door location, appropriate room size and lighting plans.

Interview and Select an Architect and Builder

This is the time to test the fit between what you want, what you need and what you can spend. It is advisable to interview two or three architects and builders and check their references before making a firm decision.

Site Selection

If you don't already own the land, meet with a realtor of your choice to describe the parameters of your future house. Also discuss future sites with your architect and builder.

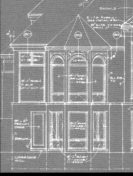

MONTH 1 .... MONTH 4

Design/Build Firms

A design/build firm is a company that employs architects, builders, estimators and sometimes interior designers and realtors. Read more about them in the Architects section.

• **Your architect and builder must work together.** The architect and contractor must be continually matching their budget and timelines. The architect converts the vision into buildable drawings. The contractor uses the drawings to make the plan work.

• **Final decisions:** Once you've received the initial drawings for the front, back and both sides of your house plus floor plans, you must make final decisions. You must decide on the exact footage of every level of your house and decide what unique elements you may want to include. For example, do you want your own home theater and entertainment center? Home automation and lighting?

Project
Description

uilding an upscale, one-acre property, single-family home. This work includes planning the project (selecting an architect and builder), executing the project (the steps from breaking the ground to finishing the interior work) and finishing the project (closing on your new home).

FINISHED PROJECT

● **Releasing the contractor**
The client does a walk-through inspection and provides a "punch list"— a list of miscellaneous items the contractor needs to do to finish the work.

● **Final Close**
Representatives for both the builder and the client will attend, along with a staff person from the closing company.

● **Final Inspection**
Independent appraisals take place at this time.

MONTH 16

• **There are certain laws that protect the client.** Experts other than independent appraisers may be called upon to ensure that all agreements and building codes have been met. The client can, of course, make notes and have miscellaneous details taken care of.

• **Warranty:** Most states provide warranty protection for the client. The builder's warranty is typically one year for construction. Specific manufacturer warranties can last as long as five to 10 years.

Additional Information
For more information, contact the National Association of Home Builders (NAHB) 1201 15th St. NW Washington, DC 20005-2800 202-266-8111.

Mechanical Work Begins

This includes the rough plumbing, HVAC, electrical and low-voltage work. Allow two to three weeks each for the mechanical steps.

Interior Work Begins

Once the rough mechanical work is completed, the insulation and drywall can be installed. The hardwood floors and tile can be worked on concurrently. Next up are the stairs and the cabinets. Then the millwork (trim around the doors and windows) takes shape. The painting of trim, walls and ceilings follows. Then the mechanical work can be finalized.

Finishing the Work

Final sanding, sealing, carpeting and closet shelving complete the job. Allow three to four months for the interior work and final items to take place.

MONTH 10　　　　MONTH 11　　　　MONTH 15

• **Environmental and energy concerns:**
Of course, you will want to save on energy consumption, so make sure the builder doesn't forget these issues. Consider the selection of furnaces and water heaters. Ask your builder what their standard efficiency ratings are. Your initial investment might be more, but you could reap the benefit of lower energy costs in the long run. Where the sun rises and sets may seem inconsequential. But you'll want to make sure some key rooms allow natural light at particular times (for example, the greenhouse effect).

Also, as you build your house, you may want to ask your builder about different ways to protect the outside of the house using some sort of protective covering or wrap. That helps address your concerns about water intrusion.

Keeping on Schedule

Make sure the builder provides you with a schedule and completion date. The duration of the project should be clearly defined in the contract. However, you can almost depend on the schedule changing due to unforeseen delays such as weather-related items. But the homeowner can also affect the schedule by making late selections and desiring personal changes.

In Conclusion

Your new house started as a dream with a piece of land. Now your custom-designed home has become a reality. It's time to start living in the special place you've created. Enjoy!

Special thanks to Orren Pickell Designers and Builders, Bannockburn, IL, and Centurian Development, Scottsdale, AZ, for their contributions to this article.

Produced by The Ashley Group
847.390.2882
www.theashleygroup.com

continued from page **228**

JMD BUILDERS, INC...**(847) 945-9670**
444 Lake Cook Rd, Ste 10, Deerfield   Fax: (847) 945-9671
See Ad on Page: 216, 217, 260, 261   *800 Extension: 1144*
Principal/Owner: Jerry Dardick
e-mail: jerry@jmdbuilders.com

KERKSTRA PRECAST/SPANCRETE GREAT LAKES ....**(800) 434-5830**
1330 Chicago Dr., Jenison   Fax: (616) 224-2651
See Ad on Page: 285   *800 Extension: 1160*
Principal/Owner: Henry Hofman
Website: www.kerkstra.com   e-mail: hhofman@kerkstra.com
Additional Information: Spancrete uses hollow-core floor planks, so a homeowner
can utilize the space beneath their garage for storage or living

LA DESIGN ....**(847) 615-0707**
1088 W. Everett Rd., Lake Forest   Fax: (847) 615-9678
See Ad on Page: 208, 209   *800 Extension: 1168*
Principal/Owner: Randolph F. Liebelt
e-mail: RLiebeltArch@aol.com
Additional Information: We offer: Design/Build Services, Smart Homes, Period
Architecture and "Green" Architecture.

LICHTENBERGER HOMES ....**(630) 293-9660**
27W031 North Avenue, West Chicago   Fax: (630) 293-9683
See Ad on Page: 252, 253   *800 Extension: 1186*
Principal/Owner: Joseph Lichtenberger

LUCAS - ANDRE BUILDERS..**(847) 735-1264**
725 N. McKinley Road, Ste. 2C, Lake Forest   Fax: (847) 735-1267
See Ad on Page: 254, 255   *800 Extension: 1197*
Principal/Owner: Jeff Andre

MIHOVILOVICH BUILDERS, INC. ....**(847) 395-4795**
24977 Nicklaus Way, Antioch   Fax: (847) 395-4935
See Ad on Page: 273   *800 Extension: 1202*

251

CHARLES L. PAGE ARCHITECT ....**(847) 441-7860**
100 Evergreen Lane, Winnetka   Fax: (847) 441-7862
See Ad on Page: 114, 115, 288, 289   *800 Extension: 1048*
Principal/Owner: Charles Page

"A rock pile ceases to be a
rock pile the moment
a single man contemplates
it, bearing within him
the image of a cathedral.**"**

— *Antoine de Saint- Exupery*

continued on page **262**

LUCAS-ANDRE
BUILDERS
Design • Development • Construction

725 N. McKinley Road, Suite 2C
Lake Forest, IL 60045

P: 847.735.1264 • F: 847.735.1267

GLEN ELLYN HOMES

489 Taft Avenue Glen Ellyn, Illinois 60137   630.469.1070

415 W. Golf Road Suite 6
Arlington Heights, Illinois 60005

Phone: 847.952.1100
Fax: 847.952.1158
Web: www.group-a-architects.com

A

**ARCHITECTS
BUILDERS**

JMD
BUILDERS, INC

444 Lake Cook Rd. Suite 1C
Deerfield Illinois 60015

847.945.9670

Custom Home Builders

ORREN PICKELL DESIGNERS & BUILDERS ....(847) 914-9629
2201 Waukegan Road, Suite W-285, Bannockburn   Fax: (847) 914-9781
See Ad on Page: 263- 270, 294, 295, 487   *800 Extension: 1221*
Principal/Owner: Orren Pickell
Website: www.pickellbuilders.com
Additional Information: Named by Custom Home Magazine as the Nation's "2001 Custom Builder of the Year". Winner of Over 100 Key Awards for Excellence.

THE POULTON GROUP ....(847) 615-1178
268 Market Square, Lake Forest   Fax: (847) 615-1177
See Ad on Page: 194, 229   *800 Extension: 1323*
Principal/Owner: David J. Poulton, AIA
Additional Information: A small, exclusive, high-end residential design/build firm providing new construction, renovation, preservation and interior design services.

REESE CLASSIC RESIDENCE, INC.....................................(847) 913-1680
350 Old McHenry Road, Long Grove   Fax: (847) 913-1684
See Ad on Page: 218   *800 Extension: 1247*
Principal/Owner: Mark Farrahar
Website: www.rclassicres.com e-mail: mark@rclassicres.com
Additional Information: Reese Classic has completed over 80 homes since being established in 1992 and is known for exceptional commitment to customers' needs.

ROBERTS ARCHITECTS LTD. ....(847) 251-7193
2610 Old Glenview Road, Wilmette   Fax: (847) 251-7234
See Ad on Page: 202   *800 Extension: 1254*
Principal/Owner: David Roberts
Website: robertsarchitectsltd.com e-mail: robertsarch@ameritech.net

RUGO/RAFF LTD. ARCHITECTS ....(312) 464-0222
20 W. Hubbard Street, Chicago
See Ad on Page: 148, 149   *800 Extension: 1261*
Principal/Owner: Steven Rugo
e-mail: Steve@RugoRaff.com

SEBERN HOMES, INC...(630) 377-7767
PO Box 1306, St. Charles   Fax: (847) 464-4527
See Ad on Page: 287   *800 Extension: 1271*
Principal/Owner: Ken Bernhard
Website: www.sebernhomes.com

SEVVONCO INC. ....(847) 359-3591
201 East Dundee Road, Palatine   Fax: (847) 359-5123
See Ad on Page: 232, 233   *800 Extension: 1274*
Principal/Owner: Scott Sevon
Website: www.sevvonco.com e-mail: sevvonco@mindspring.com
Additional Information: Illinois First American Lung Association Health House Builder and Remodeler.

SKIFFINGTON ARCHITECTS, LTD. ....(847) 438-3714
250 North Trail, Hawthorn Woods   Fax: (847) 438-3714
See Ad on Page: 185   *800 Extension: 1279*
Principal/Owner: David Patrick Skiffington, AIA
Website: www.skiffingtonarchitects.com e-mail: dskiff@quixnet.net

262

continued on page **280**

It may have begun in your childhood, somewhere in your imagination. Your home, just as you want it. Life without compromise, every single day.

Your Orren Pickell professionals give form to your custom homebuilding or remodeling fantasies and bring your dreams into sharp focus. We guide you through every detail. We never skimp, using only master craftsmen and the finest materials every step of the way. Just look at the results.

lders.c

THE COMPLETE DESIGN EXPERIENCE.
AT ORREN PICKELL DESIGNERS & BUILDERS, WE HAVE THE RESOURCES AND EXPERTISE TO TAKE YOU THROUGH EVERY PHASE OF THE CUSTOM HOMEBUILDING PROCESS.

Site Selection

We will help you find your ideal site. If you already have a site, our designs will reflect the terrain and surrounding neighborhood.

Architectural Design

Our award-winning professional architects use computer-aided design and virtual reality technology. Watch your dreams materialize.

Landscaping

Experts will guide you through every consideration, from the driveway approach to the type of grass, from the vistas to the positioning of trees, shrubs, and trees.

Kitchen and Cabinetry

Award-winning interior designers and master carpenters are on the staff of CabinetWerks, an Orren Pickell company. Their only job is to help you.

Construction Group

You'll experience the dedication of our talented and experienced craftsmen. You'll find that their commitments to highest quality work, on time and within budget, are renewed every day.

Maintenance Division

Your one-year service guarantee begins the day you move into your new home. Many homeowners are so happy with this program that they extend it, assuring that everything is kept fine-tuned for years to come.

Remodeling and Renovation

You'll appreciate the cleanliness, reliability, and painstaking attention to detail of our master craftsmen. Their pride and professionalism extend to highest quality remodeling, renovation, and/or restoration projects.

Behind-the-Scenes

Yours will be the ultimate designing/building experience. Our estimators will keep you on budget while the team guides you through this exciting creative process. We're all there to ensure that your home meets your, and our, highest standards.

Do this for yourself

Call Orren Pickell Designers & Builders today.
Spend the rest of your life in the home of your dreams.

ORREN PICKELL
DESIGNERS & BUILDERS

2201 Waukegan Road • Suite W-285 • Bannockburn, IL 60015
Ph: 847.914.9629 Fax: 847.914.9781
www.pickellbuilders.com

Ullman & Fill, Architects
Wayne Cable Photographer

General Contractor
Construction Management
Fine Home Building
Upscale Condominium Alterations

Ullman & Fill, Architects
Hedrich Blessing Photographers

Ullman & Fill, Architects
Hedrich Blessing Photographers

8322 Lincoln Ave Skokie, IL 60077
847-673-5000 Fax 847-673-5005

Wujcik Construction Group, Inc.

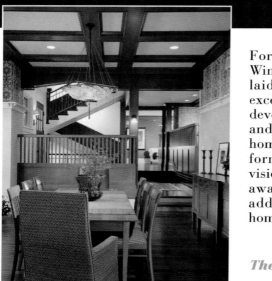

SPEND THE REST OF YOUR LIFE IN THE HOME OF YOUR DREAMS.

ellbuil

Pick

You've waited for this your whole life

DISTINCTIVE CUSTOM HOMES, INC.

611 Rockland Road, Suite 2   Lake Bluff, Illinois 60044
Tel: 847.295.4500 Fax: 847.295.1914

WWW.DISTINCTIVECUSTOMHOME.COM

J&B BUILDERS, INC.

Distinctive Homes

REMODELING / NEW HOMES / CUSTOM DESIGNS

2000 W. MAIN STREET, UNIT H   ST. CHARLES, IL 60174
(630) 587-9900   FAX (630) 587-8566   JBBUILDERS.COM

RENOVATION

BURACK
& COMPANY

DESIGNERS, BUILDERS, AND DEVELOPERS OF DISTINCTIVE PROPERTIES

RAISE YOUR EXPECTATIONS

1741 Green Bay Rd., Highland Park, IL 60035 · (847) 266-3500 · Fax (847) 266-3707

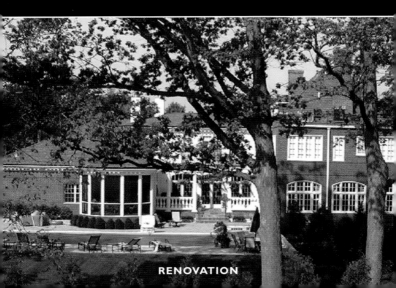

RENOVATION

Custom Home Builders

continued from page **262**

STONEGATE BUILDERS, INC. ....**(847) 579-1525**
1480 Old Deerfield Road #20, Highland Park   Fax: (847) 579-1252
See Ad on Page: 230, 231   *800 Extension: 1288*
Principal/Owner: John Stalowy
Website: www.stonegatebuilders.com   e-mail: Jstalowy@stonegatebuilders.com
Additional Information: A Design/Build firm that prides itself on its' management
style. Employs its' own finishers to maintain control over finished products.

SWANSON + DONAHUE ARCHITECTS ....**(847) 615-8055**
810 S. Waukegan Road, Lake Forest   Fax: (847) 615-2808
See Ad on Page: 154-157   *800 Extension: 1297*
Principal/Owner: Richard M. Swanson, AIA & Thomas F. Donahue, AIA
Website: rmswanson.com   e-mail: swandonarch@aol.com

SWANSON + DONAHUE ARCHITECTS ....**(847) 234-6655**
37 Sherwood Terrace, Suite 122, Lake Bluff   Fax: (847) 234-6635
See Ad on Page: 154-157   *800 Extension: 1298*
Principal/Owner: Richard M. Swanson, AIA & Thomas F. Donahue, AIA
Website: rmswanson.com   e-mail: swandonarch@aol.com

THOMAS HOMES, INC. ....**(630) 734-9693**
115 E. First Street, Hinsdale   Fax: (630) 734-9694
See Ad on Page: 284   *800 Extension: 1327*
Principal/Owner: Judith Linn
Website: www.thomashomesofhinsdale.com
e-mail: www.thomashomesofhinsdale@msn.com

TIP TOP BUILDERS ....**(847) 679-5010**
8255 N. Kimball Avenue, Skokie
See Ad on Page: 282, 283   *800 Extension: 1328*
Principal/Owner: Howard Dardick

280

WINDSOR BUILDERS, INC. ....**(847) 562-9545**
320 Melvin Drive, Suite 9, Northbrook   Fax: (847) 562-9546
See Ad on Page: 281   *800 Extension: 1345*
Principal/Owner: Matthew Kurtyka
e-mail: windsorbld@aol.com

WINDWARD BUILDERS, INC. ....**(847) 295-5132**
1492 Minthaven Road, Lake Forest   Fax: (847) 295-5137
See Ad on Page: 272   *800 Extension: 1348*
Website: www.Windwardbuilders.com

WUJCIK CONTRUCTION GROUP, INC. ....**(847) 673-5000**
8322 N. Lincoln, Skokie   Fax: (847) 673-5005
See Ad on Page: 271   *800 Extension: 1351*
Principal/Owner: Mike Wujcik
Website: wujcik.com   e-mail: wujcikcons@aol.com

WINDSOR BUILDERS, INC.

320 Melvin Dr., Suite 9 Northbrook, IL 60062 847.562.9545 Fax 847.562.9546

8255 N. KIMBALL AVE.
SKOKIE, IL 60076
847-679-5010

Historic.
Renovation

SWANSON + DONAHUE ARCHITECTS ....**(847) 615-8055**
810 S. Waukegan Road, Lake Forest   Fax: (847) 615-2808
See Ad on Page: 154-157   *800 Extension: 1299*
Principal/Owner: Richard M. Swanson, AIA & Thomas F. Donahue, AIA
Website: rmswanson.com   e-mail: swandonarch@aol.com

SWANSON + DONAHUE ARCHITECTS ....**(847) 234-6655**
37 Sherwood Terrace, Suite 122, Lake Bluff   Fax: (847) 234-6635
See Ad on Page: 154-157   *800 Extension: 1301*
Principal/Owner: Richard M. Swanson, AIA & Thomas F. Donahue, AIA
Website: rmswanson.com   e-mail: swandonarch@aol.com

**"First impressions count…
whether building a dream
home or restoring a relic
from the past, attention
to details is needed."**

— *Adams Stair Work & Carpentry , Inc.*

SeBern Homes, Inc....

AN ELITE AWARD WINNING CUSTOM HOME BUILDER

- Innovative Designs
- Personal Commitment to Quality
- Superior Craftsmanship

Building Custom Homes In Your Area.

SeBern Homes, Inc.
630.377.7767
www.sebernhomes.com

Page Builders, Inc.
100 Evergreen Lane Winnetka, IL 60093
847.441.7860

The Page Company provides complete services from site acquisition through concept, design, planning, construction, finishing and landscaping for over 35 years on the North Shore.

Charles L. Page, Architect
100 Evergreen Lane Winnetka, IL 60093
847 . 441 . 7860

Charles L. Page, Archiect is known for his authentic interpretation of French and English traditional architecture

Remodeling
Specialists

AMDEGA CONSERVATORIES ....**(847) 277-9190**
421 N. Northwest Hwy., Barrington   Fax: (847) 277-9008
See Ad on Page: 291   *800 Extension: 1007*
Principal/Owner: Bonnie Miske

ARMCOR DESIGN & BUILD/FOUR SEASONS SUNROOMS ....**(847) 487-7900**
951 N. Old Rand Rd. (Main St.), Wauconda   Fax: (847) 487-7902
See Ad on Page: 441   *800 Extension: 1014*
Website: www.armcor-fourseasons.com
Additional Information: We specialize in high performance glass structures and mon-
umental skylights, conservatories, sunrooms, greenhouses and solariums.

BRYAN ASSOCIATES, INC. - ARCHITECTS ....**(630) 920-0777**
522 Chestnut Street, Suite 2B, Hinsdale   Fax: (630) 920-0778
See Ad on Page: 206   *800 Extension: 1031*
Principal/Owner: Daniel W. Bryan
e-mail: BryanRKTEC@msn.com
Additional Information: Established in 1986, Bryan Associates offers client-centered,
thoughtful and creative expertise in architectural design of new custom homes and
historically accurate residential renovations and remodelings.

BURACK & COMPANY ....**(847) 266-3500**
1741 Green Bay Road, Highland Park   Fax: (847) 266-3707
See Ad on Page: 278, 279   *800 Extension: 1036*
Principal/Owner: Robert Burack

CEDAR ROOFING COMPANY, INC...**(847) 247-4400**
27820 N. Irma Lee Circle, Lake Forest   Fax: (847) 247-4405
See Ad on Page: 297   *800 Extension: 1042*
Principal/Owner: Matt Wilkinson
Website: www.cedarinc.com e-mail: sales@cedarinc.com

GLEN ELLYN HOMES ....**(630) 469-1070**
489 Taft Avenue, Glen Ellyn   Fax: (630) 469-1356
See Ad on Page: 256, 257   *800 Extension: 1113*
Principal/Owner: Douglas Walksler/Thomas Gale
e-mail: gehomes@aol.com
Additional Information: Custom homes and premium properties in Chicago's
Western suburbs.

KEYSTONE BUILDERS, INC...**(847) 432-4392**
3435 Old Mill Road, Highland Park   Fax: (847) 432-4395
See Ad on Page: 292, 293   *800 Extension: 1162*
Principal/Owner: Joanna & Stan Szymel
Website: www.keystone-builders.com e-mail: sales@keystone-builders.com

LICHTENBERGER HOMES ....**(630) 293-9660**
27W031 North Avenue, West Chicago   Fax: (630) 296-9683
See Ad on Page: 252, 253   *800 Extension: 1185*
Principal/Owner: Joseph Lichtenberger

LUCAS - ANDRE BUILDERS..**(847) 735-1264**
725 N. McKinley Road, Ste. 2C, Lake Forest   Fax: (847) 735-1267
See Ad on Page: 254, 255   *800 Extension: 1198*
Principal/Owner: Jeff Andre

continued on page **288**

AMDEGA

conservatories & garden buildings

421 Northwest Highway
Suite 201
Barrington, IL 60010

800.521.8990
• • •
www.amdega.com

The Sign of Excellence is in

DESIGN/BUILD,
NEW HOMES, ADDITIONS
AND RENOVATIONS.

You may have noticed our sign popping up around the neighborhood as we begin building new homes or creative renovation projects for your neighbors. If you're thinking about improving your home or building a new home, please give us a call to talk about your ideas. From a gallery of styles for your kitchens and baths, to elegant home expansions, we can help you develop ideas that will give you the best value for each dollar you invest.

AWARD WINNING EXCELLENCE IN REMODELING, RENOVATION AND RESTORATION ... FROM THE ORREN PICKELL REMODELING GROUP.

ORREN PICKELL
REMODELING GROUP

2201 Waukegan Road • Suite W-285
Bannockburn, IL 60015
Ph: 847.914.9629 Fax: 847.914.9781
www.pickellbuilders.com

Photography By Linda Oyman Bryan

Custom Home Builders

continued from page **290**

LOREN REID SEAMAN & ASSOCIATES ....**(847) 550-6363**
22742 N. Lakewood Lane, Lake Zurich   Fax: (847) 550-6464
728 W. Jackson, Chicago, IL
See Ad on Page: 336, 337   *800 Extension: 1195*
Principal/Owner: Loren Reid Seaman
Additional Information: Full service interior remodeling and design.

STONEGATE BUILDERS, INC. ....**(847) 579-1525**
1480 Old Deerfield Road #20, Highland Park   Fax: (847) 579-1252
See Ad on Page: 230, 231   *800 Extension: 1290*
Principal/Owner: John Stalowy
Website: www.stonegatebuilders.com   e-mail: Jstalowy@stonegatebuilders.com
Additional Information: A Design/Build firm that prides itself on its' management
style. Employs its' own finishers to maintain control over finished products.

W.E.S. ENTERPRISES, INC. ....**(847) 931-5491**
75 Market Street, Suite 20A, Elgin   Fax: (847) 931-8966
See Ad on Page: 481   *800 Extension: 1341*
Principal/Owner: William E. Severance
Website: www.kitchensbyWES.com   e-mail: wesenterprises@home.com
Additional Information: Professional remodeling contractors specializing in Kitchens
and Baths.

WINDSOR BUILDERS, INC. ....**(847) 562-9545**
320 Melvin Drive, Suite 9, Northbrook   Fax: (847) 562-9546
See Ad on Page: 281   *800 Extension: 1346*
Principal/Owner: Matthew Kurtyka
e-mail: windsorbld@aol.com

WINDWARD BUILDERS, INC. ....**(847) 295-5132**
1492 Minthaven Road, Lake Forest   Fax: (847) 295-5137
See Ad on Page: 272   *800 Extension: 1347*
Website: www.Windwardbuilders.com

WUJCIK CONTRUCTION GROUP, INC. ....**(847) 673-5000**
8322 N. Lincoln, Skokie   Fax: (847) 673-5005
See Ad on Page: 271   *800 Extension: 1352*
Principal/Owner: Mike Wujcik
Website: wujcik.com   e-mail: wujcikcons@aol.com

296

"Man needs a serene
architectural background
to save his sanity
in today's world."

— *Minoru Tamasaki*

Proudly Serving the North Shore for Over 20 years

Cedar Roofing Company has long been considered the North Shore's resident expert on cedar shakes and shingles.

Our expertise also includes slate and tile, cedar shingle siding, modified bitumen flat roofing, asphalt shingles, custom sheet metal, and gutters & downspouts.

27820 N. Irma Lee Circle
Lake Forest, IL 60045
(847) 247-4400
Website: www.cedarinc.com

Cedar Shake &
Shingle Bureau

Roofing
Specialists

CEDAR ROOFING COMPANY, INC...**(847) 247-4400**
27820 N. Irma Lee Circle, Lake Forest   Fax: (847) 247-4405
See Ad on Page: 297   *800 Extension: 1041*
<u>Principal/Owner:</u> Matt Wilkinson
<u>Website:</u> www.cedarinc.com <u>e-mail:</u> sales@cedarinc.com

"All architecture is shelter, all great
architecture is the design of space
that contains, cuddles, exalts, or
stimulates the persons in that space.**"**

— Phillip Johnson

INTERIOR DESIGNERS

LARSON ASSOCIATES
Interior Design • Architecture

542 SOUTH DEARBORN CHICAGO, IL 60605
312-786-2255 FAX: 312-786-2290

JANIE PETKUS INTERIORS

110 South Washington Street
Hinsdale, Illinois 60521
630.325.3242

www.janiepetkus.com

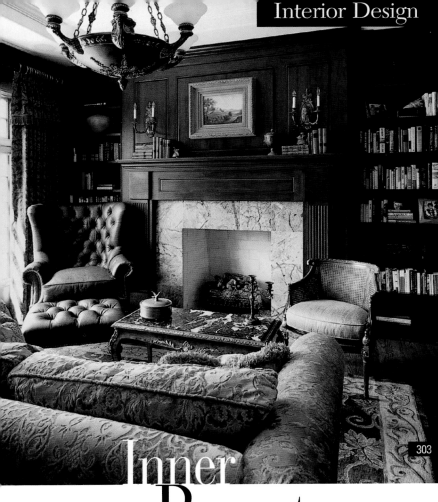

303

Inner Beauty

It may be as simple as a fresh look at the familiar. Or it may be an involved process requiring major renovation. In either case, interior designers can bring your ideas to life by demystifying the daunting task of designing a home. With their years of professional experience and the tools that they have at their fingertips, designers can orchestrate, layer by layer, design elements that compose an inviting and harmonious décor. For this collaboration to be a success, however, requires communication and trust. By listening to your dreams and by understanding your needs, designers can fashion workable rooms that are visual delights, reflecting your personality and spirit. The end result of a productive partnership should be a happy homeowner who can exclaim, "I've always known that this was a great house, but now it's home!"

Photo courtesy of **Orren Pickell Builders**

FIVE THINGS YOU SHOULD KNOW

1. Know what level of guidance you want: a person to handle every detail, someone to collaborate with you or simply an occasional consultation.

2. Know what you're trying to achieve. Start an Idea Notebook, filling it with pictures of rooms you like and don't like. This will help you define your style and stay true to your goal.

3. Know your budget. Prices of high-end furnishings know no upper limit. Adopt a "master plan" to phase in design elements if your tastes are outpacing your pocketbook.

4. Know what's going on. Always ask; don't assume. Design is not a mystical process.

5. Know yourself. Don't get blinded by beauty. Stay focused on what makes you feel "at home," and you'll be successful.

304

WHERE STRUCTURE MEETS INSPIRATION

A great interior designer, like a great architect or builder, sees space creatively, applying years of education and experience to deliver a distinguished residence at the highest level of quality in an organized, professional manner. Intensely visual, these talented individuals imprint a home with the spirit and personality of the family living there.

Creativity, that special talent to see the possibilities in a living room, library, or little reading nook, is the most important asset an interior designer will bring to a project. Particularly in upper-end interiors, where the expense of sumptuous furnishings is often a secondary concern, the creative vision is what makes a room extraordinary.

A top quality interior designer who is licensed by the state is well educated in the field of interior design, usually holding a bachelor's or master's degree in the subject. This educational background coupled with practical experience is vital. You need not know where to get the best down-filled pillows or when French fabric mills close each summer. You need not learn the difference between French Country and English Country, how to match patterns, or how to correctly balance a floor plan. Rely on a knowledgeable designer for that information.

A great interior designer also handles the "nuts and bolts" business end of the project. With skill and experience in placing and tracking orders, scheduling shipping, delivery and installation, the designer can bring your project to its perfect conclusion.

AN INTERIOR DESIGNER IS A TEAM MEMBER

Choose an interior designer when you select your architect, builder, and landscape architect. A skilled designer can collaborate with the architect on matters such as window and door location, appropriate room size, and practical and accent lighting plans. In new construction and remodeling, try to make your floor plan and furniture choices simultaneously, to avoid common design problems, such as traffic corridors running through a formal space or awkward locations of electrical outlets.

CREATE THE BEST CLIENT-DESIGNER RELATIONSHIP

Talk to the best interior designers in the area and they'll tell you how exciting and gratifying it is for them when a client is involved in the process. This is happening as more homeowners turn their attention to hearth and home, dedicating their time and resources to achieve a style they love.

To establish the most successful and pleasant

relationship with an interior designer, make a personal commitment to be involved.

Start by defining your needs, in terms of service and the end result. Have an interior designer involved during the architectural drawing phase of a new or renovation project, and get the process started early. Be clear about how much help you want from a designer. Some homeowners have a strong sense of what they want and simply need a consultant-type relationship. Others want significant guidance from a professional who will oversee the entire process.

Set up a relationship that encourages an open exchange of ideas. In pursuit of personal style, you need a trust a professional designer to interpret your thoughts and needs. You must be comfortable saying, "No, I don't like that," and receptive to hearing, "I don't think that's a good idea."

Be forthcoming about your budget. Not all interiors are guided by a budget, but the majority are. Your designer must know and respect your financial parameters and priorities. If a gorgeous dining room table is a top priority, objets d' art can be added later as you find them. Prices of exquisite furniture, custom-carved cabinets, and other high-end furnishings know no upper limit. Be realistic about what you will spend and what you expect to achieve. Do some research in furniture stores and specialty shops, starting with those showcased in this book. If your expectations temporarily exceed your budget, phase in the dÈcor over a period of time.

Be inquisitive as the design unfolds. This is a creative effort on your behalf, so let yourself enjoy it, understand it and be stimulated by it.

START THINKING VISUALLY: STOP, LOOK AND CLIP

Before you start scheduling initial interviews with interior designers, start compiling an Idea Notebook — it's the best tool for developing an awareness of your personal style. Spend a weekend or two with a pair of scissors, a notebook, and a stack of magazines, (or add a section to the Idea Notebook you made to inspire your architecture and building plans). Make this a record of your personal style. Include pictures of your favorite rooms, noting colors, fabrics, tile, carpet, fixtures, the way light filters through a curtain, anything that strikes your fancy. On those pictures, circle the design elements that you'd like to incorporate into your own home dÈcor and make comments regarding those elements you don't care for. Think hard about what you love and loathe in your current residence. Start to look at the entire environment as a rich source of design ideas. Movies, billboards, architecture, clothing - all are fascinating sources for visual stimulation.

Then, when you hold that initial meeting, you, too, will have a book of ideas to share. Although a smart

UNDERSTANDING "ECLECTIC"

Eclectic means "not following any one system, but selecting and using what seems best from all systems." Its popularity in interior design stems from the unique look it creates. Mixing the best from different styles creates a dynamic look that's totally different from an application of one chosen style. The overall effect is casual and comfortable, "dressed up" in a less formal way. Eclectic can mean a mixing of styles within one room, like a rich Oriental rug paired with a denim sofa, or between rooms, like an 18th century dining room leading into an Early American kitchen. The possibilities for accents and appointments are unlimited because there are no restrictions.

305

One Person's Project Estimate:

Time To Redesign

It's fun to imagine, but what might it actually cost to undertake a project described in this chapter? The example below describes a typical project and gives a general estimate of the costs involved.

Project Description
Redesigning a 15 x 22 sq. ft. living room in a mid-scale price range for a condo.

Initial consultation $500
During the initial consultation, dimensions of the room are measured and photos taken of the room's distinctive qualities (unusual architecture, fireplaces, French doors, etc.). Next, a floor plan is done with recommendations of furniture placement.

Cost per hour (5 hour minimum) $100/hr
These charges apply to trips to local showrooms, the design center or antique shops to choose fabrics, furniture, and accessories. After the furniture is ordered, attention is turned to window treatments (photographing the windows and using the pictures as sketchboards to design various treatments, fabrics and colors). When designing kitchens and bathrooms, time may also be spent with clients and contractors discussing styles of cabinetry, countertops and flooring.

New rug (oriental or custom) $8,000

Furniture: Transitional (contemporary upholstery, traditional wood pieces)
         Sofa $3,000
         Chairs (2) .... $1,000 ea.
         Coffee table $2,000
         End tables (2) .... $1,000 ea.
         Sofa table $2,000
         French Be'rgre chair $3,000

Lamps (1 bronze, 2 porcelain) $1,200
Lighted wall sconces $1,000
Artwork $2,000
         1 large piece over sofa
         1 smaller piece over the fireplace
New paint
         Labor and paint (one color) $1,500
Accessories $3,000
         Silver tray with crystal decanter and 2 brandy snifters,
         large candlesticks.
         Crystal vase and several unusual picture frames in sterling and brass.

TOTAL $31,700

Note: The entire cost for a room design does not necessarily have to be paid at one time. Many designers are willing to work with a client over several years, adding a few items at a time, in order to create the look that is right for the client and his/her surroundings.

Lighted wall sconces
to flank the fireplace

Contemporary
chair

IMMERSE
YOURSELF

The more
exposure you
have to good
design, the easier
it becomes to
develop your
own style.

• Haunt the
bookstores
that have large
selections of
shelter magazines
and stacks of
books on
decorating,
design and
architecture.
• Attend show
houses,
especially
the Designer
Showcase homes
presented twice
annually by
ASID, and visit
model homes,
apartments or
lofts.

designer will be able to coax this information from you, it's tremendously more reliable to have visual representations than to depend on a verbal description. It also saves a tremendous amount of time.

THE INTERIOR DESIGN PROCESS: GETTING TO KNOW YOU

Give yourself time to interview at least two interior designers. Invite them to your home for a tour of your current residence and a look at items you wish to use in the new environment. If you're building or remodeling, an interior designer can be helpful with your overall plans when he or she is given the opportunity to get involved early in the building process.

During the initial meeting, count on your intuition to guide you toward the best designer for you. Decorating a home is an intimate and very personal experience, so a comfortable relationship with a high degree of trust is absolutely necessary for a good result. You may adore what a designer did for a friend, but if you can't easily express your ideas, or if you feel he or she isn't interested in your point of view, don't pursue the relationship. Unless you can imagine yourself working with a designer two or three homes from now, keep interviewing.

You may wish to hire a designer for one room before making a commitment to do the whole house.

Some designers maintain a high degree of confidentiality regarding their clients, but if possible, get references and contact them, especially clients with whom they've worked on more than one home. Be sure to ask about the quality of follow-up service.

Be prepared to talk in specific terms about your project, and to honestly assess your lifestyle. For a home or a room to work well, function must be considered along with the evolving style. Designers ask many questions; some of them may be:

• What function should each room serve? Will a living room double as a study? Will a guest room also be an exercise area?

• Who uses the rooms? Growing children, adults, business associates? Which are shared and which are private?

• What safety and maintenance issues must be addressed? A growing family or a family pet may dictate the degree of elegance of a home.

• What kind of relationship do you want to establish between the interior and the landscape?

• Style: Formal, casual or a bit of both?

- Are you comfortable with color?

- Are you sentimental, practical?

- Are you naturally organized or disorganized?

- What kind of art do you like? Do you own art that needs to be highlighted or displayed in a certain way? Do you need space for a growing collection?

- Do you feel at home in a dog-eared, low maintenance family room or do you soothe your soul in an opulent leather chair, surrounded by rich cabinetry and Oriental rugs?

- What kind of furniture do you like? Queen Anne, contemporary, American Arts and Crafts, casual wicker, or eclectic mixing of styles?

- What words describe the feeling you want to achieve? Cheerful, cozy, tranquil, elegant, classic?

COMPUTING THE INTERIOR DESIGN FEE

Designers use individual contracts, standard contracts drawn up by the American Society of Interior Designers (ASID), or letters of agreements as legal documents. The ASID contract outlines seven project phases — programming, schematic, design development, contract documents, contract administration, project representation beyond basic services, and additional services. It outlines the designer's special responsibilities, the owner's responsibilities, the fees agreed upon, and the method of payments to the designer, including reimbursement of expenses.

Payment deadlines vary. Payments may be due at the completion of each project phase, on a monthly or quarterly basis, or as orders are made. You can usually expect to pay a retainer or a 50 percent deposit on goods as they are ordered, 40 percent upon the start of installation, and the balance when the job is completed.

Design fees, which may be based on "current market rate," are also computed in various ways. They may be charged on a flat fee or hourly basis, or may be tied to retail costs. Expect fees of approximately $100 an hour, varying by experience, reputation and workload. If an hourly rate is being used, ask if there is a cap per day, and if different rates are charged for an assistant's or drafter's time. Percentages may be figured as a certain amount above the retail or trade price, and can range from 15 to 100 percent. Make sure you understand your fee structure early on. Separate design fees may be charged by the hour, room, or entire project. It is imperative to trust your designer and rely on his or her reputation of delivering a top quality project in an honest, reliable fashion. You must feel you're being

PROFESSIONAL
DESIGNATIONS

ASID (American Society of Interior Designers)/Chicago 1647 Merchandise Mart Chicago, IL 60654 312.467.5080

IIDA (International Interior Design Association) International Headquarters 998 Merchandise Mart Chicago, IL 60654 312.467.1950 www.iida.org email: IIDAhq@iida.org Offers referrals to Chicago area homeowners.

Designers who add ASID or IIDA after their names are certified members of the organization.

309

EMBRACE THE MASTER PLAN

Gone are the days when South Florida homeowners felt the need to move into a "finished" interior. They take their time now, letting the flow of their evolving lifestyle and needs guide them along the way.

310

MAKE LIGHTING A PRIORITY

The trend toward a comprehensive lighting programs as part of good interior design is catching on in South Florida luxury homes. Appropriate light and well-designed accent lighting are very important to the overall comfort and functionality of a home. Neither the stunning volume ceiling nor the cozy breakfast nook can reach their potential if the lighting is wrong. Ask your interior designer for his or her lighting ideas. These choices need to be made in coordination with the building timeline, so plan and place orders early.

given a valuable service for a fair price.

If you work with a designer at a retail store, a design service fee ranging from $100 to $500 may be charged and applied against purchases.

FROM THE MIND'S EYE TO REALITY

Once you've found a designer who you like and trust, and have signed a clear, specific agreement, you're ready to embark on the adventure.

A good designer knows his or her way around the masses of products and possibilities. Such a person will guide you through upscale retail outlets and to craftspeople known only to a fortunate few in the trade. You can be a "kid in a candy store."

Just as you've allowed time to carefully consider and reconsider architectural blueprints, temper your enthusiasm to rush into decisions regarding your interiors. Leave fabric swatches where you see them day after day. Look at paint samples in daylight, evening light and artificial light. If possible, have everyone in the family "test sit" a kitchen chair for a week before ordering the whole set, and play with furniture placement. This small investment of time will pay handsomely in the end.

Be prepared to wait for your interiors to be installed. It's realistic to allow eight months to complete a room, and eight to 12 months to decorate an entire home.

Decide if you want your interiors to be installed piecemeal or all at once. Many designers recommend waiting for one installation, if you have the patience. Homeowners tend to rethink their original decisions when pieces are brought in as they arrive. By waiting for one installation, they treat themselves to a stunning visual and emotional thrill. ■

Project
Description

The project included redesigning every existing room along with planning and decorating a 3,500 sq. ft. addition. In all, the home has two family rooms, a great room, a theater, kitchen and dining rooms, screen porches with dining, and six bedrooms and baths. There is also a two-bedroom, two-bath guest house on the property. The project took approximately 18 months, which is a long time for a design-only project, but not long for new construction.

Creating a **Beautiful** Interior

Select an Interior Designer

Meet with several designers and ask questions. Consider personality, style and business methods when making your decision. Look at the designer's portfolio, ask for references and call them. Be sure you are comfortable with your choice—you'll be working together a long time.

MONTH 1

Create a Furniture Floor Plan

This very preliminary plan is done with furniture shapes and prototypical sizes. The purpose is to test the rooms and the lighting plan to determine such things as: Do the rooms seat the number of people you had in mind? Can you fit your existing furniture? Is traffic flow working?

MONTH 2

Review Electrical Plan

Once the preliminary floor plan is in place, review it against the electrical design of the space to be sure it will support the demand of the lighting and technology planned for the room.

Determine Flooring Type

Wood, tile, area rugs or wall-to-wall carpeting? The rest of the design of the room will evolve from the style of the flooring materials you choose.

MONTH 3

Why use an Interior Designer

A designer will help you define your style and keep your project focused to minimize costly decorating mistakes. Designers have knowledge, training and, most importantly, resources. They can handle the myriad of details while you enjoy the results.

• **As you begin,** take some time to ask yourself some questions regarding your project. For whom is the space being designed? What activities will take place there? What is your time frame for the project? What is your budget? What image do you want to project? Keep in mind, the more information you provide, the more successful the designer will be in meeting your needs and expectations.

• **Keep focused.** Your designer is responsible for providing all the information you will need to make decisions, but you must ultimately make the decisions in a timely manner to keep your project on track and meet the dates in your timeline.

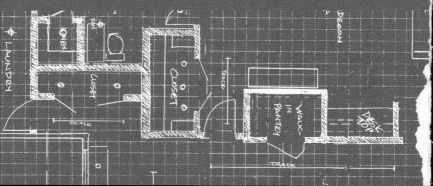

Begin Visiting Showrooms

Start looking at cabinetry, furniture, rugs, fixtures, and accessories to narrow down your choices. In some cases, clients visit the designer's studio to view selections. In others, the designer brings items, catalogs, swatches, etc. to the client's home.

Make Final Flooring, Cabinetry, Tile and Stone Selections

These items usually require professional installation, so they must be ordered first.

Workmen Begin Installation

First the flooring and tile will be installed, then cabinets and woodwork, countertops, plumbing fixtures and faucets.

MONTH 4   MONTH 5   MONTH 8

Communicate
It is important to establish parameters for updates on your project. The communication between you and your interior designer needs to be on-going.

• **Allow plenty of time.** Take as much time as you need to make your choices. You should be able to choose what you want and not be limited to choices because not enough time was allowed to view selections. Keep in mind that many decisions affect others, so once you have decided, try not to second guess or change your mind.

Creating a **Beautiful** Interior

Y ou have found your paradise. You have fallen in love with the area around your new home. The views are spectacular. The entrance is grand and suitably impressive. The great room will be a place where family, friends and visitors will all feel at ease, and all will be welcomed within. You can envision it, but how do you get from dreaming the dream to living it? Beautiful rooms do not just happen. They are the result of careful planning by the homeowner and an interior designer. While you may have an idea of what you would like, or have a desire for a particular effect, it is the interior designer who can take your dream and turn it into something magnificent.

We have taken one family's dream, to create a spectacular, yet comforting home, and followed that project from the day the client bought the home to the day the rooms they once dreamed of became rooms they now live in.

The following timeline is designed to give you an idea of how long it may take to complete an interior design project of this magnitude, and what the steps will be along the way. While the steps will most likely remain the same, the timeline may shorten or lengthen depending on your individual project. We have also included a few helpful tips and ideas, to further ensure that your project can go as smoothly as possible.

FINISHED PROJECT

● **Make Final Selections of Accessories and Artwork**
Now is the time to select the accessories that will give the rooms your personal touch.

Schedule a Thorough House Cleaning
A professional cleaning is recommended to remove construction dust before moving final furnishings into place.

MONTH 16

● **Final Installations Begin**
Workmen will be putting the final touches on the project, installing lighting fixtures, window treatments and rugs.

MONTH 18

● **Place Furniture and Accessories**
Put the furniture in place, add accessories and artwork, relax and enjoy!

• **Show off your collection.** Many homeowners have a collection, be it antique cameras, sculpture, majolica, vintage perfume bottles, glass, art, or guns and swords. A well-designed display of your collection can put the finishing touch on your decorating project. Arrange a grouping in one area for a bold statement. Divide a very large collection into subsets and display them in several rooms to create a theme in your home. Vary heights and sizes for visual appeal, place small items at eye level, larger ones on the floor.

Stay Flexible
Be aware that product availability and contractor scheduling problems may cause unavoidable delays. Building extra time into your schedule can help avoid stress between you and your designer.

SPONSORED BY:

Susan Fredman & Associates
425 Huehl Road, #6B
Northbrook, IL 60062
847.509.5121 Fax: 847.509.4111
info@susanfredman.com
www.susanfredman.com

Finishing the Work

Final sanding, sealing, carpeting and closet shelving complete the job. Allow three to four months for the interior work and final items to take place.

Make Final Furniture Selections

Order furniture in plenty of time to account for inevitable delays. Custom furniture will take more time.

Order Window Treatments

When window framing is complete, final measurements can be made for window treatments.

MONTH 11 MONTH 14 MONTH 15

• **Create a project file.** Keep carpet, fabric, wallpaper and paint samples, floor plans, a tape measure, calendar, phone list and your photo clippings together in an easy-to-carry file or project folder to reference at home and when out shopping for your rooms. With your project file in hand, decisions can be made on the spot without having to check if the upholstery matches or the piece fits into your overall plan.

Work Together

To ensure your project remains uniquely yours, continue to explore stores, websites, magazines and books for furnishings, styles, colors and accessories you like. Tell your designer your preferences. Be open to the new ideas your designer may offer, but pay attention to your gut feelings.

In
Conclusion

N ow that you have seen an interior design project guided from beginning to end, it's time to embark on your own project. Yes, it will take some time to complete. And it will require a certain amount of involvement from you and communication with the designer. But in the end, you will have a space that is uniquely yours. You will have rooms that welcome you in, views you enjoy, furnishings that fit and details that express who you are. It can be a long journey, but one with a remarkable payoff.

Thanks to Janet Mesic Mackie for her contribution of photography for this timeline.

Produced by The Ashley Group
847.390.2882
www.theashleygroup.com

DALE CAROL ANDERSON, LTD. ....**(773) 348-5200**
2030 N. Magnolia, Chicago
See Ad on Page: 340, 341
Principal/Owner: Mrs. Dale Anderson
Fax: (773) 348-5271
800 Extension: 1068

LAURA BARNETT DESIGNS ....**(312) 654-1706**
213 West Institute Place, Ste 706, Chicago
See Ad on Page: 359
Principal/Owner: Laura Barnett
e-mail: lbdesigns1@qwest.net
Additional Information: Established 1980- full service design, project supervision, specification and/or purchasing of furnishings, fabrics and accessories.
Fax: (312) 654-8706
800 Extension: 1179

CHARLES FILL ARCHITECTS, LLC ....**(773) 548-5980**
1021 E. 48th St., Chicago
See Ad on Page: 189
Principal/Owner: Charles W. Fill
Fax: (312) 944-0541
800 Extension: 1046

FLORIAN ARCHITECTS ....**(312) 670-2220**
432 North Clark, Ste. 200, Chicago
See Ad on Page: 195
Principal/Owner: Paul Florian
Website: www.florianarchitects.com e-mail: info@florianarchitects.com
Fax: (312) 670-2221
800 Extension: 1097

SUSAN FREDMAN & ASSOCIATES, LTD. ....**(847) 509-4121**
425 Huehl Rd. #6B, Northbrook
See Ad on Page: 330, 331
Principal/Owner: Susan Fredman
Website: www.susanfredman.com e-mail: info@susanfredman.com
Fax: (847) 509-4111
800 Extension: 1295

GEUDTNER & MELICHAR ARCHITECTS ....**(847) 295-2440**
711 N. McKinley Road, Lake Forest
See Ad on Page: 150, 151
Principal/Owner: Diana Melichar
Fax: (847) 295-2451
800 Extension: 1110

ELINOR GORDON DESIGN, INC. ....**(312) 335-0220**
999 N. Lake Shore Dr., Chicago
See Ad on Page: 356
Principal/Owner: Elinor Gordon
e-mail: egdesign@21stcentury.net
Fax: (312) 335-0222
800 Extension: 1080

319

GRAY & WALTER, LTD. ....**(847) 853-1940**
1018 11th Street, Wilmette
See Ad on Page: 332, 333
Principal/Owner: Kenneth Walter, ASID
Website: www.kennethwalter.com e-mail: kennethwalter@msn.com
Fax: (847) 853-9751
800 Extension: 1115

GREGGA JORDAN SMIESZNY INC. ....**(312) 787-0017**
1203 N. State Parkway, Chicago
See Ad on Page: 324, 325
Principal/Owner: Alex Jordan and Dan Smieszny
e-mail: info@gjsinc.com
Fax: (312) 787-5108
800 Extension: 1116

LOIS B. GRIES INTERIOR DESIGN ....**(312) 222-9202**
400 N. Wells Street #416, Chicago
See Ad on Page: 360
Principal/Owner: Lois Gries, ASID
Website: www.loisgries.com e-mail: loisbgries@aol.com
Fax: (312) 222-9207
800 Extension: 1192

H & R CUSTOM DESIGNS ....**(847) 562-0487**
300 Skokie Blvd., Northbrook
See Ad on Page: 364
Principal/Owner: Helene Weiner
Fax: (847) 562-9487
800 Extension: 1120

KAUFMAN SEGAL DESIGN ....**(312) 649-0680**
900 N. Franklin Street, Ste 710, Chicago
See Ad on Page: 366, 367
Principal/Owner: David Kaufman & Tom Segal
Website: www.kaufmansegaldesign.com
Fax: (312) 649-0689
800 Extension: 1153

LARSON ASSOCIATES ....**(312) 786-2255**
542 S. Dearborn, Chicago
See Ad on Page: 162, 300, 301, 334
Principal/Owner: George Larson
Fax: (312) 786-2290
800 Extension: 1176

LORI LENNON & ASSOCIATES ....**(847) 482-0165**
350 South Ashland Lane, Lake Forest
See Ad on Page: 354, 355
Principal/Owner: Lori Lennon
Fax: (847) 482-0166
800 Extension: 1196

continued on page **335**

SANDRA SALTZMAN INTERIORS

1430 NORTH ASTOR STREET
CHICAGO, ILLINOIS 60610
312.642.8381 Fax 312.642.8402
SAVGA10@AOL.COM

Sarah Van Assche Interiors

Design

Space Planning

Decoration

EVA QUATEMAN

INTERIORS • RENOVATIONS

773 • 472 • 0522

Gregga Jordan Smieszny

Bruce Gregga

Alex Jordan

Dan Smieszny

1203 N. State Pkwy
Chicago, IL 60610
Phone 312 787 0017
Fax 312 787 5108
Email info@GJSInc.com

Photography: James Yochum©

Photography: Wayne Cable©

ARLENE SEMEL & ASSOCIATES, INC.

Photography: Wayne Cable©

CHICAGO

312·644 1480

DESIGN MAGIC

MAKING A DIFFERENCE IN THE NON-PROFIT COMMUNITY

JOIN US IN SUPPORTING THE SPIRIT!

Supporting the Spirit Foundation (SSF),
is a new non-profit organization founded on
the belief that all people are entitled to live and
work within environments that seek to heal
and comfort the spirit. In alliance with
the Illinois Chapter of the American Society
of Interior Designers and the Illinois
Facilities Fund,

SSF works to enhance
the environments of non-profit
organizations such as childcare facilities,
assisted living centers, and shelters of domestic
violence by providing a wide scope of design
services and materials on a pro bono basis.
Volunteer designers and industry professionals
contribute their time and talent to tackle both
large and small projects.

For everyone at
Supporting the Spirit Foundation,
renovation truly does mean renewal!

SUPPORTING THE
SPIRIT
FOUNDATION

SSF is located in donated office space at The Merchandise
Mart. For more information or to make a donation,
please call at 312/832-9944 or 847/509-4121.

Olafsen Design Group

William D.B. Olafsen, ASID
233 East Erie, Suite 305
Chicago, Illinois 60611
312.664.4738

425 Huehl Road, #6B

Northbrook, IL 60062

847.509.4121

847.509.4111 Fax

info@susanfredman.com

www.susanfredman.com

SUSAN FREDMAN
AND ASSOCIATES

1018 11th Street • Wilmete, IL 60091
847/853-1940 • Fax 847/853-9751
159 West Kinzie Street • Chicago, IL 60610
312/329-1007 • Fax 312/527-4445
www.kennethwalter.com

GRAY & WALTER ASSOC

LARSON ASSOCIATES

Interior Design • Architecture

542 SOUTH DEARBORN   CHICAGO, IL 60605

312-786-2255   FAX: 312-786-2290

continued from page **319**

OFF THE BOLT ....**(312) 587-0046**
   1333 N. Kingsbury, Ste. 309, Chicago   Fax: (312) 587-0638
   See Ad on Page: 621   *800 Extension: 1216*
   <u>Principal/Owner:</u> Noreen Fremont

OLAFSEN DESIGN GROUP ....**(312) 664-4738**
   233 East Erie, Suite 305, Chicago
   See Ad on Page: 329   *800 Extension: 1220*

PAGE ONE INTERIORS INC. ....**(847) 382-1001**
   320 E. Main, Barrington   Fax: (847) 382-0484
   See Ad on Page: 362   *800 Extension: 1226*
   <u>Principal/Owner:</u> Adele Lampert, ASID
   <u>Website:</u> interiorspageone.com <u>e-mail:</u> pageoneinteriors@aol.com
   <u>Additional Information:</u> Beautiful showroom with antiques, reproductions and accessories. Full design sevices including architectural & CAD, residential & commercial.

PAGE ONE INTERIORS INC. ....**(312) 587-8490**
   707 N. Wells, Chicago
   See Ad on Page: 362   *800 Extension: 1229*
   <u>Principal/Owner:</u> Adele Lampert, ASID
   <u>Website:</u> interiorspageone.com <u>e-mail:</u> pageoneinteriors@aol.com
   <u>Additional Information:</u> Beautiful showroom with antiques, reproductions and accessories. Full design services including architectural & CAD, residential & commercial.

JANIE PETKUS INTERIORS ....**(630) 325-3242**
   110 S. Washington, Hinsdale   Fax: (630) 325-9351
   See Ad on Page: 302   *800 Extension: 1142*
   <u>Principal/Owner:</u> Janie Petkus

GAIL PRAUSS INTERIOR DESIGN, LTD. ....**(708) 524-1233**
   421 N. Marion Street, Oak Park   Fax: (708) 524-1237
   See Ad on Page: 365   *800 Extension: 1105*
   <u>Principal/Owner:</u> Gail Prauss
   <u>Website:</u> www.praussinteriors.com <u>e-mail:</u> gpid@msn.com

EVA QUATEMAN INTERIORS, LTD. ....**(773) 472-0522**
   399 W. Fullerton Parkway, Chicago   Fax: (773) 665-8615
   See Ad on Page: 323   *800 Extension: 1086*
   <u>Principal/Owner:</u> Eva Quateman

335

QUINTESSENTIAL DESIGN ....**(773) 529-6131**
   1133 W. Lill Avenue, Chicago   Fax: (773) 529-6132
   See Ad on Page: 368   *800 Extension: 1246*
   <u>Principal/Owner:</u> Lori M. Quint
   <u>Website:</u> www.quintessentialdesign.com <u>e-mail:</u> Quintproqo@aol.com

LESLIE REILLY STUDIO ....**(847) 934-4100**
   1201 W. Northwest Hwy., Palatine   Fax: (847) 934-4111
   See Ad on Page: 370   *800 Extension: 1182*
   <u>Principal/Owner:</u> Leslie Reilly, ASID
   <u>Website:</u> LeslieReilly.com
   <u>Additional Information:</u> Our specialty is thte kitchen, but we start with an holistic view of the home, how it functions and flows.

ELIZABETH A. ROSENSTEEL DESIGN/STUDIO............**(602) 522-0989**
   3040 N. 44th Street, Suite 1, Phoenix   Fax: (602) 522-0983
   See Ad on Page: 338, 339   *800 Extension: 1081*
   <u>Principal/Owner:</u> Elizabeth A. Rosensteel
   <u>e-mail:</u> ElizRosDes@aol.com
   <u>Additional Information:</u> 23 years of design experience, National and International clientel.

ROVITUSO STRANGE ARCHITECTS INC. ....**(630) 455-1708**
   544 W. 58th Place, Hinsdale   Fax: (630) 455-1709
   See Ad on Page: 197   *800 Extension: 1260*
   <u>Principal/Owner:</u> Frances E. Rovituso-Strange, AIA
   <u>e-mail:</u> RSArchInc@aol.com

MARY RUBINO INTERIORS, INC. ....**(847) 424-0432**
   620 Judson Avenue, No. 3, Evanston   Fax: (847) 424-0201
   See Ad on Page: 361   *800 Extension: 1200*
   <u>Principal/Owner:</u> Mary Rubino
   <u>Website:</u> www.maryrubino.com <u>e-mail:</u> mary@maryrubino.com

RUGO/RAFF LTD. ARCHITECTS ....**(312) 464-0222**
   20 W. Hubbard Street, Chicago
   See Ad on Page: 148, 149   *800 Extension: 1262*
   <u>Principal/Owner:</u> Steven Rugo
   <u>e-mail:</u> Steve@RugoRaff.com

continued on page **357**

847.550.6363

ELIZABETH A ROSENSTEEL

DESIGN / STUDIO
3040 N 44TH ST SUITE 1 PHOENIX AZ 85018
TEL 602 522 0989 ▪ FAX 602 522 0983
EMAIL ELIZROSDES@AOL.COM

ELIZABETH A ROSENSTEEL

DESIGN / STUDIO
3040 N 44TH ST SUITE 1 PHOENIX AZ 85018
TEL 602 522 0989 ▪ FAX 602 522 0983
EMAIL ELIZROSDES@AOL.COM

DALE CAROL ANDERSON LTD.

INTERIOR DESIGN

ANTIQUES

**CUSTOM DESIGN
FURNITURE**

**ALSO REPRESENTS
BERNARD AND BENJAMIN STEINITZ**

PARIS

NEW YORK

PALM BEACH

CHICAGO

2030 N. MAGNOLIA
CHICAGO, ILLINOIS 60614
TEL 773. 348. 5200

JANIE PETKUS
INTERIORS

Janie Petkus: "When my client decided to build a vacation house, the challenge was to create a home that was totally different from their primary residence. Their beautiful setting on a lake in Wisconsin inspired us to design a rustic lodge that was reminiscent of nineteenth century Adirondack hunting and fishing lodges. A variety of natural materials — slate, stone, iron and wood, were blended with colorful rugs, textured fabrics and leathers. Each item was carefully selected to ensure guests of all ages would feel comfortable and welcome."

Desi

SUSAN FREDMAN
AND ASSOCIATES

Susan Fredman: "In designing this great room, balance was our most important element. This room has a two-story fireplace, which was used as a design element to balance and 'hold' the space. Balance was needed to make sure that the space was not overpowering for people seated. The upholstery is large and overstuffed to provide weight and balance. The attention to detail was planned carefully to make the space feel warm, interesting, and very livable."

343

Photo by **Janet Mesic-Mackie**

ners

KAUFMAN SEGAL DESIGN

David Kaufman: "To add interest and definition to this bedroom we created a multi-dimensional elevation. The upholstered wainscot helps soften the hard lines of the geometric headboard. It also serves as a picture rail and support for floating nightstands. By mixing a combination of soft and luxurious materials such as cashmere and wool sateen with natural walnut we established a contemporary atmosphere that is both warm and inviting."

Photo by **Bruce Van Inwegen**

344

VISBEEN ASSOCIATES, INC.

Wayne E. Visbeen: "This sophisticated wine cellar and entertainment/tasting room, joined by a stone arch, exemplifies the elegance of rich material, texture, and color in an Old World-themed environment. The gold-toned cabinetry with the beautiful glass doors and shelving also reflect the homeowner's taste and lifestyle."

Desi

LORI LENNON & ASSOCIATES

Lori Lennon: "This 1920s dining room, with its tall, handsome oak wainscot and large, white marble fireplace, needed an important subject to connect within the narrow wall space. Sand, a complementary shade for the wood trim, is bordered by a mural of Napoleon's expedition to Egypt. This room creates romance and the flexibility for numerous styles of dining experiences."

Photo by **Rich Sistos**
Interior Photo by **Rich Mauer**

SARAH VAN ASSCHE INTERIORS

Sarah Van Assche: "Our 93-year-old client needed to scale down his current 4,000 sq. ft. vintage residence to this 1,100 sq. ft. apartment in a contemporary high-rise. The new 'white box' started with a furniture plan that could incorporate his most memorable antiques and showcase his beloved paintings and collectibles. Existing lighting conditions were drastically improved with the addition of low-voltage lighting fixtures. Above all, the use of intense, warm color and texture were key factors in making the client's transition to his new home a great success."

Photo by **Kennedy Photography**

ners

LARSON ASSOCIATES

George Larson: "The goal in designing my international style home was to make a functional floor plan with a sense of light and privacy. The house is 35 ft. by 48 ft. and sited to take maximum advantage of the narrow lot, providing a front and a back garden. Entering on the north side of the house, the front garden is accessible from the kitchen and breakfast room, which face east. The entrance hall encompasses a dining room and opens onto the 35 ft. by 20 ft. living room, which faces the garden at the back of the house. An 8 ft. diameter skylight brings light into the center of the entrance hall."

Photo by **Scott McDona**

Photo by **Jessie Walker**

346

Desi

GRAY
& WALTER

Kenneth Walter: "My client previously lived in a striking, contemporary condominium in a premier building. The Landmarks Preservation Commission protected the façade of the house. The assignment was to keep the home comfortable while remaining in concert with the grandeur of the spaces. This vignette represents a corner of the master bedroom suite which fronts the house, flanked by two turrets. The homeowner needed a bedroom space that could be a home within a home."

ıners

ELIZABETH ROSENSTEEL
DESIGN/STUDIO

Elizabeth Rosensteel: "I use simple, structural elements to create natural elegance and quiet sophistication, such as this bathroom. By blending organic shapes and materials with clean lines, I create environments that exude serenity and functional beauty. The result is exquisite strength, uncompromising design and bold sophistication."

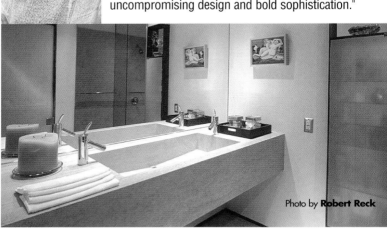

Photo by **Robert Reck**

348

Photo by **Judy A. Slagle**

LAURA
BARNETT
DESIGNS, INC.

Laura Barnett: "The floor in this octagonal room already had a diamond insert. We decided to play up that strong 'central' influence, since it draws one's eye through the room to the fabulous lake view. By adding wood molding, we were able to reflect the floor image to the ceiling plane. We wrapped the walls and ceiling right up to the molding in a silver-gray wall covering. We kept all the materials in the silver/gray/ black palette so that the mahogany table would be yet another focus on the center."

Desi

YOUNGMAN & COMPANY, INC.
WITH DAVID HANSEN, AIA

Angie Youngman: "The ultimate design is a fully expressed interpretation of an ongoing conversation between client, architect, and designer. This design is clear, highly functional, and has long-lasting aesthetic quality."

ɡners

Photo by **Joe Gutt**

ELINOR GORDON DESIGN

Elinor Gordon: "Our challenge was to design a breakfast room/home office in a newly constructed Gold Coast apartment. The allocated space was nothing more than two bare walls. We felt the key was organization. The result was built-ins. We chose a vanilla color paint finish for the unit and the walls. This lent a desired lightness to the space. Open shelves are used for a television, computer, books and collectibles. A mail slot and a corkboard keep correspondence organized and at hand. The closed bottom cabinets hold files and adds much-needed storage space."

GAIL PRAUSS INTERIOR DESIGN, LTD.

Gail Prauss: "This Arts & Crafts dining room has come to life with color. The walls received a special textured finish with a final stain to blend with and complement the dark wood wainscoting. The artistic blending of classic and contemporary furnishings in rich wood, metal and stone give the room a special ambiance."

Photo by **James Yochum**

Desi

Photo by **Wayne Cable**

351

ARLENE SEMEL
& ASSOCIATES

Arlene Semel: "A colorful patchwork antique hooked rug became artwork for the floor in the design of this modern farmhouse. Special folk-inspired furniture complements the rug to create a warm, one-of-a-kind sitting room for daily use and pleasure."

jners

SANDRA
SALTZMAN
INTERIORS

Sandra Saltzman: "Having a classical knowledge of design allows me the various possibilities to experiment with modern elements in creating a clean environment per the request of my clients. My minimalism is influenced by those masters from the 50s through the 70s and utilizes neutral colors, mixed textures and sharp crisp lines."

Desi

PAGE ONE INTERIORS

Adele Lampert: "Our task was to create an efficient, high-tech study with a Tusan feeling — all in a space with a 20 ft. high ceiling and only 11 ft. wide. The detailed cabinetry designs allowed a leather/tapestry sofa to be "shoe-horned" into place with plenty of space for paper storage, file drawers, television and computer support equipment. Dramatically lit areas were used to display the treasured art and antiques. The uplit ceiling and beams were painted in ancient Roman style with garlands, urns and festoons. An antique French bronze chandelier was added."

Photo by **Kristine Wolf**

OLAFSEN DESIGN GROUP

William D.B. Olafsen: "Our client requested the design of a study with ample room for display of books, trophies and photographs. Within the confined area, we created a sleek space and desk, the whole room reminiscent of a 1930s French library. By accent-uating the radiused walls, high gloss maple and restrained detailing, we achieved a room with glamour, yet warmth."

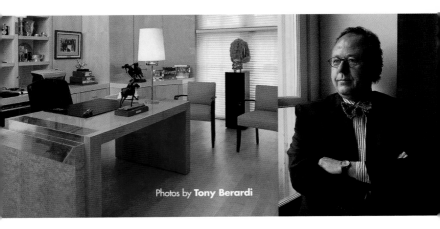

Photos by **Tony Berardi**

*Concentrating on meeting the client's complete needs
from interior architectural planning and furnishings to
accessories, for lasting design excellence.*

ELINOR GORDON DESIGN, inc.

Interior design • Space planning
Furniture design

Photography by Joe Gutt©

*"Design is a process that evolves from
following the architecture of a space,
its function and the client's dreams.
Add to this communication and trust,
and the outcome will be success."*

Elinor Gordon

999 N. Lake Shore Drive   Chicago, IL 60611
Tel 312.335.0220   Fax 312.335.0222
egdesign@21stcentury.net

continued from page 335

S & B INTERIORS, INC. ....**(877) 666-2616**
11270 SW 59th Avenue, Pinecrest
See Ad on Page: 358
Principal/Owner: Sandi Samole, ASID
Website: sandbinteriors.com e-mail: sandi@sandbinteriors.com
Additional Information: From conception to completion, we design and build your dreams nationwide.
Fax: (305) 661-2722
800 Extension: 1264

SANDRA SALTZMAN INTERIORS ....**(312) 642-8381**
1430 North Astor Street, Chicago
See Ad on Page: 320, 321
Principal/Owner: Sandra Saltzman
e-mail: sam2productions@aol.com
Fax: (312) 642-8402
800 Extension: 1268

LOREN REID SEAMAN & ASSOCIATES ....**(847) 550-6363**
22742 N. Lakewood Lane, Lake Zurich
728 W. Jackson, Chicago, IL
See Ad on Page: 336, 337
Principal/Owner: Loren Reid Seaman
Additional Information: Full service interior remodeling and design.
Fax: (847) 550-6464
800 Extension: 1194

A. WILLIAM SEEGERS ARCHITECTS...................................**(312) 454-0099**
117 N. Jefferson Street, Chicago
See Ad on Page: 199
Principal/Owner: A. William Seegers
e-mail: AWSeegers@aol.com
Additional Information: Provide high quality, personalized services for all projects of varying size and range.
Fax: (312) 454-1456
800 Extension: 1001

ARLENE SEMEL & ASSOCIATES, INC. ....**(312) 644-1480**
445 N. Franklin, Chicago
See Ad on Page: 326, 327
Principal/Owner: Arlene Semel
e-mail: asemel@asachicago.com
Additional Information: We, at Arlene Semel & Associates, Inc., believe that good interior design solves the practical problems of function and comfort, while defining and enriching the art of every day living.
Fax: (312) 644-8157
800 Extension: 1010

357

TOM STRINGER INC. ....**(312) 664-0644**
62 West Huron, Chicago
See Ad on Page: 368, 369
Principal/Owner: Thomas D. Stringer
Fax: (312) 664-2611
800 Extension: 1329

SARAH VAN ASSCHE INTERIORS ....**(773) 529-4269**
3000 N. Sheridan Road, Chicago
See Ad on Page: 322
Principal/Owner: Sarah Van Assche
e-mail: svainteriors@aol.com
Additional Information: Specialize in clean classic design with an emphasis on interpreting client's personal style.
Fax: (773) 529-4272
800 Extension: 1269

VISBEEN ASSOCIATES INC. ....**(616) 285-9901**
4139 Embassy Dr. S.E., Grand Rapids
See Ad on Page: 203
Principal/Owner: Wayne A. Visbeen, AIA, IIDA
e-mail: visbeenaia@aol.com
Additional Information: Visbeen Associates Inc. specializes in architecture, offering full design services from concept to finished project, including interior design.
Fax: (616) 285-9963
800 Extension: 1337

WICKETS FINE CABINETRY...**(847) 835-0868**
708 Vernon Avenue, Glencoe
See Ad on Page: 488
Website: wicketscabinetry.com e-mail: anita@wicketscabinetry.com
Fax: (847) 835-0867
800 Extension: 1344

J.A. WILSON & ASSOCIATES ARCHITECTS ....**(312) 337-4688**
230 West Huron, Chicago
See Ad on Page: 204
Principal/Owner: John A. Wilson
e-mail: jawilsonarchitects@earthlink.net
Additional Information: Custom residential architects with a feel for detail, aesthetics and comfort.
Fax: (312) 337-4689
800 Extension: 1141

S & B INTERIORS, INC.
FL. LIC IB0000056

"From conception to completion, we design and build your dreams!"
-Sandi Samole, ASID
President/Designer

Residential - Commercial - Space Planning

Website
www.sandbinteriors.com
e-mail
sandi@sandbinteriors.com
Phone
(305) 661-1577
Toll Free
(877) 666-2616
Fax
(305) 661-2722

Laura Barnett Designs

emphasizing the creation of a total environment

Photography by Judy A. Slagle

Photography by Judy A. Slagle

213 west institute place suite 706
chicago, illinois 60610
312.654-1706
lbdesigns1@qwest.net

Lois B. Gries Interior Design
400 N. Wells, Suite 416
Chicago, IL 60610

Lois Gries, ASID
T: 312.222.9202
F: 312.222.9207

www.loisgries.com

MARY RUBINO INTERIORS, INC.

design and purchasing

Photographed by Douglas Fogelson

Translating personalities into homes...
classic modern style
international influences
mixing periods and regions
innovative approach, thoughtful service

M.A. University of Chicago
L'Universita Degli Studi di Bologna
A.B. Brown University

EVANSTON, ILLINOIS TELEPHONE 847.424.0432 WWW.MARYRUBINO.COM

RESIDENTIAL  COMMERCIAL

Tel: (773) 529-6131   Fax: (773) 529-6132

quintproqo@aol.com

Create more than beautiful windows with
H&R Custom Designs

Specializing in: **HunterDouglas** WINDOW FASHIONS

- Duette® Honeycomb Shades • Silhouette® Window Shadings
- Luminette Privacy Sheers® • Country Woods®
- Plantation Shutters • Vertical & Mini Blinds • Cornices
- Fabrics • Bedspreads • Headboards • Pillows • Wallpaper
- Faux Texturing • Draperies • Specialty Valances • And More!

H&R Custom Designs
Commercial • Residential
300 Skokie Blvd • Northbrook Illinois
847.562.0487 • 630.323.6800
Hours M - F 10 - 4
www.handrdesigns.com

GAIL PRAUSS INTERIOR DESIGN, LTD.
GAIL PRAUSS ASID

TRADITIONAL   CONTEMPORARY   HISTORICAL

421 N. MARION STREET   OAK PARK, IL 60302
708.524.1233   FAX 708.524.1237
VISIT OUR WEBSITE @ WWW. PRAUSSINTERIORS.COM

Home Books
12 Tips
For Pursuing Quality

1. Assemble a Team of Professionals During Preliminaries.
Search out and value creativity.

2. Educate Yourself on What to Expect.
But also be prepared to be flexible in the likely event of set-backs.

3. Realize the Value and Worth of Design.
It's the best value for your investment.

4. Be Involved in the Process.
It's more personally satisfying and yields the best results.

5. Bigger Isn't Better – Better is Better.
Look for what produces quality and you'll never look back.

6. Understand the Process.
Be aware of products, prices and schedules, to be a productive part of the creative team.

7. Present a Realistic Budget.
Creative, workable ideas can be explored.

8. Create the Right Environment.
Mutual respect, trust and communication get the job done.

9. There Are No Immediate Miracles.
Time is a necessary component in the quest for quality.

10. Have Faith in Yourself.
Discover your own taste and style.

11. Plan for the Future.
Lifestyles and products aren't static.

12. Do Sweat the Details.
Establish the discipline to stay organized.

CHICAGO
HOME
BOOK

1350 E. Touhy Ave. Des Plaines, IL 60018 800-645-1848 847-390-2882 fax 847-390-2902

KAUFMAN SEGAL *DESIGN*

Van Inwegen Photography

Van Inwegen Photography

TOM·STRINGER·INC
INTERIOR DESIGN

CHICAGO | LOS ANGELES

62 WEST HURON

CHICAGO, IL 60610

312.664.0644

101 SOUTH ROBERTSON BLVD

LOS ANGELES, CA 90048

310.385.9399

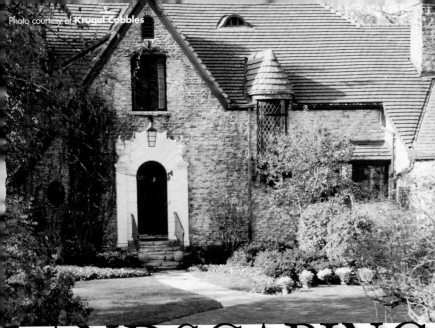

Photo courtesy of **Krugel Cobbles**

LANDSCAPING

LANDSCAPE ARCHITECTS & CONTRACTORS

ILT VIGNOCCHI   tel 847 487 5200

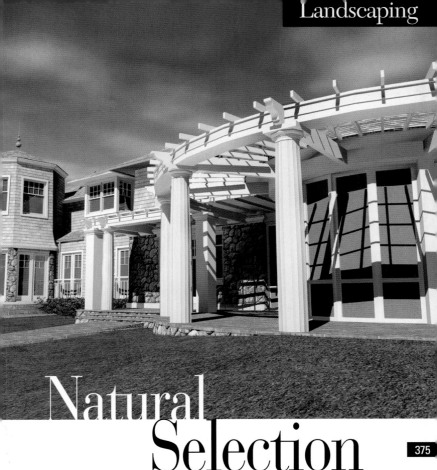

Natural
Selection

Landscaping is the only design area that is by nature intended to evolve over time. The philosophy behind landscape design has evolved as well. From traditional European formality to the naturalism of Prairie Style, to the simplicity and order of Far Eastern influences, your landscape should be as unique a design statement as your home itself.

More and more people are blurring the divisions between inside and outside environments, with expanses of windows, patios designed to act as "outdoor rooms," and various types of glass and screened enclosures to enjoy the outdoors whatever the weather. Landscape becomes almost an architectural element at times, creating an interplay and synthesis of indoors and outdoors.

Water gardens are growing in popularity as people learn that they are ecosystems in their own right, requiring little additional time or attention once they are established. Think of it: the soothing splash of a waterfall or babbling brook right in your own backyard!

Photo courtesy of **Gregory Maire Architects, Inc.**

VIEWS AND VISTAS

First you choose your views, then you build your home. To create a harmonious balance between your home and its surroundings, your architect should be invited to visit the site of your new home, and to meet with your landscape architect. The site can often serve as a catalyst, inspiring a design that responds to the uniqueness of the site. When all the team members are included, important details (like the location of your air conditioning units) can be discussed and settled, making for the best results for you and your family.

A PARTY OF GARDENS

As gardening attracts more devotees in South Florida, people are rediscovering the satisfaction of creating imaginative gardens. Some ideas: one-color gardens, fragrance gardens, native plant gardens, Japanese gardens.

GETTING BACK TO THE GARDEN

Think of the land as a canvas for a work of environmental art. Think of the landscape professional as an artist who uses nature to translate your needs and desires into a living, breathing reality. A formal English garden or seemingly artless arrangements of native plantings, a winding cobblestone walkway leading from a hand-laid brick driveway or dramatically lit oak trees above a steaming spa - these are the kinds of possibilities you can explore. When you work with a professional who is personally committed to superior work and service, designing a landscape is full of creativity, new ideas and satisfying results.

GETTING A LANDSCAPE STARTED

Selecting a landscape professional to create and maintain a distinctive landscape is one of the most important decisions you'll make as a homeowner. In making your decision, consider these questions:

• Are you landscaping a new construction home? There are critical decisions to be made early in the home building planning process that concern the landscape. Interview and work with professionals who have considerable experience in doing excellent work with new construction projects. Make them part of your team and have them meet with your architect, interior designer and builder early in the project.

• Do you want to hire a landscape architect or a landscape designer? Landscape architects have met the criteria to be registered by the state. Many hold university degrees in landscape architecture. A landscape designer generally has had training and/or experience in horticulture and landscaping and may also have a background in art.

• Do you want full service? If you want to work with one source, from design through installation to maintenance, only consider those who offer comprehensive service.

Allow time to interview at least two professionals before making a decision. Start early, especially if you plan to install a swimming pool, which should be dug the same time as the foundation of a new home.

Invite the professional to your home to acquaint him or her with your tastes and personality through observing your choices in interior design as well as the current landscape. Have a plat of survey available. Be prepared to answer questions like:

• Do you prefer a formal or informal feel? The formality of symmetrical plantings or the informal look of a natural area?

• Is there a place or feeling you'd like to recreate? Somewhere where you've vacationed, or the place where you grew up?

• What colors do you like? This will impact the flowers chosen for your gardens.

• Are you a gardener? Would you like to be? If you're fond of flower, herb or vegetable gardening, your landscape professional will build the appropriate gardens.

• How will you use the space? Will children use the backyard for recreation? Will you entertain outdoors? If so, will it be during the day or at night? Do you envision a pool, spa, gazebo or tennis court?

• Are you fond of lawn statuary, fountains or other ornamental embellishments?

• What architectural features must be considered? A wrap-around porch, large picture windows? Brick or stone exteriors?

• To what extent will you be involved in the process? Most landscape architects and designers are happy to encourage your involvement in this labor of love. There is a great deal of pleasure to be derived from expressing your personality through the land. A lifelong hobby can take root from this experience. Landscapers say their clients often join garden clubs after the completion of their project, and that many of their rehabbing projects are done for clients who are already avid gardeners.

Landscape professionals expect that you will want to see a portfolio, inquire about their styles, and their experience. You may wish to request permission to visit sites of their installed landscapes. If you have special concerns, such as environmental issues, ask if the landscape professional has any experience in such areas.

COMPUTING LANDSCAPE FEES

It's important to create a workable budget. It's easy to be caught off guard when you get a landscape proposal — it is a significant investment.

To make sure you give the outside of your home the appropriate priority status, plan to invest ten to 25 percent of the cost of a new home and property in the landscaping. Although landscape elements can be phased in year after year, expect that the majority of the cost will be incurred in the first year. Maintenance costs must also be considered.

THE LANDSCAPE BUDGET

Basic:
10% of the cost of your home & property
In-depth:
The 10 to 25% rule of thumb applies to your landscapes too.
Starting at $90,000:
• Finish grading
• Sodded lawns
• Foundation plantings (around the house) including some smaller trees
• Walkways of pavers or stone
City Dwellers!
• Soft atmospheric lighting up to the front door and in the back yard
• Asphalt driveway
• Concrete unit pavers or stone patio, or deck
• Perimeter plantings of trees and shrubs for privacy and finished look

377

OUTDOOR DECOR

As homeowners get more involved in their yards and gardens, they learn to "see" outdoor rooms and take deep pleasure in decorating them. Arbors, sculpture, tables, benches, water features, or any piece of whimsy add delightful decorating. Hedges or fences create natural partitions. The results are appealing, comfortable and richly rewarding.

The Price of Being Green

It's fun to imagine, but what might it actually cost to undertake a project described in this chapter? The example below describes a typical project and gives a general estimate of the costs involved.

PROJECT DESCRIPTION

Landscape development of a typical property consisting of new paver patio and walk, retaining wall and approximately 600 sq. ft. of new planting beds along front foundation.

Initial consultation 0

Design contract fees...$500

Hardscape construction
Cut Lanonstone retaining wall (85 face sq. ft.) $4,130
Concrete paver patio and walkway (480 sq. ft.) $7,785

Planting development
Bed preparation (600 sq. ft.) $9,000
Includes: Assorted foundation shrubs
    Four mid-size shade trees
    Assorted perennials
    Annual beds
    New sod for lawn areas

Landscape management...$3,648
One season (April – November) of maintenance of about one-half acre site.
Includes: Weekly mowing and trimming of maintained turf areas
    Monthly pavement edging of sidewalks, patios and driveway
    Weekly landscape debris clean-up of maintained areas
    Monthly cultivation of open bed areas
    Manual weeding
    Preventative weed control
    Granular fertilization of maintained bed areas
    Spade edging of beds
    Selective pruning of oriental trees (less than 12 feet high), shrubs and hedges
    Weekly perennial dead heading of faded flowers
    Groundcover maintenance and pruning
    Spring and Fall clean-up of maintained areas
    Weekly off-site disposal of landscape waste and grass clippings
    Turf fertilization program
    Broadleaf weed control in late Spring and late Summer

TOTAL: $25,063

Assorted annuals, perennials and shrubs

Cut Lanonstone retaining wall

Herringbone pattern for concrete patio pavers

Landscaping

LIGHTING YOUR LOT

"Less is more" is the best philosophy when designing an outdoor lighting system. Today's beautiful, functional fixtures are themselves worthy of admiration, but their purpose is to highlight the beauty of your home while providing safe access to your property. Well-established lighting companies and specialty companies offer extensive landscape lighting product lines.

380

DREAM POOLS

Yours for $60,000: Custom-designed mid-sized pool with a deep end, spa, custom lighting, cleaning system, remote control functions, cover, deck.
   Yours for $200,000: A custom-designed Roman-style pool with bar stools, a small wading pool, elevated spa and elaborate waterfall. Special-ized lighting, built-in planters, auto-mated hydraulic cover, top-of-the-line automated cleaning system, all with remote control functions.

Billing practices vary among professionals and depend on the extent of the services you desire. Some charge a flat design fee up front, some charge a one-time fee for a contract that includes everything, some charge a design fee which is waived if you select them to complete the project, and some build a design fee into the installation and/or maintenance cost.

A PROFESSIONAL DEVELOPS AN ENVIRONMENT

While you're busy imagining glorious flowers waving a welcome to you from your expertly designed tiered gardens, your landscaper will be out walking around your property, assessing practical issues like grading and drainage, the location of sewers, utility lines, and existing trees, where and when the sun hits the land, and the quality of the soil.

This important first step, the site analysis, should take place before construction has even begun, in the case of a new house. Site work helps ensure that the blueprints for your house won't make your landscape dreams impossible to achieve, and vice versa. If you've told your builder you want a breakfast nook, you'll probably get one regardless of the fact that it requires taking out a tree you value.

If you're considering installing a custom driveway or sidewalk, this early stage is the time to inform your builder. Ask your builder not to do construction outside the building envelope. You and your landscape professionals will design and build your driveway and walkways.

Expect the design process to take at least six weeks. During this time, the designer is developing a plan for the hardscape, which includes all of the man-made elements of your outdoor environment, and the many layers of softscape, which are the actual plantings. You can expect to be presented with a plan view that is workable and in harmony with your home, as well as your budget.

Hardscape elements, like irrigation systems and pavements, will be installed first, before a new house is completely finished. Softscape will go in later.

During this landscape project, you most likely have begun to appreciate the special nature of landscape and will not be surprised if your completed project does not look "complete." A landscape should be given time in the hands of nature to come to maturity: three years for perennials, five years for shrubs, and 15 years for trees.

LUXURY LIVING WITH A CUSTOM-DESIGNED POOL

The beauty and value of a custom-designed swimming pool are unmatched. A welcome design element to the landscape, a pool adds to the overall property value of the residence, and creates greater use and enjoyment of the yard. As area families spend more and more of their leisure time at home, a pool answers their dreams of living well at home.

Deciding to build a swimming pool is best done as a new home is being designed so the pool can enhance the home and landscape architecture. By integrating the pool into the overall scheme, you'll be able to establish a realistic budget. One of the biggest mistakes homeowners make when purchasing a pool is not initially getting all the features they want. It's difficult and costly to add features later.

The design process is time-consuming. You may have four or more meetings with your pool professional before finalizing the design. The building process takes about two months, after obtaining permits. You should plan to have your pool dug at the same time as the home foundation. Pool construction is integrated with surrounding decking, so make sure your landscape architect, pool builder, or hardscape contractor is coordinating the effort.

OUTDOOR LIVING

Today's homeowners, having invested the time and resources to create a spectacular environment, are ready to "have it all" in their own backyards.

Decks, gazebos, and increasingly, screened rooms, are popular features of today's upscale homes. The extended living space perfectly suits our "cocooning" lifestyle, offering more alternatives for entertaining, relaxation, and family time at home. Many new homes tout outdoor living space as a most tantalizing feature.

Decks and terraces offer extra living space and are functional enough to host almost any occasion. With thoughtful and proper design, it fulfills our dreams of an outdoor getaway spot. A multi-level deck built up and around mature trees can feel like a treehouse. A spa built into a cedar deck, hidden under a trellis, can make you believe you're in a far-off paradise.

With so many options available, building a new deck provides a unique opportunity for homeowners to give their creativity free rein.

EVERY KID'S FANTASY

In a yard with plenty of flat area: A wood construction expandable play system with: Several slides, including a spiral slide, crawl tunnels and bridges to connect fort and structures, a tic-tac-toe play panel, three swings, climbing ropes, fire pole, gymnastics equipment (trapeze, turning bar), sandbox pit, and a built in picnic table with benches. Price Tag: Around $12,000

In a smaller yard: A wood construction expandable play system with: A small fort, two swings and a single slide. Price Tag: Around $1,400

THE FINAL EVALUATION

When the landscape is installed, conduct a final, on-site evaluation. You should evaluate the finished design, find out what elements will be installed later and learn more about how the plan will evolve over time.

381

Landscaping

THINKING ABOUT OUTDOOR LIVING

An on-site meeting with a licensed contractor who is an expert in landscape building or a landscape architect is the first step in designing and building a deck, patio, or any outdoor structure. An experienced professional will guide you through the conceptualization by asking questions like these:

• Why are you building the structure? For business entertaining, family gatherings, child or teen parties, private time?

• Do you envision a secluded covered area, a wide open expanse, or both?

• Do you want a single level, or two or more levels (the best option for simultaneous activities)?

• Will it tie in with current or future plans?

• How do you want to landscape the perimeter?

• Do you want benches, railings, trellises, or other stylish options, like built-in counters with gas grills, or recessed lighting under benches or railings?

Don't let obstacles block your thinking. Your gas grill can be moved. Decks are often built around trees and can convert steep slopes into usable space.

Once a design has been settled upon, expect three to four weeks to pass before a deck or gazebo is completed. The time required to get a building permit (usually two to four weeks) must also be considered.

If you're landscaping during this time, be sure to coordinate the two projects well in advance. Building can wreak havoc on new plantings and your lawn will be stressed during construction.

DISTINCTIVE OUTDOOR SURFACES

Driveways, walkways, patios, decks, and wood terraces, and hardscape features were once relegated to "last minute" status, with a budget to match. Today they are being given the full and careful attention they deserve. A brick paver driveway can be made to blend beautifully with the color of the brick used on the house. Natural brick stairways and stoops laid by master crafters add distinctive detail and value. Custom-cut curved bluestone steps, hand selected by an experienced paving contractor, provide years of pride and pleasure.

Hardscape installation doesn't begin until your new home is nearly complete, but for your own budgeting purposes, have decisions made no later than home mid-construction phase.

A TYPICAL LANDSCAPE DESIGN TIMETABLE

• One to two weeks to get the project on the boards
+
• One to two weeks to do the actual site and design work and prepare plans
+
• One week to coordinate calendars and schedule presentation meeting
+
• One to two weeks to leave the plans with the client and get their feedback
+
• One week to incorporate changes, create and get approval on a final design
=
FIVE TO EIGHT WEEKS

THE TIGHT SQUEEZE.

When homes get bigger, back yards get smaller. A landscape architect will be attentive to keeping all aspects of your plan in proper balance.

382

To interview a paving or hardscape contractor, set up an on-site meeting so you can discuss the nature of the project and express your ideas. Be ready to answer questions like:

• Will the driveway be used by two or three cars, or more? Do you need it to be wide enough so cars can pass? Will you require extra parking? Would you like a circular driveway? A basketball court?

• Will the patio be used for entertaining? Will it be a family or adult area, or both? How much furniture will you use? Should it be accessible from a particular part of the house?

• Do you have existing or future landscaping that needs to be considered?

• Would you like to incorporate special touches, like a retaining wall, a small koi pond, or a stone archway?

If you're working with a full service landscape professional, and hardscape is part of the landscape design, be certain a hardscape expert will do the installation. A specialist's engineering expertise and product knowledge are vital to the top quality result you want. ■

WHY YOU NEED AN ARBORIST.

It's not just your kids, dogs and the neighborhood squirrels trampling through your yard during construction. Excavation equipment, heavy trucks and work crews can spell disaster for your trees. Call an arborist before any equipment is scheduled to arrive and let him develop a plan that will protect the trees, or remove them if necessary.

GARDENER'S EDENS

Visit these artistic gardens for ideas and inspiration.

Chicago Botanic Garden
Glencoe, IL 847.835.5440
www.chicago-botanic.org

Lincoln Park Conservatory
Chicago, IL 312.742.7736

Morton Arboretum
Lisle, IL 630.968.0074
www.mortonarb.org

Landscape
Architects

THE CHALET LANDSCAPE DIVISION ....**(847) 688-0561**
3132 Lake Avenue, Wilmette   Fax: (847) 688-0567
See Ad on Page: 394, 395   *800 Extension: 1310*
Principal/Owner: Lawrence J. Thalmann, III
Website: www.chaletnursery.com
Additional Information: Since 1917, it is our commitment and focus to meet the
needs and exceed the expectations of our clients.

DON FIORE COMPANY, INC. ....**(847) 234-0020**
28846 Nagel Court, Lake Bluff   Fax: (847) 234-0922
See Ad on Page: 414, 415   *800 Extension: 1075*

HEYNSSENS + GRASSMAN ....**(847) 360-0440**
PO Box 1152, Libertyville   Fax: (847) 630-0491
See Ad on Page: 388, 389   *800 Extension: 1127*
Principal/Owner: Rene Grassman Heynssens and Chris J. Heynssens
Additional Information: Registered landscape architects, specializing in the design,
construction and maintenance of residential gardens.

ILT VIGNOCCHI ....**(847) 487-5200**
25865 W. Ivanhoe, Wauconda   Fax: (847) 487-5265
See Ad on Page: 372, 373, 391   *800 Extension: 1134*
Principal/Owner: Donna Vignocchi
Website: www.iltvignocchi.com

384

**"When heaven falls to Earth,
it becomes a Garden."**

— *Stouffer*

continued on page **390**

Poul's Landscaping
& Nursery, Inc.

Since 1966

Landscape Architecture

Landscape Construction

Landscape Maintenance

754 W. Indian Creek Road • Long Grove, IL 6004?

(847) 949-6667 • www.pouls.com

do you dream in color?

Landscape
Architecture

Design

Construction

Maintenance

Ponds & Fountains

Driveways

Patios

Walkways

so do we.

BUHRMAN
design group

Full Service Landscape Design, Construction & Maintenance

(847) 680-6120

Libertyville, Illinois
lance@buhrmandesigngroup.com

HEYNSSENS +
GRASSMAN

Landscape Architecture, Construction and Maintenance

TIMELESS

BEAUTY

continued from page **384**

KEMPER CAZZETTA, LTD. ....**(847) 256-2584**
412 Green Bay Road, Kenilworth
See Ad on Page: 168, 169   *800 Extension: 1156*
<u>Principal/Owner:</u> John Cazzetta

KEMPER CAZZETTA, LTD. ....**(847) 382-8322**
209 E. Franklin Street, Barrington   Fax: (847) 382-4852
See Ad on Page: 168, 169   *800 Extension: 1158*
<u>Principal/Owner:</u> John Cazzetta

MILIEU DESIGN INC. ....**(847) 465-1160**
48 East Hintz Road, Wheeling   Fax: (847) 465-1159
See Ad on Page: 392, 399   *800 Extension: 1204*
<u>Principal/Owner:</u> Peter Wodarz

POUL'S LANDSCAPING & NURSERY, INC. ....**(847) 949-6667**
6754 W. Indian Road, Long Grove   Fax: (847) 949-6668
See Ad on Page: 385   *800 Extension: 1242*
<u>Principal/Owner:</u> William Bach
<u>Website:</u> www.pouls.com <u>e-mail:</u> info@pouls.com

ROSBOROUGH PARTNERS, INC. ....**(847) 549-1361**
15849 W. Buckley Road, Libertyville   Fax: (847) 549-1392
See Ad on Page: 393   *800 Extension: 1256*
<u>Principal/Owner:</u> Philip A. Rosborough
<u>e-mail:</u> RPI@rosboroughpartners.com

TECZA ENVIRONMENTAL GROUP ....**(847) 742-3320**
12N442 Switzer Road, Elgin   Fax: (847) 742-3171
See Ad on Page: 411   *800 Extension: 1307*
<u>Principal/Owner:</u> Ted Tecza

"With childlike credulous affection We behold their tender buds expand."

— Longfellow

ILT's trademark remains our unique sense of artistry in design, our impeccable craftsmanship and services, and our unwavering integrity and loyalty to our employees and customers.

Landscape Architecture   Landscape Construction   Landscape Maintenance

Milieu Design Inc.

GROUNDS FOR CHANGE?

48 EAST HINTZ ROAD
WHEELING, ILLINOIS 60090
PHONE: 847.465.1160
FAX: 847.465.1159
LANDSCAPE ARCHITECTURE CONSTRUCTION MAINTENANCE

RP
ROSBOROUGH PARTNERS, INC.
LANDSCAPE ARCHITECTS

"Creative and Thoughtful garden design,
quality garden construction to last detail,
and garden management providing unparalleled service.
We would like to have the opportunity to serve you."

15849 W. BUCKLEY ROAD
LIBERTYVILLE, ILLINOIS 60048
847-549-1361
847-433-9370

Landscape
Designers

COTTAGE GARDENER, LTD. ....**(708) 386-1920**
129 Wesley Ave, Oak Park   Fax: (708) 524-8311
See Ad on Page: 397   *800 Extension: 1061*
<u>Principal/Owner:</u> Michael Patek
<u>Additional Information:</u> Landscape Design/Build Services for the residential market.

"Nature is the art of God.**"**

— *Religio Medici*

Cottage Gardener Ltd.

Landscape Design, Installation & Maintenance

Oak Park, Illinois
708-386-1920

Landscape
Contractors

BUHRMAN DESIGN GROUP, INC. ....**(847) 680-6120**
2088 Bob-O-Link Lane, Libertyville   Fax: (847) 680-6124
See Ad on Page: 386, 387, 419   *800 Extension: 1034*
Principal/Owner: Lance Buhrman
e-mail: lance@buhrmandesigngroup.com

THE CHALET LANDSCAPE DIVISION ....**(847) 688-0561**
3132 Lake Avenue, Wilmette   Fax: (847) 688-0567
See Ad on Page: 394, 395   *800 Extension: 1309*
Principal/Owner: Lawrence J. Thalmann, III
Website: www.chaletnursery.com
Additional Information: Since 1917, it is our commitment and focus to meet the
needs and exceed the expectations of our clients.

DON FIORE COMPANY, INC. ....**(847) 234-0020**
28846 Nagel Court, Lake Bluff   Fax: (847) 234-0922
See Ad on Page: 414, 415   *800 Extension: 1076*

HINSDALE NURSERIES..**(630) 323-1411**
7200 S. Madison St., Hinsdale   Fax: (708) 323-0918
See Ad on Page: 410   *800 Extension: 1129*
Principal/Owner: Richard Theidel

ILT VIGNOCCHI ....**(847) 487-5200**
25865 W. Ivanhoe, Wauconda   Fax: (847) 487-5265
See Ad on Page: 372, 373, 391   *800 Extension: 1135*
Principal/Owner: Donna Vignocchi
Website: www.iltvignocchi.com

398

**"A beautiful garden
is a work of heart."**

— *Anonymous*

continued on page **409**

Milieu Design Inc.

GROUNDS FOR CHANGE?

48 EAST HINTZ ROAD
WHEELING, ILLINOIS 60090
PHONE: 847.465.1160
FAX: 847.465.1159
LANDSCAPE ARCHITECTURE CONSTRUCTION MAINTENANCE

Only
If You
Want the Very
Best...

The
Ashley
Group

1350 E. Touhy Avenue, Des Plaines, Illinois 60018
888.458.1750   Fax 847.390.2902

www.theashleygroup.com • www.homebook.com

Landscaping Your **Dream** Home

A n important part of your dream home will be your outside surroundings, so, of course, you will want a beautiful landscape to complement your home. A great deal of thought will need to go into your landscaping project – this type of project does not solely consist of planting gorgeous flowers or deciding where to place trellises. The following guide will give you an idea of the steps and time that go into landscaping an upscale residential project.

Inspecting the Progress

Throughout the construction process, keep an eye on the progress. Be checking for items listed on your contract. When you are completely involved with the process, you will be able to be vocal about it.

● Inspection

Your landscaper will first have to inspect, evaluate and map out your site. He or she will take site measurements, which may include extensive grading details. The process should take about one to two weeks to complete.

WK16

● Designing

If all goes smoothly, the landscape architect or designer will be able to complete the final designs of your project within a week. Keep in mind that modifications will likely have to be made, so you will need to leave time for negotiation.

WK18

● Ordering Materials

Once you've had the pleasure of choosing the plants and hardscape you desire, let your landscaper order them. This way, the responsibility for any problems is theirs alone.

WK19

Garden Styling

Imaginative theme gardens are becoming popular. Some ideas: a garden of native plants, a one-or two-color garden, a fragrance garden, a Zen garden, a moonlight garden. Don't forget to consider including arbors, sculpture, benches or water features.

• **Pretty Pathways:** Depending on where and how it's quarried, natural stone can vary in color, and brick can vary as well. To be certain that your bricks, cobbles or specialty stones perfectly match, have your contractor buy them from the same lot. There's nothing quite as disconcerting as a pathway where the bricks or stones are slightly different colors.

PLANNING

Landscaping a *Custom* House

Develop Your Vision
You will have to spend a large part of your planning stage deciding what will be most flattering to your home, what plants will work best in the climate you live in, what aspects will require the most upkeep and what is most cost effective. Plan on spending at least two to three months developing ideas for your landscape project.

Research Landscapers
You may find the architect, designer or developer who can create your dreams, but plan on spending at least one month looking for that perfect fit. At this point, if you want to be fully involved with the overall process, it would be best to inform landscapers.

Choosing Subcontractors
The landscaper usually chooses the subcontractors who will assist on the project, but there are situations in which the client will choose. This process should take approximately one month.

WK 1   WK8   WK12

Design/Build Landscapers
A design/build landscaping firm offers its clients both the design of the project and the services to construct it. It differs from firms that may offer just design or construction services.

• **Who does what?** A landscape architect and a landscape designer perform similar tasks for projects, including surveying the land, discussing ideas with clients and drawing up plans. Due to an architect's more technical education, however, he or she is more eligible to handle the complicated projects. A landscape contractor installs the plants, trees, shrubs and hardscape of the project.

• **Who chooses the subcontractors?** This is a tedious process, because subcontractors are on other job sites and the new job has to be explained to each one. If you feel more comfortable meeting those who will potentially be working on your project, talk to your landscaper about being present at the interviews.

Project
Description

L andscaping an upscale, one-acre property, single family home. This project includes the installation of a swimming pool, masonry walls, fence, lighting, brick paving, a patio, and an assortment of shade trees and plants.

FINISHED PROJECT

● **Final Inspection**

Take an initial walk-through and get an overall sense of the finished project. Let your surroundings soak in and then take a second inspection. Bring your landscape architect along so you can let him or her know immediately if something just isn't right.

● **Payment**

When it comes to making the final payment of your landscaping bill, be sure to review the charges carefully. Additions, rare plants and specialty products all add on to the final cost of your project. An estimated price for the landscape project described here is around $200,000.

WK30

Grows on You: Keep in mind that some aspects of your completed landscape project may not be at their fullest potential when first implemented. Although good planning alleviates many surprises, it often takes one to three years for a landscape to mature. So if the flowers or shrubbery don't complement the walkway as you thought they would, give them some time. The flowers you want may not be available for another year, but you can always add a different variety. Larger, more permanent aspects of the landscape project, such as the swimming pool or a greenhouse, are, of course, much harder to change or alter, but can be done.

A Work in Progress

Landscapers expect their clients to freshen their landscaping every few years. So if you'd like to add more color or even move plants, don't be shy about giving your landscape professional a call.

The Pool

The installation of your swimming pool should take about five to six weeks. However, a pool with bar stools, an elevated spa or special water features may take longer.

Hardscape

The materials used for hardscape, such as brick paver paths, patios and retaining walls, will dictate the time needed to create them: brick or cobblestone paths take more time than flagstone stepping paths, and mortarless flagstone patios take more time than those joined with mortar.

Softscape

Softscape includes all your plantings and sodding. Once the hardscape is finished, the softscaping can begin. Depending on the amount of detail in your plan, a one-acre area may take from six days to two weeks. Water features and lighting are not considered part of the softscape; they are added last.

Lighting

After the major aspects of your landscaping project are complete, the installation of lighting will begin. The overall process of lighting installation is fairly straightforward and will take a few days at the most to complete. Keep in mind, though, that setbacks do arise.

• **Bumps in the Road:** There are many reasons why your project may be delayed: materials are scarce or not in season, your new plants may not transplant well, or the specialty stones for your masonry walls are not available. Various problems can arise in the construction of a pool. And there will be numerous subcontractors working on your construction, who also work on other projects at the same time. For example, if the concrete layers are delayed two days and the electrician has other jobs scheduled, the added time could be significant. These setbacks are not pleasant, but they are realistic. Being emotionally prepared for such setbacks helps.

Types of Lighting

There are many ways to illuminate your garden. Do you entertain often? Try torches or tiki lights. Will you have a moonlight garden? Chinese hanging lanterns, floating candles in a glass bowl and lamp posts complement it well. Solar-powered lights are also popular now.

TIMELINE

In
Conclusion

The actual completion of a landscaping project varies greatly – a small project could take as little as one week and a large project can take as long as one year. There is no definite timeframe for a project like this. Talk to your landscaper in the initial interviewing and hiring process about timeframes. Ask if you can speak with past clients to find out how long their projects took to complete. This is not a small aspect of the overall completion of your dream home. Therefore, plan on dedicating a significant amount of time to the landscaping of your home. Eventually you will have a finished product that you can be proud of for years to come!

Special thanks to the American Society of Landscape Architects and Van Zelst Inc., Wadsworth, Illinois, for their contribution to this timeline and to Linda Oyama Bryan for her photography.

Produced by The Ashley Group
847.390.2882
www.theashleygroup.com

continued from page **398**

MILIEU DESIGN INC. ....**(847) 465-1160**
48 East Hintz Road, Wheeling
See Ad on Page: 392, 399
Principal/Owner: Peter Wodarz
Fax: (847) 465-1159
800 Extension: 1203

POUL'S LANDSCAPING & NURSERY, INC. ....**(847) 949-6667**
6754 W. Indian Road, Long Grove
See Ad on Page: 385
Principal/Owner: William Bach
Website: www.pouls.com e-mail: info@pouls.com
Fax: (847) 949-6668
800 Extension: 1241

PUGSLEY & LAHAIE, LTD...**(847) 438-0013**
24414 N. Old McHenry Road, Lake Zurich
See Ad on Page: 413
Principal/Owner: Robert A. LaHaie
e-mail: pandlgroup@cs.com
Fax: (847) 438-0084
800 Extension: 1244

ROSBOROUGH PARTNERS, INC. ....**(847) 549-1361**
15849 W. Buckley Road, Libertyville
See Ad on Page: 393
Principal/Owner: Philip A. Rosborough
e-mail: RPI@rosboroughpartners.com
Fax: (847) 549-1392
800 Extension: 1255

SPECIAL TOUCH LANDSCAPING, INC....**(815) 467-9066**
15320 Jughandle Road, Minooka
See Ad on Page: 412
Principal/Owner: Rob Lombardo
Fax: (815) 467-9065
800 Extension: 1283

TECZA ENVIRONMENTAL GROUP ....**(847) 742-3320**
12N442 Switzer Road, Elgin
See Ad on Page: 411
Principal/Owner: Ted Tecza
Fax: (847) 742-3171
800 Extension: 1306

409

VAN ZELST, INC. ....**(847) 623-3580**
39400 N. Hwy 41, Wadsworth
See Ad on Page: 416, 417
Principal/Owner: David Van Zelst
Website: www.vanzelst.com e-mail: info@vanzelst.com
Fax: (847) 623-7546
800 Extension: 1336

"He who plants a garden
plants happiness.**"**

— *Anonymous*

tecza environmental group

12 N. 442 Switzer Road • Elgin, Il 60123
847 • 742 • 3320

LANDSCAPE DESIGN
A Complete Master Plan

LANDSCAPE INSTALLATION
Ideas Come to Life

LANDSCAPE MAINTENANCE
Professional Service, Care & Attention

Special Touch Landscaping Inc.

Turning Dreams -

Into Reality.

15320 Jughandle Road
Minooka, IL 60447
815.467.9066

ILCA
ILLINOIS LANDSCAPE
CONTRACTORS ASSOCIATION

*residential and commercial
design/ build*

PUGSLEY & LAHAIE, LTD.
landscape architects and contractors
Lake Zurich, Illinois
phone: 847/438-0013 fax: 847/438-0084

For over thirty years we have been
helping nature beautify the North Shore

DESIGN

The following design books represent the premier works of selected designers, luxury homebuilders and architects.

This book is divided into 10 chapters, starting with design guidelines in regards to color, personality and collections. In these chapters, interior designer Perla Lichi presents beautiful, four-color photographs of the design commissions she has undertaken for clients accompanied by informative editorial on the investment value of professional interior design.

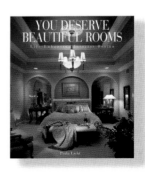

YOU DESERVE BEAUTIFUL ROOMS
120 pages, 9.75" x 14"
Home Design, Architecture
1-58862-016-6 $39.95   Hardcover

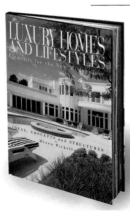

Orren Pickell is renowned as one of the nation's finest builders of custom homes. In this collection of more than 80 beautiful four-color photos and drawings, Pickell shows off some of his finest creations to give homeowners unique ideas on building a new home or adding to an existing one.

LUXURY HOMES & LIFESTYLES
120 pages, 9.75" x 14"
Architecture, Home Design
0-9642057-4-2 $39.95   Hardcover

Designer Susan Fredman has spent 25 years creating interiors, which, in one way or another, have been inspired by nature. In this book, she takes readers through rooms which reflect elements of our surroundings as they are displayed throughout the year.

AT HOME WITH NATURE
136 pages, 11.25" x 11.25"
Home Design, Architecture
1-58862-043-3 $39.95   Hardcover

The Ashley Group is proud to present these speci

CALL TO ORDE

BOOKS

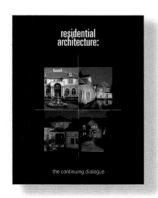

Michigan-based architect Dominick Tringali uses the skill and knowledge that has brought him over 20 industry awards to share strategies on building the ultimate dream house. By combining unique concepts with innovative techniques and materials, Dominick's portfolio displays an array of homes noted for their timeless appeal. This $45 million collection of elite, custom homes contains the residences of notable CEOs, lawyers, doctors and sports celebrities including Chuck O'Brien, Joe Dumars, Tom Wilson, Larry Wisne and Michael Andretti's estate in Pennsylvania.

**RESIDENTIAL
ARCHITECTURE:
LIVING PLACES
May 2002.
128 pages.
9" x 12"
Art & Architecture
1-58862-088-3
$39.95   Hardcover**

Across the nation, homeowners often enlist the services of landscapers. Within this group lies an elite sector which specializes in breaking the mold on traditional landscaping. In this book, you will find truly groundbreaking approaches to the treatment of outdoor space.

**PORTFOLIO SERIES:
GARDEN DESIGN
June 2002.
150 pages.
10" x 10"
Gardening,
Home Design
1-58862-087-5
$29.95   Hardcover**

es on luxury home style, design and architecture

888.458.1750

Hardscape
Contractors

BUHRMAN DESIGN GROUP, INC. ....**(847) 680-6120**
2088 Bob-O-Link Lane, Libertyville   Fax: (847) 680-6124
See Ad on Page: 386, 387, 419   *800 Extension: 1033*
Principal/Owner: Lance Buhrman
e-mail: lance@buhrmandesigngroup.com

HIRSCH BRICK & STONE ....**(847) 623-0063**
15187 Primrose Lane, Wadsworth   Fax: (847) 623-3367
See Ad on Page: 424   *800 Extension: 1130*
Principal/Owner: Greg Hirsch

J. B. BRICKWORKS ....**(847) 634-6437**
1414 Armour Blvd., Ste. B, Mundelein   Fax: (847) 816-6540
See Ad on Page: 422   *800 Extension: 1139*
Principal/Owner: Brent Shad

KRUGEL COBBLES ....**(847) 234-7935**
3337 West Berwyn Ave., Lake Bluff   Fax: (847) 785-9202
See Ad on Page: 420, 421   *800 Extension: 1167*
Principal/Owner: Hans Hirsch
Website: www.krugel.com

POUL'S LANDSCAPING & NURSERY, INC. ....**(847) 949-6667**
6754 W. Indian Road, Long Grove   Fax: (847) 949-6668
See Ad on Page: 385   *800 Extension: 1240*
Principal/Owner: William Bach
Website: www.pouls.com e-mail: info@pouls.com

SPECIAL TOUCH LANDSCAPING, INC...**(815) 467-9066**
15320 Jughandle Road, Minooka   Fax: (815) 467-9065
See Ad on Page: 412   *800 Extension: 1282*
Principal/Owner: Rob Lombardo

UNILOCK ....**(630) 892-9191**
301 E. Sullivan, Aurora   Fax: (630) 892-9215
See Ad on Page: 423, 722, 723   *800 Extension: 1333*
Principal/Owner: Tracy Walsh, Inside Sales
Website: www.unilock.com

**❝Nothing is more
the child of art
than a garden.❞**

— *Sir Walter Scott*

Through creative use of designs, colors and textures, thousands of Chicagoland home exteriors have been beautified with the use of Unilock products.

Finally...
Chicago's Own
Home & Design
Sourcebook

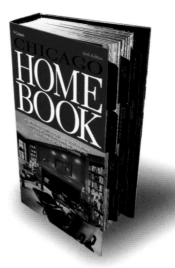

The **Chicago Home Book** is your final destination when searching for home remodeling, building and decorating resources. This comprehensive, hands-on sourcebook to building, remodeling, decorating, furnishing and landscaping a luxury home is required reading for the serious and discriminating homeowner. With more than 700 full-color, beautiful pages, the **Chicago Home Book** is the most complete and well-organized reference to the home industry.

This hardcover volume covers all aspects of the process, includes listings of hundreds of industry professionals, and is accompanied by informative and valuable editorial discussing the most recent trends.

Ordering your copy of the **Chicago Home Book** now can ensure that you have the blueprints to your dream home, in your hand, today.

O R D E R   F O R M

Swimming Pools,
Spas & Sport

BARRINGTON POOLS, INC. ....**(847) 381-1245**
Box 3906, Barrington   Fax: (847) 551-1318
See Ad on Page: 428, 429   *800 Extension: 1024*
Principal/Owner: Dale Overson
Website: www.barrington-pools.com

DOWNES SWIMMING POOL CO., INC. ....**(847) 465-0895**
433 Denniston Court, Wheeling   Fax: (847) 465-0970
See Ad on Page: 427   *800 Extension: 1077*
Principal/Owner: Lou Downes
Website: downespool.com   e-mail: downespool@aol.com
Additional Information: Custom pool builder serving the area for 32 years. Named one of the top 49 Pool Builders in April 2001.

FENCEWORKS ....**(847) 432-0900**
2356 Skokie Valley Road, Highland Park   Fax: (847) 432-1189
See Ad on Page: 432   *800 Extension: 1095*
Principal/Owner: Stan Ascher
Website: www.theguyon41.com   e-mail: stan@theguyon41.com
Additional Information: Fenceworks provides custom-built fences, stationary and adjustable basketball systems and backyard redwood playscapes. Delivery and installation available.

POOL CRAFT, INC. ....**(847) 776-5278**
1509 W. Dundee Road, Palatine   Fax: (847) 776-5299
See Ad on Page: 430, 431   *800 Extension: 1239*
Additional Information: Specialists in custom pools, spas and waterfalls.

SPORT COURT ....**(630) 682-5500**
1547 Orchard Road, Wheaton   Fax: (630) 682-5109
See Ad on Page: 433   *800 Extension: 1284*
Principal/Owner: Dave Vanderveen
Website: sportcourt.com
Additional Information: World's largest builder of backyard game courts and putting greens.

426

"A thing of beauty is a joy forever."
— *Anonymous*

DOWNES SWIMMING POOL CO., INC.

QUALITY POOL CONSTRUCTION AND SERVICE

"Named one of the top 100 firms in the industry"

433 Denniston Court, Wheeling, Illinois 60090
800-939-9309 • 847-465-0895 • Fax 847-465-0970
www.downespool.com

BARRINGTON

POOLS, INC.

Tel: 847.381.1245 • Fax: 847.551.1318

Photography by: Linda Oyama Bryan

Pool Craft, Inc.

Specialists in custom pools, spas & waterfalls

847.776.5278 • Fax 847.776.5299

 Pool Craft, Inc.
1509 West Dundee Road
Palatine, Illinois 60074

Home
Golf
Center

SPORT COURT®

800.616.4321

1547 Orchard Road Wheaton, IL 60187-7201

Backyard
Game Court

Landscape
Lighting

ACTIVE ELECTRICAL SUPPLY ....**(773) 282-6300**
4240 W. Lawrence Avenue, Chicago   Fax: (773) 282-5206
See Ad on Page: 435, 634, 635   *800 Extension: 1003*
Principal/Owner: Skip Leigh

LIGHTSCAPE, INC. ....**(847) 266-7551**
3150 N. Skokie Hwy, #9, Highland Park   Fax: (847) 266-7552
See Ad on Page: 374, 436   *800 Extension: 1188*
Principal/Owner: Steve Achtemeier

"The seed is hope;
the flower is joy.**"**

— *Anonymous*

KICHLER LANDSCAPE LIGHTING

The primary function of outdoor lighting is to provide adequate illumination for the comfort and safety of your family and guests. At Fox Lighting Galleries, we will enable you to create outdoor lighting that is both functional and beautiful.

Fox Lighting Galleries

Secure your home
Beautifully

Increasing your home's safety through outdoor lighting shouldn't mean sacrificing its beauty.

Let Lightscape provide attractive, natural looking lighting to illuminate and secure your home...beautifully.

LIGHTSCAPE
INC.

Aesthetic Landscape Lighting

• 3150 NORTH SKOKIE HWY. NO.9 • HIGHLAND PARK, IL 60035
847.266.7551

Decks,
Landscape Lighting &
Architectural Elements

FENCEWORKS ....**(847) 432-0900**
2356 Skokie Valley Road, Highland Park   Fax: (847) 432-1189
See Ad on Page: 432   *800 Extension: 1094*
Principal/Owner: Stan Ascher
Website: www.theguyon41.com e-mail: stan@theguyon41.com
Additional Information: Fenceworks provides custom-built fences, stationary and
adjustable basketball systems and backyard redwood playscapes. Delivery and
installation available.

KEMPER CAZZETTA, LTD. ....**(847) 256-2584**
412 Green Bay Road, Kenilworth
See Ad on Page: 168, 169   *800 Extension: 1155*
Principal/Owner: John Cazzetta

KEMPER CAZZETTA, LTD. ....**(847) 382-8322**
209 E. Franklin Street, Barrington   Fax: (847) 382-4852
See Ad on Page: 168, 169   *800 Extension: 1157*
Principal/Owner: John Cazzetta

437

> **"**The flower is the poetry of
> reproduction. It is an example of
> the eternal seductiveness of life.**"**
>
> — *Jean Giraudoux*

The A Grou

shley
p

RESOURCE COLLECTION

home resource images, and strives to provide the highest
resources available to upscale consumers and professionals.
Group, visit our website at www.theashleygroup.com.
a member of the Reed Elsevier plc group, is a leading
vertical markets, including entertainment,
encompasses more than 140 Web sites as well as *Variety*,
market leading business to business magazines

Conservatory
Additions

AMDEGA CONSERVATORIES ....**(847) 277-9190**
421 N. Northwest Hwy., Barrington
See Ad on Page: 291
Principal/Owner: Bonnie Miske
Fax: (847) 277-9008
800 Extension: 1006

ARMCOR DESIGN & BUILD/FOUR SEASONS SUNROOMS ....**(847) 487-7900**
951 N. Old Rand Rd. (Main St), Wauconda
See Ad on Page: 441
Website: www.armcor-fourseasons.com
Additional Information: We specialize in high performance glass structures and monumental skylights, conservatories, sunrooms, greenhouses and solariums.
Fax: (847) 487-7902
800 Extension: 1015

"The physician can bury his mistakes, but the architect can only advise his clients to plant vines."

— *Frank Lloyd Wright*

Interior
Plant Design

LINDA M. MANDEL, LTD. ....**(847) 614-4875**
1450 Ridge Road, Highland Park   Fax: (847) 831-0382
See Ad on Page: 443   *800 Extension: 1190*
Principal/Owner: Linda M. Mandel

**"I like a garden
with good bones."**

— *Russell Page*

QUALITY
PLANT
CARE

Linda M. Mandel Ltd. has been providing unique and creative interior plant designs since 1982. We offer personal, reliable sales and maintenance for Chicago and surrounding suburbs. Let our professional plantscaping freshen your atmosphere and create an attractive visual experience.

Please call for an appointment

Linda M.Mandel, Ltd.
Highland Park, IL
Phone   847-614-4895
Fax   847-831-0382

Finally...
Chicago's Own
Home & Design
Sourcebook

The **Chicago Home Book** is your final destination when searching for home remodeling, building and decorating resources. This comprehensive, hands-on sourcebook to building, remodeling, decorating, furnishing, and landscaping a luxury home is required reading for the serious and discriminating homeowner. With more than 700 full-color, beautiful pages, the **Chicago Home Book** is the most complete and well-organized reference to the home industry. This hardcover volume covers all aspects of the process, includes listings of hundreds of industry professionals, and is accompanied by informative and valuable editorial discussing the most recent trends. Ordering your copy of the **Chicago Home Book** now can ensure that you have the blueprints to your dream home, in your hand, today.

Order your copy now!

CHICAGO
HOME
BOOK

Published by
The Ashley Group
1350 E. Touhy Ave, Des Plaines, IL 60018
844-390-2882 fax 847-390-2902
www.chicagohomebook.com

KITCHEN & BATH

nuHaus

1665 Old Skokie Road
Highland Park, IL. 60035
tel.: (847) 831-1330
www.nuhaus.com

K+B+Arts, Inc.

Deyan L. Wolfson
President
Kitchen and Bathroom
Home Design Specialists

Lake Point Tower
505 N. Lake Shore Drive
Suite 207
Chicago, IL 60611

773.259.8142 (direct line)
312.377.0492 (showroom)
312.377.0494 (fax)
www.kbarts.com

449

Form, Function... Fabulous!

Kitchens and baths were once designed for efficiency, with little attention to beauty. Today they are paramount to a home's comfort and style, places to nurture body and spirit. Without a doubt, today's larger kitchen is the real family room, the heart and soul of the home. Some kitchens serve as the control center in "Smart Houses" wired with the latest technology. With the kitchen as a focal point of the home, good design means the room must be both functional and a pleasure to be in, while reflecting the "feel" of the rest of the home. From the European "unfitted" look to super-high tech, there are styles and finishes to make everyone feel at home in the kitchen.

The bath has evolved into a truly multipurpose "cocooning" area as well. Sufficient room for exercise equipment, spacious master closets and spa features are in high demand, resulting in master suites to allow one to escape from the world. The emphasis on quality fixtures and luxury finishes remains, whatever the size of the room.

Photo courtesy of **Chicago Kitchen & Bath**

PLANNED TO PERFECTION
THE CUSTOM KITCHEN & BATH

In many ways, the kitchen and bath define how we live and dictate the comfort we enjoy in our everyday lives. Families continue to design their kitchens to be the heart of the home - in every way. It's the central gathering place. It's a work space. It's a command center for whole house electronic control systems. Bathrooms become more luxurious, more multi-functional. Having experienced the pleasures of pampering on vacations, in spas, beauty salons and health clubs, sophisticated area homeowners are choosing to enjoy a high degree of luxury every day in their own homes.

Homeowners building a new home, or remodeling an existing one, demand flexible and efficient spaces, custom designed to fill their needs. Reaching that goal is more challenging than ever. As new products and technologies race to keep up with the creative design explosion, the need for talented, experienced kitchen and bath designers continues to grow.

The kitchen/bath designer will be a member of your home building team, which also includes the architect, contractor, interior designer and, in new home construction, the landscape architect.

Professional kitchen and bath designers, many of whom are also degreed interior designers, possess the education and experience in space planning particular to kitchens and baths. They can deliver a functional design perfectly suited to your family, while respecting your budget and your wishes. Their understanding of ergonomics, the relationship between people and their working environments, and a familiarity with current products and applications will be invaluable to you as you plan.

SEARCH OUT AND VALUE
DESIGN EXCELLENCE

Designing a kitchen or bath is an intimate undertaking, filled with many decisions based on personal habits and family lifestyle. Before you select the kitchen/bath professional who will lead you through the project, make a personal commitment to be an involved and interested client. Since the success of these rooms is so important to the daily lives of you and those around you, it's a worthwhile investment of your time and energy.

Choose a designer whose work shows creativity and a good sense of planning. As in any relationship, trust and communication are the foundations for success. Is the designer open to your ideas, and does he or she offer information

FIVE WAYS TO SPOT A TOP QUALITY KITCHEN OR BATH

1. **A feeling of timelessness:** Sophisticated solutions that blend appropriately with the home's overall architecture & smoothly incorporate new products and ideas.
2. **A hierarchy of focal points:** Visual elements designed to enhance - not compete with - each other.
3. **Superior functionality:** Rooms clearly serve the needs they were designed to meet, eliminate traffic problems and work well years after installation.
4. **Quality craftsmanship:** All elements, from cabinets, counters, and floors, to lighting, windows and furnishings, are built and installed at the highest level of quality.
5. **Attention to detail:** Thoughtful planning is evident - from the lighting scheme to the practical surfaces to the gorgeous cabinet detailing.

450

on how you can achieve your vision? If you can't express your ideas freely, don't enter into a contractual relationship, no matter how much you admire this person's work. If these rooms aren't conceived to fulfill your wishes, your time and resources will be wasted.

What also is true, however, is that professional designers should be given a comfortable degree of latitude to execute your wishes as best as they know how. Accomplished designers earned their reputation by creating beautiful rooms that work, so give their ideas serious consideration for the best overall result.

Many homeowners contact a kitchen or bath designer a year before a project is scheduled to begin. Some come with a full set of complete drawings they simply want to have priced out. Some take full advantage of the designer's expertise and contract for plans drawn from scratch. And some want something in between. Be sure a designer offers the level of services you want - from 'soup to nuts' or strictly countertops and cabinetry.

Designers charge a design fee which often will be used as a deposit if you choose to hire them. If you expect very detailed sets of drawings, including floor plans, elevations, and pages of intricate detail, such as the support systems of kitchen islands, the toe kick and crown molding detail, be specific about your requirements. All contracts should be written, detailed, and reviewed by your attorney.

TURNING DREAMS INTO DESIGNS — GET YOUR NOTEBOOK OUT

The first step toward getting your ideas organized is to put them on paper. Jot down notes, tape photos into an Idea Notebook, mark pages of your Home Book. The second step is defining your lifestyle. Pay close attention to how you use the kitchen and bath. For example, if you have a four-burner stove, how often do you cook with all four burners? Do you need a cook surface with more burners, or could you get by with less, freeing up space for a special wok cooking module or more counter space? How often do you use your bathtub? Many upper-end homeowners are forgoing the tub in favor of the multi-head shower surround and using bathtub space for a dressing or exercise area or mini-kitchen. As you evaluate your lifestyle, try to answer questions like these:

THINKING ABOUT KITCHEN DESIGN

• What feeling do you want to create in the kitchen? Traditional feel of hearth and home? The clean, uncluttered lines of contemporary design?

THE LATEST APPLIANCES

There's a revolution in kitchen appliances, guaranteed to make your life simpler and more enjoyable: High-performance stainless steel cook-top ranges with a commercial level of performance; Cook-tops with interchangeable cooking modules (like woks, griddles); Down draft ventilation on gas cook-tops; Convection ovens with oversize capacity, and electronic touchpad controls; Refrigeration products and systems you can put wherever you could put a cabinet or drawer; Flush-design appliances; Ultra-quiet dishwashers with stainless steel interiors; Refrigerators that accept decorative door panels and handles to match your cabinets; State-of-the-art warming drawers.

451

Ingredients of a New Kitchen

It's fun to imagine, but what might it actually cost to undertake a project described in this chapter? The example below describes a typical project and gives a general estimate of the costs involved.

PROJECT DESCRIPTION

Designing and installing a high-end, prairie-style kitchen, 16' x 33' sq. ft.

Consultation: retainer, applied towards cabinet purchase $2,500

Cabinetry $44,000

Kitchen, Island, Pantry, Desk
36"- 42" high wall cabinets to ceiling
Maple w/med. stain, modified Shaker styling, custom solid wood construction
Cabinet Accessories

To allow for an ergonomic, efficient use of space, roll-out shelves, an appliance garage, a lazy susan, a trash pull-out, cutlery dividers, tray dividers, a tip-out at sink and cabinet hardware were incorporated.

452

Glass $3,500
Stained glass doors, glass shelves

Countertop $12,000
Granite, 1 1/4" thick, large beveled edge

Backsplash $2,500
Tumbled marble with accent mosaic

Appliance Package, all stainless steel $20,000
36" gas cooktop with hood
Two electric ovens, 48" built-in refrigerator,
Two dishwashers, under counter refrigerator,
Warming drawer, microwave, disposal, hot water dispenser

Plumbing Fixtures $2,900
Undermount double bowl main sink, prep sink,
pull-out faucets, soap dispensers, water filter system

Flooring $4,000
Stone-look porcelain tile

Lighting $2,500
General, task, accent, combination of low voltage, halogen and xenon

Labor $7,000
Installation of cabinets, appliances, counters,
and backsplash. Room preparation, floor installation,
electric and plumbing hook-ups, by general contractor.

TOTAL...$98,400

Note: A very similar look can be had at several price points. For a less expensive installation, custom cabinets can be replaced with stock or semi-custom. The granite tops could be made of butcher block or laminate. Clear or frosted glass can be substituted for custom glass. Depending on the choice of materials, prices could be cut back by half the quoted cost.

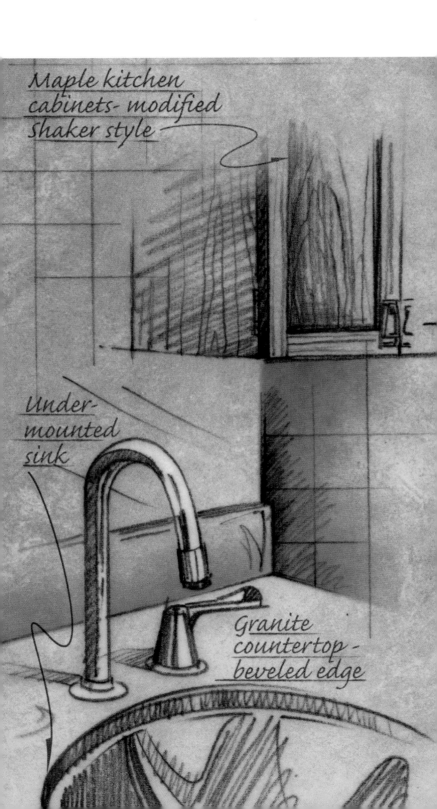

Maple kitchen
cabinets- modified
shaker style

Under-
mounted
sink

Granite
countertop -
beveled edge

WHAT DESIGNERS OFFER YOU

1. Access to the newest products: With their considerable knowledge of products and solutions, your remodeling or budget limitations can be more easily addressed.
2. Ergonomic design for a custom fit: Designers consider all the measurements - not just floor plan space - but also how counter and cabinet height and depth measure up to the needs of the individual family members.
3. A safe environment: Safety is the highest priority. As kitchens and baths serve more functions, managing traffic for safety's sake becomes more crucial.
4. Orderly floor plans: When an open refrigerator door blocks the path from the kitchen to the breakfast room, or you're bumping elbows in the bathroom, poor space planning is the culprit.
5. Smart storage: Ample storage in close proximity to appropriate spaces is essential.

• Is meal preparation the main function of the kitchen? Gourmet cooks and gardeners want a different level of functionality than do homeowners who eat out often or want to be in and out of the kitchen quickly.

• How does the family use the kitchen? How will their needs change your requirements over the next ten years? (If you can't imagine the answer to this question, ask friends who are a few years ahead of you in terms of family life.)

• Do you want easy access to the backyard, dining room, garage?

• Is there a special view you want preserved or established?

• Do you want family and friends to be involved and close to the action in the kitchen?

• What appliances and amenities must be included? Do some research on this question. Warming drawers, refrigeration zones, wine coolers, ultra-quiet dishwashers that sense how dirty the dishes are, cooktops with interchangeable cooking modules, convection ovens with electronic touchpad controls, are all available.

• What are your storage needs? If you own a lot of kitchen items, have a relatively small kitchen, or want personally tailored storage space, ask your kitchen designer to take a detailed inventory of your possessions. Top quality cabinets can be customized to fit your needs. Kitchen designers, custom cabinet makers, or space organization experts can guide you. Consider custom options such as:
  • Slotted storage for serving trays
  • Pull-out recycling bins
  • Plate racks and wine racks
  • Cutlery dividers
  • Angled storage drawer for spices
  • Pivoting shelving systems
  • Pull-out or elevator shelves for food processors, mixers, televisions or computers

• Is the kitchen also a work area or home office? Do you need a location for a computerized home management or intercom system?

THINKING ABOUT BATH DESIGN

• What look are you trying to create? Victorian, Colonial, contemporary, whimsical?

• What functions must it fill? Exercise area, sitting room, dressing or make-up area?

• Who will use the bath? Children, teens, guests, (and how many)?

• What is the traffic pattern? How do people move in and around a bathroom? (Set up your video camera in the corner one morning to get a realistic view.)

• What amenities are desired? Luxury shower systems, whirlpool tub, ceiling heat lamps, heated towel bars, spa, heated tile floors, audio and telephone systems

• What are your storage needs? Linen or clothes closets? Stereo and CD storage? Professionals will customize spaces for your needs.

• Do you want hooks for towels or bathrobes? Heated towel bars or rings?

THE SKY'S THE LIMIT

New high-end kitchen budgets can easily reach the $100,000 range, so it's important to identify your specific needs and wishes. The sky's the limit when designing and installing a luxury kitchen or bath in the 2000s, so don't get caught by surprise by the cost of high quality cabinetry, appliances and fixtures. Know what you're willing to spend and make sure your designer is aware of your budget. Projects have a way of growing along the way. If you've established a realistic budget, you have a solid way to keep the project moving forward and prioritizing your wishes. As you establish your budget, think in terms of this general breakdown of expenses:

Cabinets	40%
Appliances	15%
Faucets and Fixtures	8%
Flooring	7%
Windows	7%
Countertops	8%
Labor	15%

THE NEW KITCHEN - THE FLAVOR OF THE PAST - A TASTE OF THE FUTURE

Many of the fabulous new kitchens being built now don't look "new." The desire for an inviting, lived-in look that encourages friends and family to linger over coffee and conversation is leading homeowners to embrace European design ideas of furniture-quality cabinetry, and dedicated work zones. Consumers are investing in restaurant-quality appliances, gorgeous imported natural stone countertops and floors, and luxury options like dedicated wine coolers, stem glass holders, and plate racks. Tastes are turning to more classical, traditional detailing in cabinetry, with Georgian, Greek and Roman influence in its architecture.

"WHAT ABOUT RESALE?"

This is a question designers hear when homeowners individualize their kitchens and baths. It's only prudent to consider the practical ramifications of any significant investment, including investing in a new custom kitchen and bath. Beautiful upscale kitchens and baths will only enhance the value of your home. Indeed, these two rooms are consistently credited with recouping much of their original cost. Research by professional builders' organizations and real estate companies bears this out year after year. The greatest return, however, is in the present, in the enjoyment of the space.

455

YOUR KITCHEN.COM

Technology has arrived in the kitchen. On-line grocery shopping, computers, multiple phone lines, intercom, security system & "smart house'" controls. Right by the breakfast table.

A STEP UP

Custom counter height is an idea whose time has arrived in new and remodeled homes in the Chicago area. Multiple heights, appropriate to the task or the people using the particular area, are common. When one permanent height doesn't work as a solution to a problem, consider asking for a step to be built in to the toe kick panel of the cabinetry.

GET TWO
DISHWASHERS

**Homeowners today are installing extra dishwashers:
1. To make clean up after a party a one-night affair.
2. To serve as a storage cabinet for that extra set of dishes.
They're also installing dishwashers at a more friendly height to eliminate unnecessary bending.**

This is not to say that homeowners no longer demand state-of-the-art features; quite the contrary. New, smart ideas play an ever more important role in a kitchen's daily life. Kitchens are often equipped as a central hub in a computer automated home, with everything from ovens and entertainment systems accessible by remote control. Home office or homework areas equipped with telephones, computers, printers, and fax machines are included in most every new project. With advances in refrigeration technology, homeowners now have separate integrated refrigerators and freezer drawers installed near the appropriate work zone - a refrigerated vegetable drawer near the sink, a freezer drawer by the microwave, dedicated refrigerators to keep grains or cooking oils at their perfect temperatures. Ultra-quiet dishwashers, instant hot water dispensers, roll-out warming drawers and versatile cooktops are just some of the products that meet the demands of today's luxury lifestyle.

THE NEW BATH - PRACTICALITY DRENCHED WITH PANACHE AND POLISH

Imagine it's a Thursday night at the end of a very busy week. You come home, have a great work out while listening to your favorite CDs over the loudspeakers in your private exercise room, then jump into an invigorating shower where multiple shower heads rejuvenate your tired muscles, and a steaming, cascading waterfall pulls all the stress from your body. You wrap yourself in a big fluffy bath sheet, toasty from the brass towel warmer as you step onto the ceramic tile floor that's been warmed by an underfloor radiant heating unit. You grab something comfortable from your lighted, walk-in closet, and then head out of your luxurious bathroom to the kitchen to help with dinner.

A master bath such as this, built in custom luxury homes, fills a growing demand for private retreats replete with nurturing indulgences.

Master bathrooms are being rethought, with the emphasis shifting from form to function. These baths are still large, up to 400 sq. ft., but the space is organized differently. The newly defined master bath is actually an extension of the master suite, often including his-and-her walk-in closets, mirrored exercise space (in remodeling projects, carved out of a spare bedroom), and separate areas for dressing, applying make-up, listening to music or making coffee.

Large whirlpool tubs are often replaced with custom shower systems with built-in seats and steam capabilities. Other stylish alternatives are Victorian-style claw-foot tubs or smaller whirlpool tubs.

THE REALITY OF REMODELING

Dollar-smart homeowners know that in cost versus value surveys, kitchen renovations and bath additions or renovations yield a very high return on the original investment. These homeowners rarely embark on such remodeling projects with resale in mind. However, knowing their investment is a wise one gives them the freedom to fully realize their dreams of the ultimate sybaritic bath or the friendliest family kitchen that accommodates them now and well into the future.

For more information on remodeling, see "The Second Time's The Charm" in the Custom Home Builders and Remodelers section.

CONTEXTUALISM IN THE KITCHEN AND BATH

Like any other rooms in the home, continuity and contextualism in the kitchen and bath are important to the overall appearance of the home. This is an important point to consider in a remodeling project, especially in an historic home. There often are restrictions on the materials and structural changes that may be made in historic buildings. Your kitchen or bath designer should be aware of these kinds of restrictions.

A REMODELING CONTINGENCY FUND

Kitchen and bath remodeling projects are well known for unexpected, unforeseen expenses, so put a contingency fund in your budget from the beginning. This fund can cover anything from structural changes to your sudden desire to install skylights in the kitchen.

THE BEAUTY OF TOP QUALITY SURFACES

Luxury surfaces continue to add astonishing beauty to kitchens and baths in new and remodeled homes throughout the area. Solid surfaces now are available in an ever-widening range of colors, including a granite look, with high degrees of translucence and depth. Granite and stone add a beautiful, natural look, with an abundance of choices and finishes. Tile, stainless steel, laminates, and wood - even concrete - are other possibilities. Each surface has its benefits, beyond the inherent beauty it can add to your design.

Your kitchen designer will advise you on the best choices for your project, based on overall design and budget. Use the professionals showcased in these pages to find the best quality materials and craftsmanship. ■

TAKING A TEST DRIVE

You wouldn't invest in a new car without taking it out for a test drive, so take the opportunity up front to test the individual fixtures and elements of a new kitchen or bath. Don't be hesitant to grab a magazine and climb into a bathtub, or to test sit a number of possible toilet choices or shower seats. Take your family to a showroom to evaluate counter heights and faucets. The more involved you can be in the planning, the more fun you'll have, and the better the end result will be.

457

Kitchen & Bath
Designers & Contractors

ARTISTIC KITCHEN DESIGNS ....**(630) 571-4567**
1600 W. 16th Street, Oak Brook   Fax: (630) 571-4572
See Ad on Page: 480   *800 Extension: 1017*
Principal/Owner: Cindy Goodrich

LAURA BARNETT DESIGNS ....**(312) 654-1706**
213 West Institute Place, Ste 706, Chicago   Fax: (312) 654-8706
See Ad on Page: 359   *800 Extension: 1178*
Principal/Owner: Laura Barnett
e-mail: lbdesigns1@qwest.com
Additional Information: Established 1980- full service design, project supervision,
specification and/or purchasing of furnishings, fabrics and accessories.

CHICAGO KITCHEN AND BATH, INC. ....**(312) 642-8844**
1521 N. Sedgwick, Chicago   Fax: (312) 642-2272
See Ad on Page: 484, 485   *800 Extension: 1052*
Principal/Owner: Michael Steckhan
Website: www.chicagokb.com e-mail: JC@chicagokb.com
Additional Information: Specialists in home designed solutions for the kitchen and
bath.

CIRCA B.C. INC. NATURAL STONE & DESIGN STUDIO ....**(312) 432-0303**
939 W. Randolph Street, Chicago   Fax: (312) 432-1918
See Ad on Page: 591   *800 Extension: 1055*
Principal/Owner: Spiro Tsiranois
e-mail: CircaBC@aol.com
Additional Information: Natural Stone, Glass, Mosaic Supply, Fabricator, Installer and
Distributor of Bath and Kitchen Fixtures & Hardware. Space Planner, Interior Design,
Construction.

DREAM KITCHENS, INC...**(847) 933-9100**
3437 Dempster St., Skokie   Fax: (847) 933-9104
See Ad on Page: 479   *800 Extension: 1078*
Principal/Owner: Rick Glickman
Website: www.dreamkitchens.com e-mail: Rick@DreamKitchens.com
Additional Information: "Kitchens from a Cook's Perspective" - "Winner: US Chamber
of Commerc Blue Chip Enterprise Award". Featured in *Entrepreneur* Magazine and
Woman's Day Home.

LOIS B. GRIES INTERIOR DESIGN ....**(312) 222-9202**
400 N. Wells Street #416, Chicago   Fax: (312) 222-9207
See Ad on Page: 360   *800 Extension: 1191*
Principal/Owner: Lois Gries, ASID
Website: www.loisgries.com e-mail: loisbgries@aol.com

HACKLEY/LANG & ASSOCIATES, INC. ....**(847) 853-8258**
440 Green Bay Road, Kenilworth   Fax: (847) 853-8351
See Ad on Page: 187   *800 Extension: 1122*
Principal/Owner: Chip Hackley & Bill Lang
Website: www.hackley-lang-architects.com e-mail: hackley_lang@hotmail.com

continued on page **466**

Anything Less Could Cost You More!

Howard Miller
Kitchens • Baths • Additions

3026 Commercial Ave., Northbrook, IL 60062
(847) 291-7050

<u>Showroom Hours</u>
M – F 9 am – 5 pm and Sat 10 am – 2 pm
or by appointment

A wide range of services from design to complete
remodeling and installation or product only

One of the widest selections of kitchen and bath
products in the Chicagoland area since 1986

Authorized dealer of major brand names such as
Bertch,Ultracraft and Legacy cabinets, Dupont Corian,
Barclay, Kohler, Jacuzzi, Elkay,Grohe, KWC and
ARWA plumbing products, flooring and ceramic tile

Call today to see how we can help on your project!

www.howardmillerkitchens.com

Unconventional... a marriage of form, function and beauty. The M-15 collection from Studio Becker takes kitchen style a step beyond.

Striking curved planes, cabinet interiors that unfold, doors that defy gravity, Italian design and European construction. For those who find *unconventional*, exciting.

In Chicagoland, only at Karlson Kitchens

Designers of fine Cabinetry for the Home since 1965

KARLSON KITCHENS

1815 CENTRAL STREET • EVANSTON, ILLINOIS 60201
Tel: 847-491-1300 • Fax: 847-491-0100 • www.karlsonkitchens.com

Wood·Mode
FINE CUSTOM CABINETRY

There are kitchens and there are Karlson Kitchens. Wood Mode cabinetry, customized to meet the most discriminating homeowners, and kitchen designs from Karlson Kitchens can be traditional or contemporary, painted or plain, but always in style.

When you choose Wood Mode cabinetry you are assured of quality that can last a lifetime, with maximum storage capabilities, hand rubbed finishes, select woods and superior construction.

Wouldn't you rather have a Wood Mode kitchen from Karlson Kitchens?

Designers of fine Cabinetry for the Home since 1965

KARLSON KITCHENS
1815 CENTRAL STREET • EVANSTON, ILLINOIS 60201
Tel: 847-491-1300 • Fax: 847-491-0100 • www.karlsonkitchens.com

HOME IMPROVEMENT GROUP
KITCHEN AND BATH GALLERY

18 W. 641 ROOSEVELT ROAD • LOMBARD, IL 60148
TEL: 630.705.0150 • FAX: 630.705.0151

The Finest in Kitchens and Bath.

*Expert Design
Professional Installation*

Visit our Award Winning Showroom
or look us up on the web at
www.insigniakitchenandbath.com

NKBA
The Finest
Professionals
in the Kitchen
& Bath Industry
National Kitchen & Bath Association®

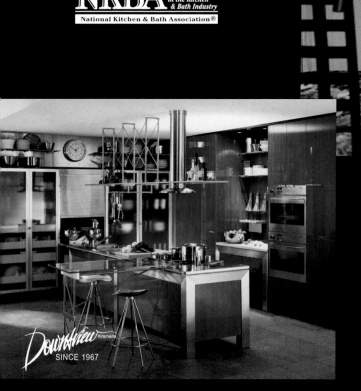

SINCE 1967

Winner of the National Kitchen and Bath Association's 2000 James H. Foster, Jr., CKD Memorial Award for excellence in design.

Showroom Hours:
M-T-W-F   10am-5pm
Th   10am-8pm
Sat   10am-4pm
Other hours by appointment

Associated with

Professional Plumbing Inc.

RESIDENTIAL COMMERCIAL INDUSTRIAL

Kitchen & Bath Design Group, Ltd.

Showroom & Design Center

1435 S. Barrington Rd • Barrington, IL 60010

tel: 847-381-7950

fax: 847-381-8904

continued from page **458**

HOME IMPROVEMENT GROUP ....**(630) 705-0150**
18 W. 641 Roosevelt Rd., Lombard   Fax: (630) 705-0151
See Ad on Page: 462, 463   *800 Extension: 1131*
<u>Principal/Owner:</u> Dimitrios Yiannopoulos
<u>Additional Information:</u> Kitchen & Bath Designs - Professional Installation - Resale
Luxury Kitchen and Bathrooms.

INSIGNIA KITCHEN & BATH DESIGN GROUP, LTD. ....**(847) 381-7950**
1435 S. Barrington Rd., Barrington   Fax: (847) 381-8004
See Ad on Page: 464, 465   *800 Extension: 1137*
<u>Principal/Owner:</u> Bryan Zolfo
<u>Website:</u> www.insigniakitchenandbath.com

K + B + ARTS, INC. ....**(312) 377-0492**
505 N. Lake Shore Dr., Suite 207, Chicago   Fax: (312) 377-0494
See Ad on Page: 448, 476, 477   *800 Extension: 1146*
<u>Principal/Owner:</u> Deyan Wolfson
<u>Website:</u> www.kbarts.com   <u>e-mail:</u> deyan@kbarts.com

KARLSON KITCHENS ....**(847) 491-1300**
1815 Central Street, Evanston   Fax: (847) 491-0100
See Ad on Page: 460, 461, 608, 654   *800 Extension: 1148*
<u>Principal/Owner:</u> David Karlson
<u>Website:</u> www.karlsonkitchens.com

KEYSTONE BUILDERS, INC. ....**(847) 432-4392**
3435 Old Mill Road, Highland Park   Fax: (847) 432-4395
See Ad on Page: 292, 293   *800 Extension: 1161*
<u>Principal/Owner:</u> Joanna & Stan Szymel
<u>Website:</u> www.keystone-builders.com   <u>e-mail:</u> sales@keystone-builders.com

LEMONT KITCHEN & BATH, INC. ....**(630) 257-8144**
106 Stephen St., Lemont   Fax: (630) 257-8142
See Ad on Page: 483   *800 Extension: 1181*
<u>Principal/Owner:</u> Gary A. Lichlyter

466

HOWARD MILLER KITCHEN BATHS ADDITIONS ....**(847) 291-7050**
3026 Commercial Avenue, Northbrook   Fax: (847) 291-7075
See Ad on Page: 459   *800 Extension: 1133*
<u>Principal/Owner:</u> Howard Miller, President
<u>Additional Information:</u> Established as a High Quality Kitchen & Bath Design Firm
serving the North Shore area since 1986.

MORGANTE WILSON ARCHITECTS ....**(773) 528-1001**
3813 N. Ravenswood, Chicago   Fax: (773) 528-6946
See Ad on Page: 140-143   *800 Extension: 1205*
<u>Principal/Owner:</u> Fred Wilson & Elissa Morgante
<u>Website:</u> www.morgantewilson.com
<u>Additional Information:</u> Morgante Wilson Architects is a comprehensive design office
committed to the individual expression of each client's needs and vision.

continued on page **475**

Building Your **Dream** Kitchen and Bath

You may live in a house you love, in a neighborhood that suits you perfectly. However, your home may not fit your changing lifestyle or desires. The following timeline shows the steps involved in planning, executing, and finishing the major remodeling of a kitchen and full bath. It will help you to see the major tasks involved, and give you helpful information to make this process go more smoothly.

Mechanical Work & Whirlpool Bath

All electrical, plumbing, heating, ventilating and air conditioning work is finished. Low-voltage work is completed and whirlpool bath is installed.

Demolition

Walls, flooring, etc. are torn up and removed. Generally takes three days.

Framing

Rough framing and room modifications are completed.

Interior Work

Drywall is installed, walls are taped and primed.

Flooring

Floors are completed. Depending on the complexity of the materials used, this may take up to three more days than anticipated.

WK12   WK13   WK14   WK15   WK16

Windows

Attempt to keep existing window locations during any remodeling project. Moving windows is not a cost-saving endeavor.

• **Whenever you are adding on** new space to a home, have a heating contractor determine whether your existing heating system can accommodate and heat the extra space. You don't want to overwork and thereby damage your existing equipment and be forced to replace the entire unit.

• **Consider your cabinet options carefully.** Those choices will drive the overall price. You can add some options at a later date to defray some of the initial cost. Some that are easy to add include tilt front doors, spice racks and slide-out wire baskets. However, if you decide to wait, make certain that the option you want will be available and can be added after installation.

Building Your **Dream** Kitchen and Bath

Examine your Options

Contact three to five remodelers. Make appointments to discuss ideas and begin the basis for a cost estimate.

WK 1

Narrow the Field

Hold initial meetings with the remodelers. These visits to the house include a walking inspection with measurements taken of specific rooms, etc.

Select Your Partner

Choose a designer/remodeler and blueprints will be created. Expect that it will take three weeks for a project of this size. A retainer will probably be required.

WK5

Review Designs

Meet with your remodeler to review the designs. Establish a budget per design.

Approve Drawings

Finalize and sign off on drawings and hold a "rough budget" meeting.

Approve budget and sign the contract.

WK9

Your Vision

The first appointment is the time to discuss your vision and the remodeler's suggestions for potential layout of the rooms, such as how to squeeze more features into an existing space, etc.

• In some cases, designers and remodelers are employed by the same firm; in other cases, they could be separate firms. There are advantages to going to a company that has both services under one roof, but you are not obligated to hire a design/build firm for both services. Many firms are willing to do one or the other.

• To prevent ending up with an addition that doesn't fit the style of your home, look at pictures of a company's work and make certain to visit homes that it has remodeled.

Project Description

The remodeling of a kitchen and full bath. For the kitchen, the cabinets will be replaced, an island added, new flooring installed, and a breakfast nook with a bay window constructed. For the bath, a whirlpool will be installed, new flooring and new countertops will replace the old, and a closet will be carved out of the existing space.

FINISHED PROJECT

Project Completed!

After the final clean-up, be sure to make a final inspection to ensure that everything is done to your satisfaction.

WK21

• While most states provide warranty protection for the client, the remodeler will include a warranty as well. This may last as long as five years for general items and as long as 10 years for manufacturing products. Certain laws also protect the client. Experts may be called upon to ensure that all agreements and building codes have been made.

Additional Information

For more information, contact the National Association of the Remodeling Industry (NARI), 780 Lee Street, Suite 200 Des Plaines, IL 60016 847-298-9200.

SPONSORED BY:

Neff Design Centre
1376 Merchandise Mart
Chicago, IL 60654
(312) 329-0486
Fax: (312) 329-0487
www.neff.com

Cabinetry and Kitchen Island

Kitchen island and all cabinetry are installed. Complicated cabinetry may take up to three more days than anticipated.

WK17

Countertops, Plumbing & Back Splash

It only takes a day to install countertops but you must wait two weeks after the cabinetry is installed before you can begin. If, during the wait, you change your mind and order different countertops, this will delay installation by three extra weeks. All plumbing is hooked up.

Depending on the materials used, it can take from one to four days to complete the back splash.

WK19

All painting is completed.

WK20

• **If you are going to add a large jetted tub** to your project, consider adding a water heater dedicated to that tub. A large jetted tub can hold up to an average of 75 gallons or more, which can easily overextend your existing water heater and cause problems down the road.

Gaining Space

Examine how you are utilizing space. You may be able to steal some space from a neighboring room or closet. If your bathroom space is limited, purchase a jetted tub and shower combination or install a pedestal lavatory instead of a vanity cabinet with a sink.

In
Conclusion

The process of remodeling a kitchen and bath can be somewhat mysterious, sometimes perplexing, and often frustrating. At the end of the process, however, will be two of the most beautiful, comfortable, and enjoyable rooms of your home well into the future!

Special thanks to Neff Kitchens (Toronto, Ontario, Canada), the National Association of the Remodeling Industry, Inc. and the Design Guild of Chicago, Illinois for their contributions to this article.

Produced by The Ashley Group
847.390.2882
www.theashleygroup.com

continued from page **466**

NEFF DESIGN CENTRE ....**(312) 329-0486**
1376 Merchandise Mart, Chicago
Fax: (312) 329-0487
See Ad on Page: 467-474
800 Extension: 1208
Principal/Owner: Terrell Goeke
Website: www.neffdesign.com e-mail: terry@neffdesign.com

NUHAUS ....**(847) 831-1330**
1665 Old Skokie Road, Highland Park
Fax: (847) 831-1337
See Ad on Page: 446, 447, 478
800 Extension: 1213
Principal/Owner: Doug Durbin
Website: www.nuhauscabinetry.com

PAGE ONE INTERIORS INC. ....**(847) 382-1001**
320 E. Main, Barrington
Fax: (847) 382-0484
See Ad on Page: 362
800 Extension: 1227
Principal/Owner: Adele Lampert, ASID
Website: interiorspageone.com e-mail: pageoneinteriors@aol.com
Additional Information: Beautiful showroom with antiques, reproductions and accessories. Full design services including architectural & CAD, residential & commercial.

PAGE ONE INTERIORS INC. ....**(312) 587-8490**
707 N. Wells, Chicago
See Ad on Page: 362
800 Extension: 1228
Principal/Owner: Adele Lampert, ASID
Website: interiorspageone.com e-mail: pageoneinteriors@aol.com
Additional Information: Beautiful showroom with antiques, reproductions and accessories. Full design services including architectural & CAD, residential & commercial.

ORREN PICKELL DESIGNERS & BUILDERS....................**(847) 914-9629**
2201 Waukegan Road, Suite W-285, Bannockburn
Fax: (847) 914-9781
See Ad on Page: 263- 270, 294, 295, 487
800 Extension: 1223
Principal/Owner: Orren Pickell
Website: www.pickellbuilders.com
Additional Information: Named by Custom Home Magazine as the Nation's "2001 Custom Builder of the Year". Winner of Over 100 Key Awards for Excellence.

GAIL PRAUSS INTERIOR DESIGN, LTD. ....**(708) 524-1233**
421 N. Marion Street, Oak Park
Fax: (708) 524-1237
See Ad on Page: 365
800 Extension: 1106
Principal/Owner: Gail Prauss
Website: www.praussinteriors.com e-mail: gpis@msn.com

ELIZABETH A. ROSENSTEEL DESIGN/STUDIO..............................**(602) 522-0989**
3040 N. 44th Street, Suite 1, Phoenix
Fax: (602) 522-0983
See Ad on Page: 338, 339
800 Extension: 1082
Principal/Owner: Elizabeth A. Rosensteel
e-mail: ElizRosDes@aol.com
Additional Information: Twenty three years of design experience, National and International clientele.

continued on page **482**

K+B+Arts, Inc.

We create kitchens and baths to enhance your lifestyle.

K+B+Arts. Inc.

yan L. Wolfson
esident
chen and Bathroom
me Design Specialists

Lake Point Tower
505 N. Lake Shore Drive
Suite 207
Chicago, IL 60611

773.259.8142 (direct l
312.377.0492 (showro
312.377.0494 (fax)
www.kbarts.com

Dream Kitchens, inc

Consultation, Design, and Installation
3437 Dempster St. Skokie, IL 60076
847-933-9100   Fax 847-933-9104

Visit our award winning web site **www.dreamkitchens.com**

ARTISTIC

KITCHEN DESIGNS

"Professional Design Through Complete Installation"

SHOWROOM

1600 W. Sixteenth Street
Oak Brook, IL

630.571.4567
fax 630.571.4572

www.artistickitchendesigns.com

W.E.S. ENTERPRISES, INC.
Professional Kitchen & Bath
Remodeling & Design.

Let our professional design staff create your
dream kitchen or bathroom suite.
Utilizing the latest design trends & innovations available.
Visualize your kitchen or bath project with our state
of the art design software.
- •Design Services
- •Cabinetry Sales
- •Appliances
- •Complete Remodeling Services

oud member of:

NKBA The Finest
Professionals
in the Kitchen
& Bath Industry
ational Kitchen & Bath Association℠

KraftMaid
Cabinetry

847-931-5491

75 Market St. Suite #20A
Elgin, IL 60103

e-mail wesenterprises@home.com
www.KitchensbyWES.com

continued from page **475**

S & B INTERIORS, INC. ....**(877) 666-2616**
11270 SW 59th Avenue, Pinecrest   Fax: (305) 661-2722
See Ad on Page: 358   *800 Extension: 1266*
Principal/Owner: Sandi Samole, ASID
Website: sandbinteriors.com e-mail: sandi@sandbinteriors.com
Additional Information: From conception to completion, we design and build your
dreams nationwide.

DAVID A. SCHAEFER ARCHITECTS PC ....**(630) 928-0122**
2603 W. 22nd Street, Suite 17, Oak Brook   Fax: (630) 928-0181
See Ad on Page: 212   *800 Extension: 1069*
Principal/Owner: David Schaefer
Website: www.das-architects.com e-mail: dasarch2603@aol.com

ARLENE SEMEL & ASSOCIATES, INC. ....**(312) 644-1480**
445 N. Franklin, Chicago   Fax: (312) 644-8157
See Ad on Page: 326, 327   *800 Extension: 1012*
Principal/Owner: Arlene Semel
e-mail: asemel@asachicago.com
Additional Information: We, at Arlene Semel & Associates, Inc., believe that good
interior design solves the practical problems of function and comfort, while defining
and enriching the art of every day living.

STONEGATE BUILDERS, INC. ....**(847) 579-1525**
1480 Old Deerfield Road #20, Highland Park   Fax: (847) 579-1252
See Ad on Page: 230, 231   *800 Extension: 1289*
Principal/Owner: John Stalowy
Website: www.stonegatebuilders.com e-mail: Jstalowy@stonegatebuilders.com
Additional Information: A Design/Build firm that prides itself on its' management
style. Employs its' own finishers to maintain control over finished products.

W.E.S. ENTERPRISES, INC. ....**(847) 931-5491**
75 Market Street, Suite 20A, Elgin   Fax: (847) 931-8966
See Ad on Page: 481   *800 Extension: 1342*
Principal/Owner: William E. Severance
Website: www.kitchensbyWES.com e-mail: wesenterprises@home.com
Additional Information: Professional remodeling contractors specializing in Kitchens
and Baths.

WICKETS FINE CABINETRY ....**(847) 835-0868**
708 Vernon Avenue, Glencoe   Fax: (847) 835-0867
See Ad on Page: 488   *800 Extension: 1343*
Website: wicketscabinetry.com e-mail: anita@wicketscabinetry.com

WOODWORKING UNLIMITED INC. ....**(630) 871-1282**
150 Easy Street, Carol Stream   Fax: (630) 871-1283
See Ad on Page: 539   *800 Extension: 1350*
Principal/Owner: G. Thomas Kennard
e-mail: woodworking150@hotmail.com
Additional Information: Custom cabinet manufacturer with experience in all aspects
of the project, from design concept to completion.

Lemont Kitchen & Bath
— Inc —

Quality is in the Details

630.257.8144

lemontkb@ameritech.net

Chicago Kitchen+Bath™

Designed Solutions

1521 N. SEDGWICK
CHICAGO, IL 60610
TEL 312.642.8844
FAX 312.642.2272
www.chicagokb.com
Showroom Hours: Mon.– Sat. 10-4
Parking

Kitchen & Bath
Cabinets

ORREN PICKELL DESIGNERS & BUILDERS......................................**(847) 914-9629**
2201 Waukegan Road, Suite W-285, Bannockburn   Fax: (847) 914-9781
See Ad on Page: 263- 270, 294, 295, 487   *800 Extension: 1223*
Principal/Owner: Orren Pickell
Website: www.pickellbuilders.com
Additional Information: Named by Custom Home Magazine as the Nation's "2001
Custom Builder of the Year". Winner of Over 100 Key Awards for Excellence.

WICKETS FINE CABINETRY..**(847) 835-0868**
708 Vernon Avenue, Glencoe   Fax: (847) 835-0867
See Ad on Page: 488   *800 Extension: 1343*
Website: wicketscabinetry.com e-mail: anita@wicketscabinetry.com

❝A house is not a home
unless it contains food
and fire for the mind
as well as the body.**❞**

— Benjamin Franklin

CabinetWerks
An Orren Pickell Company

185 Milwaukee Avenue, Suite 110, Lincolnshire, IL 60069
Phone: 847.821.9421   Fax: 847.821.9460
E-mail: dheig@pickellbuilders.com   Web: www.pickellbuilders.com

All work shown features

Wood·Mode
FINE CUSTOM CABINETRY

fine custom cabinetry.

Photography by Linda Oyama Bryan

Custom Cabinetry as unique as your Signature.
Featuring Crystal cabinets and Wickets Signature Series cabinetry.
708 Vernon Avenue, Glencoe, Illinois 847.835.0868

W&T
WICKETS
FINE CABINETRY

Fixtures
& Hardware

BARTLETT SHOWER DOOR CO. ....**(773) 975-0069**
2219 N. Clybourn, Chicago
See Ad on Page: 490
Principal/Owner: John Klemptner
Fax: (773) 975-0099
800 Extension: 1025

CIRCA B.C. INC. NATURAL STONE & DESIGN STUDIO ....**(312) 432-0303**
939 W. Randolph Street, Chicago
See Ad on Page: 591
Principal/Owner: Spiro Tsiranois
e-mail: CircaBC@aol.com
Fax: (312) 432-1918
800 Extension: 1053
Additional Information: Natural Stone, Glass, Mosaic Supply, Fabricator, Installer and Distributor of Bath and Kitchen Fixtures & Hardware. Space Planner, Interior Design, Construction.

DECORATOR HARDWARE & BATH ....**(847) 677-5533**
3921 W. Touhy Ave., Lincolnwood
See Ad on Page: 554
Website: www.decoratorhardware.com
Fax: (847) 677-7491
800 Extension: 1073

489

"An idea is salvation
by imagination.**"**

— *Frank Lloyd Wright*

Kitchen & Bath
Surfaces

EXOTIC MARBLE & TILE ....**(847) 763-1863**
8055 Monticell Avenue, Skokie — Fax: (847) 763-1865
See Ad on Page: 594 — *800 Extension: 1092*
<u>Website:</u> www.exoticmarble.com <u>e-mail:</u> sales@exoticmarble.com

PARKSITE SURFACES ....**(630) 761-9490**
1563 Hubbard Avenue, Batavia — Fax: (630) 761-6820
See Ad on Page: 492, 558, 559 — *800 Extension: 1231*
<u>Website:</u> parksite.com
<u>Additional Information:</u> Parksite Surfaces is an authorized distributor and marketer of DuPont Corian and DuPont Zodiaq. Through our efforts, we are able to obtain insights on current needs which we share with DuPont to create better solutions for our customers.

FRANK ZANOTTI TILE & STONE CO., INC.......................................**(847) 433-3636**
6 Walker, Highwood — Fax: (847) 433-8950
See Ad on Page: 588, 589 — *800 Extension: 1102*
<u>Principal/Owner:</u> Frank Zanotti
<u>Additional Information:</u> "Old World Charm can be evoked with materials such as limestone, slate or tumbled marble, while stainless steel or glass bends perfectly in a high tech home."

491

"The color of the world
is changing day by day.**"**

— *Les Miserables*

Standards of Living.

DuPont Zodiaq®.

Zodiaq® quartz surfaces will infuse your bathroom with bold sophistication and enlightened luxury. Create a breathtaking sanctuary with its subtle shimmer and crystalline clarity.

DuPont Corian®.

Transform the private retreat of your bathroom into an inviting escape of warmth and comfort. Corian® solid surfaces give you the freedom to create anything you can imagine.

800.338.3355

For inspiration, visit www.parksite.com

Kitchen & Bath
Appliances

DACOR ....**(847) 303-9600**
2330 North Hammond Dr., Ste. A, Schaumburg   Fax: (847) 303-9623
See Ad on Page: 494, 495   *800 Extension: 1065*
<u>Principal/Owner:</u> Mike Joseph
<u>Website:</u> www.dacor.com

LAKE VIEW APPLIANCE DISTRIBUTING, LLC. ....**(630) 238-1280**
1071 Thorndale Ave., Bensenville   Fax: (630) 238-1926
See Ad on Page: 505   *800 Extension: 1171*
<u>Principal/Owner:</u> Philip Gafka
<u>e-mail:</u> pgafka@lakeviewdist.com

OAKTON DISTIBUTORS, INC. ....**(847) 228-5858**
780 Lively Blvd., Elk Grove
See Ad on Page: 496-504   *800 Extension: 1214*
<u>Website:</u> www.oakton.com

493

❝Nothing we use or hear
or touch can be expressed
in words that equal what
is given by the senses.**❞**

— Hannah Arendt

dacor®

The life of the kitchen™

A legendary leader in cooking technology
for over 35 years! Furnishing the finest
built-in contemporary & commercial-style
appliances for your lifestyle.

BOSCH

GAGGENAU

Featuring live demonstrations of all appliances.

Bosch also offers cooking equipment
that features:

- Elegant simplicity in design and controls
- True European convection cook system
- 27"/30" wall ovens and 30"/36" cooktops

Gaggenau is Convection Perfection.

Gaggenau combines high-quality materials, precision manufacturing and design simplicity to bring you simply outstanding appliances with:

- Universal heating - up to 10 cook modes
- Side opening doors
- Professional quality baking stones
- Multi-level baking with no flavor transfer
- Rotisserie
- Meat probe for precision roasting
- Heat insulated glass door with full interior viewing

I think I've died and gone to the kitchen.

Viking products are marketed under the Ultraline® brand name in Canada.

The complete Viking kitchen is a chef's paradise. From the range to the refrigerator, every appliance offers the same superior performance and features you'd find in a professional kitchen.

And with 14 designer finishes to choose from, your kitchen is sure to be a vision.

Ahhh, heaven.

NUHAUS
Workstations by Cheng Design:
Cheng Design introduces its Geocrete Pangea Series, a new line of workstations, each fitting a unique application. These small (25 in. deep by 30 in. wide or 25 in. deep by 48 in. wide) modules plug into new or existing kitchens, adding a wonderful accent to contemporary or traditional designs. With a pastry table, integral brass or stainless trivets, fitted cutting board or integral fruit bowl feature, all are produced with Cheng signature artwork and in-lays. Each of the six module designs is 2.5 in. thick, and available in eight earthy colors: Noir, Slate, Lapis, Plumb, Moss, Blaze, Veldt and Silt.

LEMONT KITCHEN & BATH
Rösle Open Kitchen Rail System:
Since accessories are an important element in kitchen design, the new Rösle gourmet utensils and 'open kitchen' rail system are now available. The stainless steel rail system is perfect for hanging your most often used cooking utensils. Glass shelves and spice shelves, utensils and wine holders are among some of the additional items offered. This rail system complements either contemporary or traditional kitchens.

Photo by **Stocker Photography**

KARLSON KITCHENS
Wood-Mode Cabinetry:
Wood-Mode cabinetry paints a room with beauty and durability. The solid feel and rich warmth of this cabinetry is hard to surpass. It is customized to meet the needs of bookworms or crystal collectors. Homeowners can find Wood-Mode cabinetry in traditional styles, innovative details, and advanced concepts.

Showroom

K & B ARTS, INC.

SCIC-Cantini Line:
The SCIC-Cantini line features post-formed shaped doors that make opening cabinet doors easier; steel, aluminum, and cherry wood; open pantry columns; and 200 available colors for some styles of cabinet doors. These kitchens value absolute simplicity and linearity. We also feature Bench Mark, a totally custom traditional cabinet line, the sophisticated, contemporary Hill Craft kitchens, and Merit kitchens, which are a bit of everything.

CABINETWERKS

Arts and Crafts Kitchen::
More homeowners are moving toward transitional kitchens. This Arts and Crafts kitchen was built to fit into a smaller space-an architectural "jewel box." Note the horizontal lines of the Prairie style Brookhaven cabinetry, the honed granite countertops, the antique seeded glass inserts and the natural stone floor and backsplash. Incorporated into the cabinetry are a refrigerator/freezer, warming drawer, microwave, stove, double oven, dishwasher, waste bin and plenty of floor-to-ceiling storage.

Photo by **Linda Oyama Bryan**

The Ashley Group Luxury Home Resource Collection

The **Ashley Group (www.theashleygroup.com)** is pleased to offer as your final destination when searching for home improvement and luxury resources the following **Home Books** in your local market. Available Now: *Chicago, Washington D.C., South Florida, Los Angeles, Dallas/Fort Worth, Detroit, Colorado, New York, Atlanta, Arizona, Philadelphia, San Diego, North Carolina,* and *Las Vegas.* These comprehensive, hands-on guides to building, remodeling, decorating, furnishing, and landscaping a luxury home, are required reading for the serious and selective homeowner. With over 700 full-color, beautiful pages, the **Home Book** series in each market covers all aspects of the building and remodeling process, including listings of hundreds of local industry professionals, accompanied by informative and valuable editorial discussing the most recent trends.

Order your copies today and make your dream come true!

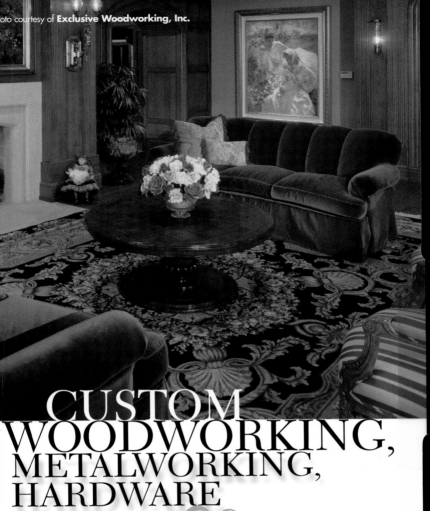

CUSTOM WOODWORKING, METALWORKING, HARDWARE & GLASS

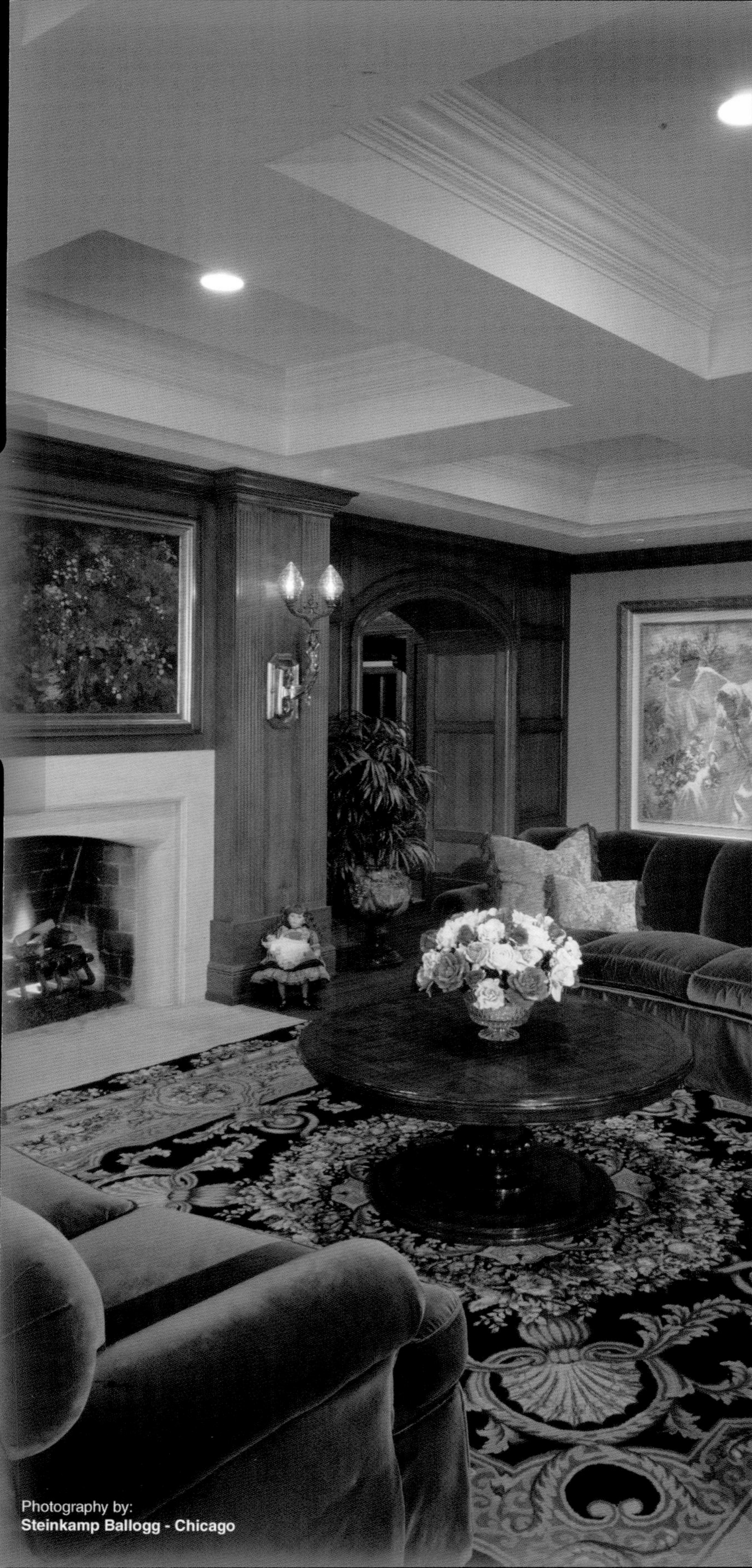

Photography by:
Steinkamp Ballogg - Chicago

- Quality Products
- Personalized expert advice & service
- Complete Showroom

- Free in-home estimates
- Free quotes from blueprints
- Free delivery

- Expert installation available
- Two convenient locations
- Family owned and operated

KONSLER LTD.

WINDOWS • DOORS • MILLWORK
www.konslerltd.com

Libertyville

631 E. Park Ave. (Rt. 176)
Libertyville, IL 60048
(847) 816-7979 Fax (847) 816-7990

Barrington

557 N. Hough St. (Rts. 59 & 14)
Barrington, IL 60010
(847) 277-7979 Fax (847) 277-7990

513

Elegant
Touches

Fine, handcrafted interior architectural elements are the details that distinguish the highest quality custom-designed homes. They lend richness and elegance, infusing a home with character and originality. Even an empty room can speak volumes about the personal taste and style of its owners with cabinetry, moldings, ceiling medallions, chair rails, staircases, mirrors and mantels. Windows, doors, and hardware must endure the rigors of regular use, synthesizing beauty and function into high quality design statements made to stand the test of time. Bring your eye for detail as you explore the finest in architectural elements on the following pages.

Photo courtesy of **Lange Custom Woodworking, Inc.**

WALL TO WALL ELEGANCE

Nowhere is the commitment to elegant living through quality materials more apparent than in the selection of cabinets and millwork. Representing a significant percentage of the overall cost of a new or renovated home, sophisticated homeowners use this opportunity to declare their dedication to top quality.

Architectural millwork, made to order according to a set of architectural drawings, is becoming an increasingly popular luxury upgrade. Such detailing creates a richly nostalgic atmosphere that reminds homeowners of the comfort and security of a grandparents' home or the elegance of a club they've been in.

Elegant libraries, dens or sitting rooms dressed with fashionable raised panel cabinetry and special moldings are often included in the plans for new homes and remodeling projects. As a homeowner considering how and where to install millwork, ask yourself questions like these:

• How is the room used? Will a study be used for work or for solitude? Entertaining or a second office? Will it have to function as both a working office and an elegant room?

• How are the cabinets and shelves used? Books, collectibles, audio-video equipment, computer, fax or copy machines?

• What look do you want? You may want to consider "dressing" your rooms in different woods. You may like the rich look and feel of cherry paneling in your library, mahogany in the foyer, oak in a guest room and plaster in a dining room.

• Will the interior millwork choices work with the exterior architecture? A colonial home reminiscent of Mount Vernon should be filled with authentic details, like "dog-ear" corners, that create classic luxury. Using millwork inside a modern home can add interest and warmth to one or many rooms.

TIME IS OF THE ESSENCE

Hand-crafted high quality woodwork cannot be rushed. Millwork specialists encourage clients to contact them as early as possible with a clear idea of what kind of architectural statement they wish to make. The earlier you plan these details, the more options you'll have. Wainscoting with raised panels has to be coordinated with electrical outlets, window and door openings; beamed ceilings with light fixtures, and crown moldings with heating vents.

Hold a preliminary meeting before construction begins while it's early enough to incorporate innovative or special requirements into your plans.

PRICING A POWER LIBRARY

• A 15- by 16-foot library, fully paneled in cherry, mahogany or oak, some cabinets, with moldings, desk with hidden computer, coffered ceilings: $20,000 to $30,000.

• In a 16- by 24-foot two-story study, less paneling and more cabinetry of cherry, mahogany or oak, heavy with moldings, and radius work, desk with more pull out and hidden compartments for fax machine, small copier, bar with leaded glass cabinet fronts and a marble top, built-in humidor, and heavily coffered ceilings with multiple steps: $40,000.

514

The more time you can devote to design (two to three weeks is recommended), the better your result will be. You're creating a custom millwork package that's never been designed for anyone before. Investments made on the front end are the most valuable. Ask about design fees, timelines and costs per revision. Keep your builder up to date on all of your millwork plans.

Drawings can be as detailed as you require. If you want to see the intricacies of a radius molding before you contract for it, let the millwork specialist know your requirements. Ask to see wood samples, with and without stain or paint.

Try to visit installed projects to get a firsthand feel for the quality of a specialist's work and to develop clearer ideas for your own home.

Changes made after an order is placed are costly. Therefore, if you're unsure, don't make a commitment. Add accessory moldings and other details as you see the project taking shape.

Expect a heavily laden room to take at least five to eight weeks to be delivered, about the time from the hanging of drywall to the installation of flooring. Installation takes one to three weeks, depending on the size and scope of the project.

THE ELEGANT REFINEMENT OF CUSTOM CABINETRY

Handcrafted custom cabinets are a recognizable standard of excellence which lend refinement and beauty to a home. Built in a kitchen, library, bathroom, or closet, or as a free-standing entertainment system or armoire, custom cabinets are a sophisticated signature statement.

There are no limits to the possibilities of custom cabinets. The requirements of any space, no matter how unusual, can be creatively met. The endless combinations of style and detail promise unique cabinetry to homeowners who are searching for an individual look, while the first class craftsmanship of experienced, dedicated woodworkers promises unparalleled quality.

DESIGNING HANDSOME CABINETRY

Cabinetry is a major element in your dream home, so let your imagination soar. Collect pictures of cabinets, noting the particular features you like. Cabinet makers appreciate visual examples because it's easier to interpret your desires from pictures than from words. Pictures crystallize your desires.

When you first meet with a cabinet maker, take your blueprints, and if possible, your builder, architect or designer. Be prepared to answer questions like:

HOW TO RECOGNIZE CUSTOM CABINET QUALITY

1. Proper sanding which results in a smooth, beautiful finish.
2. Superior detail work, adding unexpected elegance.
3. Classic application of design features and architectural details.
4. Beautiful, functional hardware selections.
5. High-quality hinges and drawer glides.
6. Superior overall functionality.

WHY YOU WANT A PROFESSIONAL DESIGNER

515

• They rely on experience to deliver you a custom product. Computer tools are great, but nothing replaces the experienced eye.
• They have established relationships with other trades, and can get top-quality glass fronts for your cabinets, or granite for a bar top.
• Their design ability can save you significant dollars in installation.
• They know how to listen to their clients and help them get the results they dream of.

One Person's Project Estimate:

Adding a Winding Elegance

It's fun to imagine, but what might it actually cost to undertake a project described in this chapter? The example below describes a typical project and gives a general estimate of the costs involved.

Project Description

Construction of a high-end, cherry wood circular staircase, 16-rise (stairs)

Scenario I
Staircase is constructed as part of a new home construction, based on previous blueprint renderings.

Raw Materials (lumber)..$ 9,630

Labor (Shop time)..$34,295

Labor (Installation)..$ 4,680

Total:...$48,605

Scenario II
Staircase is constructed as an addition to an existing home.
In addition to the above prices, the following quotes would be added.

Consultation (Quote)...$265

Field measurement..$210
    Job site measurements are taken

Preliminary drawings.. $0

Estimating $360
    Processing the information from a blueprint and
    determining the cost of the raw materials, labor and any
    other type of subtiers (paint, special material).

Proposal $100

Engineering...$360

Total:...$50,030

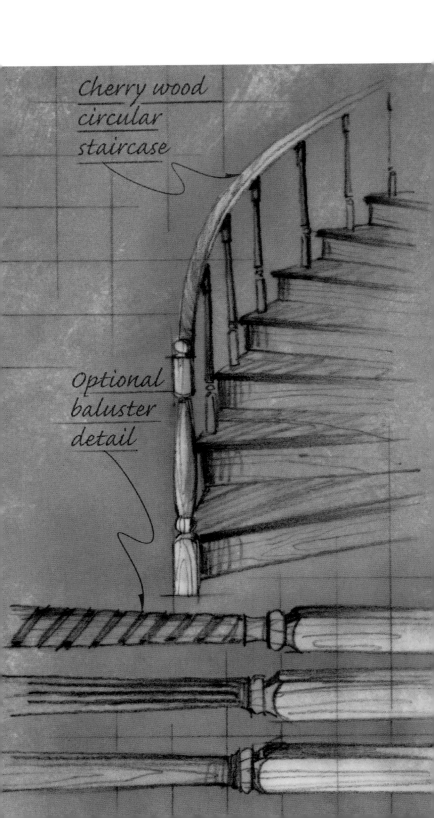

Cherry wood circular staircase

Optional baluster detail

PRICING OF CUSTOM KITCHEN CABINETS

• **Deluxe Kitchen - Face frame-style cabinets or oak, maple or pine, with raised panel doors; crown molding on upper cabinetry, decorative hardware, wood nosing (cap) around counter tops: $10,000 - $20,000**
• **Upgrade to - Shaker inset-style cabinets in cherrywood, painted finish: $20,000 additional.**

518

• What is the exterior style of your home and do you want to continue that style inside?

• How will you the use the cabinets? Cutlery trays, pull-out bins? Shelves for books, CDs, computer software, collections?

• What styles and embellishments do you like? Shaker, Prairie, Country English, contemporary? Fancy moldings, wainscoting, inlaid banding? Use your Idea Notebook to communicate your preferences.

• Do you prefer particular woods? Cherry, oak, sycamore, or the more exotic ebony, Bubinga or Swiss pearwood? (Species must be selected on the basis of the finish you want.)

• Will cabinetry be visible from other rooms in the house? Must it match previously installed or selected flooring or countertops? (Take samples.)

MANAGING THE LENGTHY PROCESS OF A CUSTOM CABINET PROJECT

With plenty of unhurried time, you can be more creative, while allowing the woodworkers the time they need to deliver a top quality product. Take your blueprints to a cabinet maker early. Although installation occurs in the latter part of the construction, measuring usually takes place very early on.

If your project is carefully thought out, you won't be as likely to change your mind, but a contingency budget of 10 to 15 percent for changes (like adding radiuses or a lacquered finish) is recommended.

Custom cabinets for a whole house, (kitchen, butler's pantry, library, master bath, and three to four additional baths) may take 10 to 15 weeks, depending on the details involved (heavy carving adds significant time). Cabinets for a kitchen remodeling may take two months.

THE DRAMATIC EFFECT OF EXCEPTIONAL STAIRCASES

Take full advantage of the opportunity to upgrade your new or remodeled home with a spectacular staircase by contacting the stairmakers early in the design phase. Their familiarity with products, standards and building codes will be invaluable to you and your architect, contractor or interior designer.

Visit a stair showroom or workroom on your own or with your architect, interior designer or builder during the architectural drawing phase of your project. Discuss how you can achieve what you want at a cost-conscious price. Choosing a standard size radius of 24 inches, in place of a custom 25 1/2 inch radius, for example, will help control costs.

Although your imagination may know no bounds in designing a staircase, hard and fast local building codes may keep your feet on the ground. Codes are not static, and stairmakers constantly update their files on local restrictions regarding details like the rise and run of a stair, and the size and height of rails.

THE STAIR-BUILDING PROCESS

The design of your stairs should be settled in the rough framing phase of the overall building project. If you work within this time frame, the stairs will be ready for installation after the drywall is hung and primer has been applied to the walls in the stair area.

Stairs can be built out of many woods. The most popular choice is red oak, but cherry, maple, walnut and mahogany are also used. If metal railings are preferred, you'll need to contact a specialist.

A top quality stair builder will design your stairs to your specifications. Consider the views you want of the house while on the stairs, and what kind of front entrance presentation you prefer. You may want to see the stairs from a particular room. An expert also can make suggestions regarding comfort and safety, and what styles will enhance the overall architecture.

Plans which are drawn on a computer can be changed with relative ease and can be printed at full size. This is very helpful to homeowners who want to see exactly what the stairs will look like in their home. The full-size plans can be taken to the job site and tacked to the floor to be experienced firsthand.

THE POLISHED ARTISTRY OF CUSTOM GLASS AND MIRROR

A room can be transformed through the use of custom decorative glass and mirrors. Artists design intricately patterned, delicately painted glass to add light and architectural interest in all kinds of room dividers and partitions. Glass artistry can be based on any design, playing on the texture of carpet, the pattern of the brick, or repeating a fabric design. A glass block wall or floor panel can add the touch of distinction that sets a home above the others. Stained glass, usually associated with beautiful classic styling, can be designed in any style - from contemporary to art deco to traditional.

Top specialists, like those presented in the following pages, take great care in designing and delivering unique, top quality products. They work with top quality fabricated products, with the highest quality of beveling and edge work.

USING PLASTER DETAILING

Plaster architectural detailing and trim add a distinctive look to any home. Most often used in out of the way places, like in ceiling medallions or crown moldings, the high relief detailing is especially impressive.

PRICES OF CUSTOM STAIRS

Stairs can cost anywhere from $200 to $95,000, depending on size, materials and the complexity of design:
- **Red Oak spiral staircase, upgraded railing: $10,000**
- **Red Oak circle stairs, standard railings on both sides and around upstairs landing: $13,000**
- **Six flights of Red Oak circle stairs stacked one atop the next, with landings at the top of each stair: $95,000**
- **Walnut or mahogany adds 50 percent to the overall cost.**

519

THE ARTISTIC PROCESS

Glass specialists will visit your home or building site to make recommendations and estimate costs and delivery time. Study their samples and if they have a showroom, go take a look. Perhaps you could visit an installed project. Seeing the possibilities can stimulate your imagination and open your eyes to new ideas in ways pictures simply cannot.

Allow a month to make a decision and four weeks for custom mirror work delivery, and ten to 14 weeks for decorated glass.

In order to have the glass or mirror ready for installation before the carpet is laid, decisions must be made during the framing or rough construction phase in a new home or remodeling job. Mirrored walls are installed as painting is being completed, so touch-ups can be done while painters are still on site.

Expect to pay a 50 percent deposit on any order after seeing a series of renderings and approving a final choice. Delivery generally is included in the price.

THE DRAMATIC EFFECT OF CUSTOM WINDOWS AND DOORS

Just as we're naturally drawn to establish eye contact with each other, our attention is naturally drawn to the "eyes' of a home, the windows, skylights and glass doors.

These very important structural features, when expertly planned and designed, add personality and distinction to your interior while complementing the exterior architectural style of your home.

After lumber, windows are the most expensive part of a home. Take the time to investigate the various features and qualities of windows, skylights and glass doors. Visit a specialty store offering top of the line products and service and take advantage of their awareness of current products as well as their accumulated knowledge.

Visit a showroom with your designer, builder or architect. Because of the rapidly changing requirements of local building codes, it's difficult for them to keep current on what can be installed in your municipality. In addition, the dizzying pace of energy efficiency improvements over the past five years can easily outrun the knowledge of everyone but the window specialist. Interior designers can help you understand proper placement and scale in relation to furnishings and room use.

As you define your needs ask questions about alternatives or options, such as energy efficiency, ease of maintenance, appropriate styles to suit the exterior architecture, and interior.

Top quality windows offer high energy efficiency,

DOOR #1, #2, OR #3?

- Door #1 - Six panel oak door with sidelights of leaded glass: $1,700 - $2,000
- Door #2 - Six panel oak door with lead and beveled glass: $3,000
- Door #3 - Oversized, all matched oak, with custom designed leaded glass and brass, sidelights, elliptical top over door: $15,000
- Allow $500 to $1,500 for doorknobs, hinges and other hardware.

520

THREE TIPS FOR DOOR HARDWARE

1. Use three hinges to a door - it keeps the door straight.
2. Match all hardware - hinges, knobs, handles, all in the same finish. Use levers or knobs - don't mix.
3. Use a finish that will last.

the best woodwork and hardware, and comprehensive service and guarantees (which should not be pro-rated). Good service agreements cover everything, including the locks.

Every home of distinction deserves an entry that exudes a warm welcome and a strong sense of homecoming. When we think of "coming home," we envision an entry door first, the strong, welcoming look of it, a first impression of the home behind it. To get the best quality door, contact a door or millwork specialist with a reputation for delivering top quality products. They can educate you on functionality, and wood and size choices and availability, as well as appropriate style. Doors are also made of steel or fiberglass, but wood offers the most flexibility for custom design.

Since doors are a permanent part of your architecture, carefully shop for the design that best reflects the special character of your home. Allow two to three weeks for delivery of a simple door and eight to 12 weeks if you're choosing a fancy front door. Doors are installed during the same phase as windows, before insulation and drywall.

FABULOUS HARDWARE ADDS DESIGN FLAIR

Door and cabinet hardware, towel bars and accessories add style and substance to interiors. Little things truly do make the difference - by paying attention to the selection of top quality hardware in long-lasting, great-looking finishes, you help define your signature style and commitment to quality in a custom home. There are hundreds of possibilities, so when you visit a specialty showroom, ask the sales staff for their guidance. They can direct you towards the products that will complement your established design style and help you stay within the limits of your budget. When a rim lock for the front door can easily cost $500, and knobs can be $10 each, the advice of a knowledgeable expert is priceless.

Most products are readily available in a short time frame, with the exception of door and cabinetry hardware. Allow eight weeks for your door hardware, and three to four weeks for cabinetry selections. Since accessory hardware is usually in stock, changing cabinet knobs, hooks and towel bars is a quick and fun way to get a new look. ■

LUXURY GLASS & MIRROR

• **Mirrored Exercise Room:** Floor to ceiling, wall to wall mirrors, on two or three walls. Allow at least a month, from initial measuring, to squaring off and balancing walls, to installation. Price for polished mirror starts around $9 per square foot. Cut-outs for vent outlets cost extra.
• **Custom Shower Doors:** Frameless, bent or curved shower doors are popular luxury upgrades. Made of clear or sandblasted heavy glass - 1/2" to 3/8" thick. $2,000 and up.
• **Stained Glass Room Divider:** Contemporary, clear on clear design, with a hint of color. Approximately 4' x 6', inset into a wall. $4,500.
• **Glass Dining Table:** Custom designed with bevel edge, 48" x 96" with two glass bases. $1,200.

521

Millwork

EXCLUSIVE WINDOWS INC./EXCLUSIVE MILLWORK CO. ....**(630) 655-1898**
545 Willowbrook Centre Parkway, Willowbrook   Fax: (630) 655-1954
See Ad on Page: 526, 527   *800 Extension: 1088*
Principal/Owner: Tom Lavins
Website: www.exclusivewindows.com   e-mail: chardy4exclusivewindows.com

EXCLUSIVE WOODWORKING, INC...**(847) 831-1330**
1665 Old Skokie Road, Highland Park   Fax: (847) 831-1337
See Ad on Page: 510, 511, 523   *800 Extension: 1089*
Principal/Owner: Doug Durbin

LANGE CUSTOM WOODWORKING INC. ....**(262) 249-0576**
6035 E. Hwy 50, Lake Geneva   Fax: (262) 249-0449
See Ad on Page: 524, 525   *800 Extension: 1174*
Principal/Owner: Larry Lange
e-mail: w.w.w.lange@genevaonline.com
Additional Information: A name known for superior craftsmanship and diverse product lines. When only the finest will do.

"God is in the details.**"**

— *Ludwig Mies van der Rohe*

Lange Custom Woodworking

Lange Custom Woodworking

Jessica Lagrange Interiors, L.L.C.

Olafsen Design Group

Lange Custom Woodworking

- Custom Furniture

- Architectural Millwork

- Liturgical Furnishings

- Kitchens & Baths

- Home Theaters

- Libraries

- Office Furnishings

- Design Services

ange Custom Woodworking

A name known for superior craftsmanship
and diverse product lines.

"When only the finest will do."

LANGE CUSTOM WOODWORKING, *Inc.*

6035 E. Hwy 50 (2 1/2 miles east of Rt 12)
Lake Geneva, WI. 53147
Phone: (262) 249-0576   Fax: (262) 249-0449
E-Mail: lange@genevaonline.com

Exclusive Windows, Inc.
Window and Door Company

Exclusive Millwork, Co.

Division of Exclusive Windows, Inc.

www.exclusivewindows.com

Stairs &
Custom Metalworking

ADAMS STAIR WORKS AND CARPENTRY INC. ....**(847) 223-1177**
1083 S. Corporate Circle, Grayslake   Fax: (847) 223-1188
See Ad on Page: 535   *800 Extension: 1004*
Principal/Owner: Douglas Adams
Website: www.adamsstair.com   e-mail: Adams@adamsstair.com

CREATIVE STAIRS AND WOODWORKING, INC. ....**(630) 963-5050**
440-450 Ogden Ave, Lisle   Fax: (630) 963-3666
See Ad on Page: 530, 531   *800 Extension: 1062*
Principal/Owner: Eliot Del Longo
Website: www.creativestairs.com

CUSTOM WELDING ....**(630) 355-3696**
475 North River Road, Naperville   Fax: (630) 355-3653
See Ad on Page: 536, 537   *800 Extension: 1064*

LAKE SHORE STAIR COMPANY ....**(847) 362-3262**
615 E. Park Ave., Libertyville   Fax: (847) 362-3349
See Ad on Page: 532, 533   *800 Extension: 1170*
Website: www.lakeshorestair.com

NEIWEEM INDUSTRIES ....**(815) 759-1375**
21 Greenwood Drive, Oakwood Hills   Fax: (815) 759-1377
See Ad on Page: 529   *800 Extension: 1209*
Principal/Owner: Kurt Neiweem

" Less is only more
where more is no good. **"**

— *Frank Lloyd Wright*

WOODWORKING, INC.

L A K E
S H O R E
S T A I R
C O M P A N Y

615 E. Park Avenue • Libertyville, Illinois 60048
(847)-362-3262 • Fax: (847)-362-3349
www.lakeshorestair.com

Custom Builders of Fine Traditional &
Contemporary Ornamental Stair & Rail Systems.
A Family Tradition Since 1932.

Finally...
Chicago's Own
Home & Design
Sourcebook

The **Chicago Home Book** is your final destination when searching for home remodeling, building and decorating resources. This comprehensive, hands-on sourcebook to building, remodeling, decorating, furnishing, and landscaping a luxury home is required reading for the serious and discriminating homeowner. With more than 700 full-color, beautiful pages, the **Chicago Home Book** is the most complete and well-organized reference to the home industry. This hardcover volume covers all aspects of the process, includes listings of hundreds of industry professionals, and is accompanied by informative and valuable editorial discussing the most recent trends. Ordering your copy of the **Chicago Home Book** now can ensure that you have the blueprints to your dream home, in your hand, today.

Order your copy now!

Published by
The Ashley Group
1350 E. Touhy Ave. Des Plaines, IL 60018
847-390-2882 fax 847-390-2902
www.chicagohomebook.com

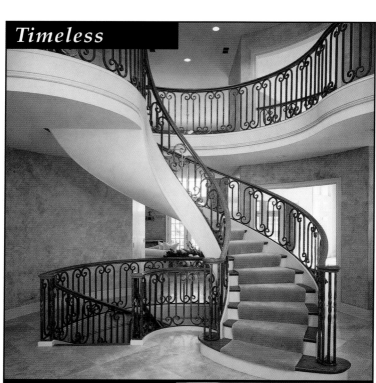

Timeless

Forever

Custom
Cabinets

EXCLUSIVE WOODWORKING, INC....**(847) 831-1330**
1665 Old Skokie Road, Highland Park   Fax: (847) 831-1337
See Ad on Page: 510, 511, 523   *800 Extension: 1090*
Principal/Owner: Doug Durbin

NEFF DESIGN CENTRE ....**(312) 329-0486**
1376 Merchandise Mart, Chicago   Fax: (312) 329-0487
See Ad on Page: 467-474   *800 Extension: 1207*
Principal/Owner: Terrell Goeke
Website: www.neffdesign.com   e-mail: terry@neffdesign.com

S & B INTERIORS, INC....**(877) 666-2616**
11270 SW 59th Avenue, Pinecrest   Fax: (305) 661-2722
See Ad on Page: 358   *800 Extension: 1265*
Principal/Owner: Sandi Samole, ASID
Website: sandbinteriors.com   e-mail: sandi@sandbinteriors.com
Additional Information: From conception to completion, we design and build your
dreams nationwide.

SANDELL CABINETS, INC....**(708) 754-0087**
323 W. 195th Street, Glenwood
See Ad on Page: 540   *800 Extension: 1267*
Principal/Owner: Carol Lynn Miller, Vice President
Website: www.sandellcabinets.com   e-mail: cmiller@sandellcabinets.com

538

WOODWORKING UNLIMITED INC........................................**(630) 871-1282**
150 Easy Street, Carol Stream   Fax: (630) 871-1283
See Ad on Page: 539   *800 Extension: 1349*
Principal/Owner: G. Thomas Kennard
e-mail: woodworking150@hotmail.com
Additional Information: Custom cabinet manufacturer with experience in all aspects
of the project, from design concept to completion.

YORK ORIGINALS ....**(630) 851-4985**
24W947 Ramm Drive, Naperville   Fax: (630) 851-4988
See Ad on Page: 546, 547   *800 Extension: 1355*
Principal/Owner: Morgan York
Website: www.yorkoriginals.com   e-mail: myork@yorkoriginals.com

Woodworking Unlimited Inc.
Quality-crafted cabinetry
From Concept to Installation
150 Easy St. Carol Stream, IL. 60188
(630) 871-1282   Fax (630) 871-1283

Sandell Cabinets, Inc.

CUSTOM MADE CABINETS

323 W. 195th St.
Glenwood, IL 60425
(708) 754-0087 • Fax (708) 754-8775

1-800-956-1199

Decorative
Glass & Mirrors

CHARDONNAY DESIGNS, INC...**(847) 808-7272**
15 E. Palatine #118, Prospect Heights   Fax: (847) 808-7373
See Ad on Page: 542, 543, 647   *800 Extension: 1043*
<u>Principal/Owner:</u> Charmaine D. Nilles
<u>Website:</u> www.chardonnaydesigns.com
<u>Additional Information:</u> As well as custom art glass, we are a full service design
source for home or office.

EXCLUSIVE WINDOWS INC./EXCLUSIVE MILLWORK CO. ....**(630) 655-1898**
545 Willowbrook Centre Parkway, Willowbrook   Fax: (630) 655-1954
See Ad on Page: 526, 527   *800 Extension: 1087*
<u>Principal/Owner:</u> Tom Lavins
<u>Website:</u> www.exclusivewindows.com <u>e-mail:</u> chardy4exclusive@msn.com

IMPERIAL GLASS BLOCK CO. ....**(847) 647-8770**
7412 N. Milwaukee Ave., Niles   Fax: (847) 647-0922
See Ad on Page: 544   *800 Extension: 1136*
<u>Principal/Owner:</u> Thomas G. Pomykala
<u>Additional Information:</u> We are a distributor of Pittsburgh Corning Glass Block. We
carry a large variety of patterns, sizes and styles.

JOE'S GLASS & MIRROR WORKS, INC. ....**(708) 453-7496**
2637 N. Erie Street, River Grove   Fax: (708) 453-7498
See Ad on Page: 545   *800 Extension: 1145*
<u>Principal/Owner:</u> Joe Corsei

541

KONSLER, LTD. ....**(847) 816-7979**
631 E. Park Avenue, Libertyville   Fax: (847) 816-7990
See Ad on Page: 512   *800 Extension: 1164*
<u>Principal/Owner:</u> Connie Konsler
<u>Website:</u> www.konslerltd.com

" Mirrors in a room, water in a
landscape, eyes in a face—
those are what give character. **"**

— *Brooke Astor*

SGO is a patented process bonding mylar and lead to a solid sheet of glass, allowing for greater design intricacies and seamless one piece construction. 300 colors and textures make it the ultimate creative solution to all your decorative glass projects.

Doors
Windows
Mirrors
Cabinetry
Ceiling panels

Make an appointment to visit our showroom

Chardonnay Designs

SGO of the North Shore

Stained Glass Overlay
Interior Design
Custom Window Treatments

▲

CREATIVE DESIGN SOLUTIONS
RESIDENTIAL & COMMERCIAL

15 East Palatine Road Suite 118
Prospect Heights, IL 60070
Tel. 847.808.7272

The largest selection of glass block in the Midwest.
Add statement making form and function to your personal design.

Joe's Glass & Mirror Works, Inc.
Known For Custom Quality Work

- ➤ Custom Euro Style Glass Enclosures
- ➤ Glass Tabletops & Countertops
- ➤ Glass Walls & Dividers
- ➤ Mirrored Closet Doors
- ➤ Mirrored Wall Designs
- ➤ Store Fronts

Hours: Mon.-Fri. 9-5 Sat. 8-12 **Showroom:** 2637 N. Erie St. River Grove

For a free estimate call us at **708-453-7496**

york Moriginal
cabinet & woodwork

fine cabinetry and furniture
designed and crafted by:

morgan york **630 851 4985**

w947 ramm drive naperville IL 6056
630 851 4988 www.yorkoriginals.cc

American Art Glass
for "lasting elegance"

599 Ogen Avenue
Lisle, Illinois 60532
(630) 241-2578

Hardware

BEMMCO ARCHITECTURAL PRODUCTS ....**(630) 960-5540**
1909 Ogden Avenue, Lisle   Fax: (630) 960-5574
See Ad on Page: 552, 553   *800 Extension: 1027*

CHICAGO BRASS ....**(847) 926-0001**
7 Prairie Avenue, Highwood   Fax: (847) 432-1178
See Ad on Page: 550, 551   *800 Extension: 1049*
Principal/Owner: C.J. Schnakenberg
Website: www.chicagobrass.com   e-mail: cj@chicagobrass.com

DECORATOR HARDWARE & BATH ....**(847) 677-5533**
3921 W. Touhy Ave., Lincolnwood   Fax: (847) 677-7491
See Ad on Page: 554   *800 Extension: 1071*
Website: www.decoratorhardware.com

KATONAH ARCHITECTURAL HARDWARE ....**(312) 670-1313**
1324 Merchandise Mart, Chicago   Fax: (312) 670-4297
See Ad on Page: 549   *800 Extension: 1152*

"Form follows function."

— *Louis Henri Sullivan*

CABINET
for your I

At Crystal Cabinets nothing is more important th
cabinetry styles and designs. Using only the fine
handcrafted, custom-designed and backed by a
Crafts to Ultra-Contemporary, your local Crystal
room in the home as well as every lifestyle. ESPE

ESTYLE

Val Constantin

, able to offer our customer a large variety of
ials and the latest innovations, each cabinet is
mited warranty. From Old World to Arts &
ffers a full line of cabinetry perfect for every
RS.

BEMMCO
Architectural Products

1909 OGDEN AVE., LISLE, IL 60532
(630) 960-5540 FAX (630) 960-5574

DECORATOR HARDWARE
& BATH CO.

THE SOURCE FOR SERVICE •QUALITY • SELECTION

3921 W. TOUHY AVE. LINCOLNWOOD, IL 60712
PHONE 847-677-5533 FAX 847-677-7491
DECORATORHARDWARE.COM

Finally...
Chicago's Own
Home & Design
Sourcebook

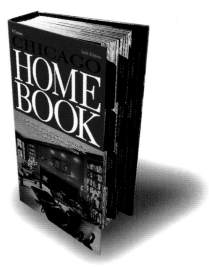

The ***Chicago Home Book*** is your final destination when searching for home remodeling, building and decorating resources. This comprehensive, hands-on sourcebook to building, remodeling, decorating, furnishing and landscaping a luxury home is required reading for the serious and discriminating homeowner. With more than 700 full-color, beautiful pages, the ***Chicago Home Book*** is the most complete and well-organized reference to the home industry. This hardcover volume covers all aspects of the process, includes listings of hundreds of industry professionals, and is accompanied by informative and valuable editorial discussing the most recent trends.

Ordering your copy of the ***Chicago Home Book*** now can ensure that you have the blueprints to your dream home, in your hand, today.

O R D E R   F O R M

THE CHICAGO HOME BOOK

☐ YES, please send me _____ copies of the CHICAGO HOME BOOK at $39.95 per book, plus $3 Shipping & Handling per book.

Total amount enclosed: $_____   Please charge my: ☐ VISA   ☐ MasterCard   ☐ American Express

Card # _____   Exp. Date _____

Name _____   Phone: (____) _____

Address _____   E-mail: _____

City _____   State _____   Zip Code _____

Send order to: Attn: Marketing Department–The Ashley Group, 1350 E. Touhy Ave., Suite 1E, Des Plaines, Illinois 60018
Or Call Toll Free: 888-458-1750   Fax: 847-390-2902   E-mail ashleybooksales@cahners.com

All orders must be accompanied by check, money order or credit card # for full amount.

Location, Location, Location!

What better LOCATION for your advertisement than the CHICAGO HOME BOOK!

Just as our readers realize how important location is when choosing a home, we realize that it's just as important to you when allocating your advertising dollars. That's why we have successfully positioned the CHICAGO HOME BOOK to reach the high-end consumers you want as clients.

Call 847-390-2882 to find out about our unique marketing programs and advertising opportunities.

Published by
The Ashley Group
1350 E. Touhy Ave. Des Plaines, IL 60018
847-390-2882 fax 847-390-2902
www.chicagohomebook.com

FLOORING

&

COUNTERTOPS

ZODIAQ® QUARTZ SURFACES

DUPONT

CORIAN® SOLID SURFACES

DUPONT

Reflect the facets of your individuality.

Corian® solid surfaces.

Warm and inviting, Corian® expresses beauty that is approachable and practicality that's desirable. With the comfortable style of Corian® you can live your mood as it unfolds. Your surroundings are the canvas of self expression, and Corian® is the palette of endless possibilities.

Zodiaq® quartz surfaces.

Throughout your kitchen, Zodiaq® quartz surfaces attract attention and reflect the facets of your individuality. Adding Zodiaq® to you home creates a cool and confident expression open to unlimited interpretation. The bold and sophisticated look of Zodiaq® is the reflection of who you are and what you've achieved.

Express yourself by combining the bold expression of Zodiaq® quartz surfaces with the innovative design versatility with Corian® solid surfaces.

Parksite
surfaces

800.338.3355

For inspiration, visit
www.parksite.com

More home owners trust us do their kitchen counter tops everyday.

More professionals trust us with their client's hon than ever before

It might be something in the air. But we think it is because we deliver better value, better quality all the time. And everyone knows it.

561

Tops 'N Bottoms

T he solid surfaces of a home, the floors and countertops are show-stopping design elements that add beauty and distinction to each room. From exquisite marble slabs, richly polished woods and luxurious carpets, to fabulous granites and ceramic tiles, the possibilities for color, style and combination are unlimited.

Custom homeowners are well traveled and sophisticated in their tastes and preferences, as shop owners and craftsmen who cater to this clientele will attest. Their strong desire for quality and beauty make for educated choices that add value and personality to the home.

The following pages will introduce you to some of the most distinguished suppliers and artisans working with these products.

Photo courtesy of **Mary Rubino Interiors**

ORIENTAL RUGS

The decision to invest in an Oriental rug should be made carefully. Buying a rug purely for its decorative beauty and buying for investment purposes require two different approaches. If you're buying for aesthetics, put beauty first and condition second. Certain colors and patterns are more significant than others; a reputable dealer can guide you. Check for quality by looking at these features:

562

- **Regularity of knotting.**
- **Color clarity.**
- **Rug lies evenly on the floor.**
- **Back is free of damage or repair marks.**

FLOOR COVERINGS OF DISTINCTION...CARPETS & RUGS

From a room-sized French Aubusson rug to a dense wool carpet with inset borders, "soft" floor treatments are used in area homes to make a signature statement, or blend quietly into the background to let other art and furnishings grab the attention.

Selecting carpeting and rugs requires research, a dedicated search, and the guidance of a well established design plan. Because the floor covers the width and depth of any room, it's very important that your choices are made in concert with other design decisions-from furniture to art, from window treatments to lighting.

Your interior designer or a representative at any of the fine retail stores featured in the following pages is qualified to educate you as you make your selections.

Rug and carpet dealers who cater to a clientele that demands a high level of personal service (from advice to installation and maintenance) and top quality products, are themselves dedicated to only the best in terms of service and selection. Their accumulated knowledge will be a most important benefit as you select the right carpet for your home.

THE WORLD AT YOUR FEET

Today's profusion of various fibers, colors, patterns, textures, and weights make carpet selection exciting and challenging. Your search won't be overwhelming if you realize the requirements of your own home and work within those boundaries.

Begin where the carpet will eventually end up — that is, in your home. Consider how a carpet will function by answering questions like these:

- What is the traffic pattern? High traffic areas, like stairs and halls, require a stain resistant dense or low level loop carpet for top durability in a color or pattern that won't show wear. Your choices for a bedroom, where traffic is minimal, will include lighter colors in deeper plush or velvets.

- How will it fit with existing or developing decors? Do you need a neutral for an unobtrusive background, or an eye-catching tone-on-tone texture that's a work of art in itself?

- Will it flow nicely into adjoining rooms? Carpet or other flooring treatments in the surrounding rooms need to be considered.

- What needs, other than decorative, must the carpet fill? Do you need to muffle sound or protect a natural wood floor?

• How is the room used? Do teenagers and toddlers carry snacks into the family room? Is a finished basement used for ping-pong as well as a home office?

THE ARTISTRY OF RUGS

Nothing compares to the artful elegance of a carefully selected area rug placed on a hard surface. Through pattern, design, texture and color, rug designers create a work of art that is truly enduring. If you have hardwood, marble or natural stone floors, an area rug will only enhance their natural beauty. From Chinese silk, to colorful Pakistanis, to rare Caucasian antiques, the possibilities are as varied as the world is wide.

If you're creating a new interior, it's best to start with rug selection. First, it's harder to find the 'right' rug than it is to find the 'right' fabric or paint: there are simply fewer fine rugs than there are fabrics, patterns or colors. However, don't make a final commitment on a rug until you know it will work with the overall design. Second, rugs usually outlive other furnishings. Homeowners like to hang on to their rugs when they move, and keep them as family heirlooms.

In recent years, many rug clients have been enjoying a bounty of beautiful, well-made rugs from every major rug-producing country in the world. As competition for the global market intensifies, rugs of exceptionally high caliber are more readily available. Getting qualified advice is more important than ever.

Fine rug dealers, like those showcased in the following pages, have knowledgeable staff members who are dedicated to educating their clientele and helping them find a rug they'll love. Through careful consideration of your tastes, and the requirements of your home, these professionals will virtually walk you through the process. They'll encourage you to take your time, and to judge each rug on its own merits. They'll insist on you taking rugs home so you can experience them in your own light (and may also provide delivery). And their companies will offer cleaning and repair service, which may well be important to you some day.

ELEGANCE UNDERFOOT: HARDWOOD

A hardwood floor is part of the dream for many custom homeowners searching for a warm, welcoming environment. Highly polished planks or fine parquet, the beauty of wood has always been a definitive part of luxurious homes and as the design "warming trend" continues, a wood floor figures prominently in achieving this feeling.

With new product options that make maintenance even easier, wood floors continue to add value and distinction in upscale homes

FOR SUCCESSFUL CARPET SHOPPING

1. Take along blueprints (or accurate measurements), fabric swatches, paint chips & photos.
2. Focus on installed, not retail price.
3. Take samples home to experience it in the light of the room.
4. Be aware of delivery times; most carpet is available within weeks; special orders or custom designs take much longer.
5. Shop together. It saves time in the decision-making process.

563

BUDGETING FOR WOOD FLOOR

• 2 1/4" strip oak — $10/sq. ft. Wider plank or parquet, glued & nailed — $15/sq. ft. Fancy parquet, hand-finished plank or French patterns (Versailles, Brittany) — $30/sq. ft. and up.
• Estimates include finishing and installation; not sub-floor trim.

Reflooring
with
Red Oak

It's fun to imagine, but what might it actually cost to undertake a project described in this chapter? The example below describes a typical project and gives a general estimate of the costs involved.

Project Description

Replacement of the tile floor of a kitchen and breakfast area with red oak flooring, 200 - 250 sq. ft.

Removal and disposal of old flooring..$875

Installation of red oak boards, 2 inches wide... $2,000*
(finishing fee included)

Toekick at base of cabinets $270

Inlaid vents that match the floor wood ($40 apiece)......................................$80

Threshold to different levels..$20

Furniture removed and replaced..$100

Cabinets wrapped during sanding $100

Total... $3,445

*Price is based on room with cabinets ($9/sq. ft.). If no cabinets exist, then the price is $8/sq. ft.

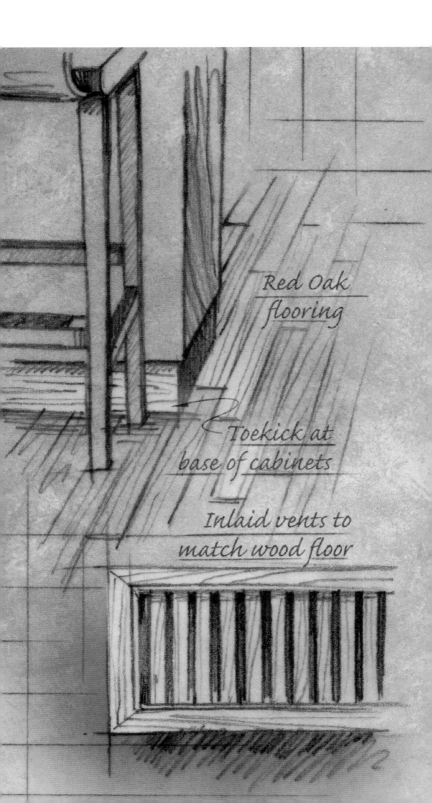

Red Oak
flooring

Toekick at
base of cabinets

Inlaid vents to
match wood floor

Flooring & Countertops

throughout the area and the suburbs. Plank, parquet, and strip wood come in a wide variety of materials, and scores of styles and tones. Consider what effect you're trying to achieve.

Plank wood complements a traditional interior, while parquet wood flooring offers a highly stylized look. Designs stenciled directly on to floorboards create an original Arts and Crafts feel.

The more exotic woods used for flooring, like Brazilian cherry wood, are often harvested from managed forests.

VINYL AND LAMINATES

Vinyl or laminated floor coverings are no longer considered candidates for immediate rehab-as a matter of fact, they're among the most updated looks in flooring. Stylish laminates are made to convincingly simulate wood, ceramic tile and other natural flooring products, and are excellent choices for heavy traffic areas. They come in hundreds of colors and patterns, and offer great compatibility with countertop materials.

THE RENAISSANCE OF CERAMIC TILE

Ceramic tile has literally come out of the back rooms and into the spotlight with its color, beauty and unique stylistic potential. As sophisticated shoppers gain a better understanding of the nature and possibilities of tile, its use has increased dramatically. Homeowners who want added quality and value in their homes are searching out hand painted glazed tiles for the risers of a staircase, quirky rectangular tiles to frame a powder room mirror, and ceramic tiles that look exactly like stone for their sun porch or kitchen. From traditional to modern, imported to domestic, ceramic tile offers a world of possibilities.

It is the perfect solution for homeowners who want floor, walls, countertops or backsplashes made of top quality, durable and attractive materials. A glazed clay natural product, ceramic tile is flexible, easy to care for, and allows for a variety of design ideas. It is easily cleaned with water and doesn't require waxing or polishing. And, like other natural flooring and counter products, ceramic tile adds visible value to a luxury home.

SELECTING CERAMIC TILE

Not all tile works in all situations, so it's imperative that you get good advice and counsel when selecting ceramic tile for your home. Ceramic tile is wear-rated, and this standardized system will steer you in the right direction. Patronize specialists who can provide creative, quality-driven advice.

THE NUMBER ONE WAY TO DECIDE ON A RUG

Do you like the rug enough to decorate around it? There's your answer.

DON'T GET COLD FEET

Stone and tile floors are known for their chilly feel. Electrical products are available now to help warm the surfaces of natural products. Installed in the adhesive layer under the flooring, these warming units are available at the better suppliers and showrooms in Chicago and the suburbs.

CERAMIC TILE AS STONE

With textured surfaces and color variations, ceramic tile can look strikingly like stone. You can get the tone on tone veining of marble, or the look of split stone, in assorted shapes, sizes and color.

566

Visit showrooms to get an idea of the many colors, shapes and sizes available for use on floors, walls and counters. You'll be in for a very pleasant surprise.

If you're building or remodeling, your builder, architect, and/or interior designer can help you in your search and suggest creative ways to enliven your interior schemes. Individual hand-painted tiles can be interspersed in a solid color backsplash to add interest and individuality. Tiles can be included in a glass block partition, on a wallpapered wall, or in harmony with an area rug.

Grout, which can be difficult to keep clean, is now being addressed as a potential design element. By using a colored grout, the grout lines become a contrast design element — or can be colored to match the tile itself.

THE SOPHISTICATED LOOK OF NATURAL STONE

For a luxurious look that radiates strength and character, the world of natural stone offers dazzling possibilities. As custom buyers look for that "special something" to add to the beauty and value of their homes, they turn to the growing natural stone marketplace. A whole world of possibilities is now open to involved homeowners who contact the master craftsmen and suppliers who dedicate their careers to excellence in stone design, installation and refurbishing.

Marble and granite, which have always been options for homeowners are more popular than ever. With luxurious texture and color, marble is often the choice to add dramatic beauty to a grand entryway or a master bath upgrade. Granite continues to grow in popularity especially in luxury kitchens — there is no better material for countertops. It's also popular for a section of countertop dedicated to rolling pastry or dough. Rustic, weathered and unpolished, or highly polished and brilliant, granite brings elegance and rich visual texture that adds easily recognizable value to a home. Beyond marble and granite, the better suppliers of stone products also can introduce homeowners to slates, soapstone, limestone, English Kirkstone, sandstone, and travertine, which can be finished in a variety of individual ways.

ADJUSTING TO STONE PRODUCTS IN THE HOME

Like Mother Nature herself, natural stone is both rugged and vulnerable. Each stone requires specific care and maintenance and homeowners often experience a period of adjustment as they become accustomed to the requirements of caring

PRICING FOR NATURAL STONE

As with all flooring and countertop materials, get an installed, not a retail quote. Installation can drive the cost up significantly. Preparing a realistic quote may take days of research, due to the tremendous variety of factors that can influence price.
As a general guideline, the installed starting price per square foot:
• **Granite: $30**
• **Tumbled marble, limestone, slate: $20**
• **Engineered stone/quartzite: $25**
• **Antique stone, with intricate installation: $75**
• **Granite slab countertop: $70**

567

Flooring & Countertops

MAKE IT CONCRETE

This material is a versatile and indestructible choice, available in a variety of colors and textures. Sealed concrete can be made with creative borders, scored, sandblasted or stained. A strong, natural material, it can be made to look like other materials and natural stone.

SOLID SURFACING SHOWS UP ON TILES

Durable, non-porous solid surface materials are now being used to make decorative wall tiles. Check with your countertop supplier for information and ideas.

for their floors or countertops.

Ask an expert about the different requirements and characteristics. Soapstone, for example, is a beautiful, soft stone with an antique patina many people love. Accumulated stains and scratches just add to the look. Granite, on the other hand, will not stain.

A professional can educate you about the specific characteristics of each stone product so you make an informed decision on what products will best serve the lifestyle of your family.

CHOOSING STONE — A UNIQUE EXPERIENCE

Once a decision to use a natural stone is made, begin your search right away. By allowing plenty of time to discover the full realm of choices, you'll be able to choose a stone and finish that brings luster and value to your home, without the pressure of a deadline. If you order imported stone, it can take months for delivery. Be prepared to visit your supplier's warehouse to inspect the stone that will be used in your home. Natural stone varies — piece to piece, box to box — a slab can vary in color from one end to the other. If you understand this degree of unpredictable irregularity is unavoidable, it will help you approach the selection in a realistic way.

STRONG AND ELEGANT COUNTERTOPS

The quest for quality and style does not stop until the countertops are selected. Today's countertop marketplace is brimming with man-made products that add high style without sacrificing strength and resiliency.

As the functions of kitchens become broader, the demand for aesthetics continues to increase dramatically. For lasting beauty with incredible design sensibilities, man-made solid surfaces are a very popular choice. The overwhelming number of possibilities and combinations in selecting countertops makes it vital to work with specialists who are quality-oriented. Countertops represent a significant investment in a custom home, and quality, performance and style must be the primary considerations in any decision. Established professionals, like those introduced in your Home Book, have a reputation for expert installation and service of the top quality products that define luxury.

MAKE COUNTERTOP CHOICES EARLY

Since decisions on cabinetry are often made far in advance, it's best to make a countertop choice concurrently.

Expect to spend at least two weeks visiting

showrooms and acquainting yourself with design and materials. Take along paint chips, samples of cabinet and flooring materials, and any pictures of the look you're trying to achieve. Expect a solid surface custom counter order to take at least five weeks to arrive.

A WEALTH OF COUNTERTOP OPTIONS

You'll face a field of hundreds of colors and textures of solid surfacing, laminates, ceramic tile, natural stone, wood and stainless or enameled steel. Poured concrete counters also are finding their way into luxury kitchens in the area.

Laminate or color-through laminate offer hundreds of colors, patterns and textures, many of which convincingly mimic the look of solid surfacing or granite. Enjoying growing popularity in countertop application, are the natural stones, those staggeringly gorgeous slabs of granite, marble or slate, which offer the timeless look of quality and luxury. Naturally quarried stone is extremely durable and brings a dramatic beauty and texture to the kitchen or bath. For endless color and pattern possibilities, ceramic tile is a highly durable option. Man made resin-based solid surfacing materials offer many of the same benefits as stone. These surfaces are fabricated for durability and beauty, and new choices offer a visual depth that is astounding to the eye. It can be bent, carved, or sculpted. Elaborate edges can be cut into a solid surface counter and sections can be carved out to accommodate other surface materials, such as stainless steel or marble. Best known for superior durability, solid surfaces stand up to scratches, heat and water.

FINDING THE BEST SOURCE FOR MATERIALS

If you're building or remodeling your home, your designer, builder or architect will help you develop some ideas and find a supplier for the material you choose. Reputable suppliers like those featured in the Home Book, are experienced in selecting the best products and providing expert installation. Go visit a showroom or office — their knowledge will be invaluable to you. The intricacies and idiosyncrasies of natural products, and the sheer volume of possibilities in fabricated surfaces, can be confounding on your own. ■

BEYOND TRADITIONAL

Solid surfacing is now being used to make custom faucets, decorative wall tiles, and lots of other creative touches for the home. Their rich colors (including granite), famed durability and versatility are perfect for bringing ideas to life. Check with your countertop supplier for information and ideas.

BE CREATIVE!

569

Mix and match counter top materials for optimum functionality and up-to-date style. Install a butcher block for chopping vegetables and slicing breads, a slab of marble for rolling pastry and bakery dough, granite on an island for overall elegance, and solid surfaces for beauty and durability around the sinks and cooktop areas.

Carpeting & Rugs

LEWIS CARPET ONE ....**(847) 835-2400**
1840 Frontage Road, Northbrook   Fax: (847) 835-1614
See Ad on Page: 571   *800 Extension: 1183*
Principal/Owner: Steven Lewis
Website: www.lewiscarpet.com e-mail: slewis@lewiscarpet.com

PEDIAN RUG ....**(847) 675-9111**
6535 N. Lincoln Avenue, Lincolnwood   Fax: (847) 675-9120
See Ad on Page: 577   *800 Extension: 1234*

RITA RUGS ....**(773) 880-0031**
3040 N. Lincoln, Chicago   Fax: (773) 880-0155
See Ad on Page: 573   *800 Extension: 1252*
Principal/Owner: Sudershan Goel
Website: www.ritarugs.com
Additional Information: Rita Rugs has been offering customers the finest selection of
oriental rugs at the best possible dollar value since 1977.

ROUZATI RUGS ....**(847) 328-0000**
1907 Central Street, Evanston   Fax: (847) 328-2306
See Ad on Page: 572   *800 Extension: 1258*
Principal/Owner: Jafar Rouzati

570

**"Vision is the art of
seeing the invisible."**

— Jonathan Swift

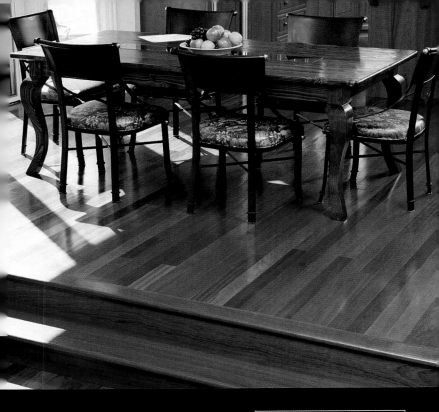

simply exquisite

incredible selection,
unparalleled service, heirloom quality,
exceptional value

RITA RUGS
Art Woven With History®

3040 North Lincoln Avenue, Chicago
Open Monday through Sat 10-6, Thursday 10-7:30, Sunday 11-4
tel: 773-880-0031   web: www.ritarugs.com

Rita Rugs is a family owned and operated business, delivering service and quality since 1979

DESIGN

**The following design books represent the premier works
of selected designers, luxury homebuilders and architects.**

This book is divided into 10 chapters, starting with design guidelines in regards to color, personality and collections. In these chapters, interior designer Perla Lichi presents beautiful, four-color photographs of the design commissions she has undertaken for clients accompanied by informative editorial on the investment value of professional interior design.

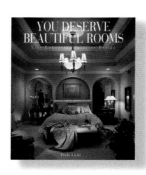

YOU DESERVE BEAUTIFUL ROOMS
120 pages, 9.75" x 14"
Home Design, Architecture
1-58862-016-6 $39.95   Hardcover

Orren Pickell is renowned as one of the nation's finest builders of custom homes. In this collection of more than 80 beautiful four-color photos and drawings, Pickell shows off some of his finest creations to give homeowners unique ideas on building a new home or adding to an existing one.

LUXURY HOMES & LIFESTYLES
120 pages, 9.75" x 14"
Architecture, Home Design
0-9642057-4-2 $39.95   Hardcover

Designer Susan Fredman has spent 25 years creating interiors, which, in one way or another, have been inspired by nature. In this book, she takes readers through rooms which reflect elements of our surroundings as they are displayed throughout the year.

AT HOME WITH NATURE
136 pages, 11.25" x 11.25"
Home Design, Architecture
1-58862-043-3 $39.95   Hardcover

The Ashley Group is proud to present these spec

CALL TO ORDE

BOOKS

Michigan-based architect Dominick Tringali uses the skill and knowledge that has brought him over 20 industry awards to share strategies on building the ultimate dream house. By combining unique concepts with innovative techniques and materials, Dominick's portfolio displays an array of homes noted for their timeless appeal. This $45 million collection of elite, custom homes contains the residences of notable CEOs, lawyers, doctors and sports celebrities including Chuck O'Brien, Joe Dumars, Tom Wilson, Larry Wisne and Michael Andretti's estate in Pennsylvania.

**RESIDENTIAL
ARCHITECTURE:
LIVING PLACES
May 2002.
128 pages.
9" x 12"
Art & Architecture
1-58862-088-3
$39.95   Hardcover**

Across the nation, homeowners often enlist the services of landscapers. Within this group lies an elite sector which specializes in breaking the mold on traditional landscaping. In this book, you will find truly groundbreaking approaches to the treatment of outdoor space.

**PORTFOLIO SERIES:
GARDEN DESIGN
June 2002.
150 pages.
10" x 10"
Gardening,
Home Design
1-58862-087-5
$29.95   Hardcover**

s on luxury home style, design and architecture

388.458.1750

Finally... Chicago's Own
Home & Design
Sourcebook

The **Chicago Home Book** is your final destination when searching for home remodeling, building and decorating resources This comprehensive, hands-on sourcebook to building, remodeling, decorating, furnishing, and landscaping a luxury home is required reading for the serious and discriminating homeowner. With more than 700 full-color, beautiful pages, the **Chicago Home Book** is the most complete and well-organized reference to the home industry. This hardcover volume covers all aspects of the process, includes listings of hundreds of industry professionals, and is accompanied by informative and valuable editorial discussing the most recent trends. Ordering your copy of the **Chicago Home Book** now can ensure that you have the blueprints to your dream home, in your hand, today.

Order your copy now!

CHICAGO
HOME
BOOK

Published by
The Ashley Group
1350 E. Touhy Ave. Des Plaines, IL 60018
844-390-2882 fax 847-390-2902
www.chicagohomebook.com

Flooring

APEX WOOD FLOORS ....**(630) 963-9322**
1326 Ogden Avenue, Downers Grove   Fax: (630) 963-9320
See Ad on Page: 580, 581   *800 Extension: 1008*
Principal/Owner: John Lessick
Website: www.apexwoodfloors.com e-mail: info@apexwoodfloors.com
Additional Information: In business 20 years- no subcontractors- quality assurance-custom borders and inlays- showroom.

ERICKSON DECORATING PRODUCTS, INC. ....**(773) 539-7555**
6040 North Pulaski Road, Chicago   Fax: (773) 539-9694
See Ad on Page: 583   *800 Extension: 1084*
Principal/Owner: John Erickson
Website: www.onlinefloorstore.com e-mail: info@onlinefloorstore.com
Additional Information: Erickson's is one of The Midwest's largest hardwood flooring distributors, stocking full lines of abrasives, finishes, equipment, cleaning and flooring.

LEWIS CARPET ONE ....**(847) 835-2400**
1840 Frontage Road, Northbrook   Fax: (847) 835-1614
See Ad on Page: 571   *800 Extension: 1184*
Principal/Owner: Steven Lewis
Website: www.lewiscarpet.com e-mail: slewis@lewiscarpet.com

PIANETA LEGNO FLOORS USA, INC...**(212) 755-1414**
1100 Second Avenue, New York   Fax: (212) 755-0112
See Ad on Page: 579   *800 Extension: 1236*
Principal/Owner: Serkan Elemek
Website: www.plfloors.com e-mail: pianetalegno@cs.com
Additional Information: Pianeta Legno Floors offers the world's finest engineered and pre-finished hardwood flooring for those seeking warmth of real wood stability of engineered structure.

PMI ....**(630) 842-4540**
333 Washington Avenue, LaGrange   Fax: (708) 352-5597
See Ad on Page: 584, 585   *800 Extension: 1238*

RITA RUGS ....**(773) 880-0031**
3040 N. Lincoln, Chicago   Fax: (773) 880-0155
See Ad on Page: 573   *800 Extension: 1251*
Principal/Owner: Sudershan Goel
Website: www.ritarugs.com
Additional Information: Rita Rugs has been offering customers the finest selection of oriental rugs at the best possible dollar value since 1977.

FRANK ZANOTTI TILE & STONE CO., INC.................................**(847) 433-3636**
6 Walker, Highwood   Fax: (847) 433-8950
See Ad on Page: 588, 589   *800 Extension: 1101*
Principal/Owner: Frank Zanotti
Additional Information: "Old World Charm can be evoked with materials such as limestone, slate or tumbled marble, while stainless steel or glass bends perfectly in a high tech home."

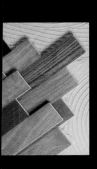

"Handscraped reclaimed oak plank"

"Classic Brazilian cherry on diagonal"

"Traditional double inlay border"

Only
If You
Want the Very
Best...

The
Ashley
Group

1350 E. Touhy Avenue, Des Plaines, Illinois 60018
888.458.1750   Fax 847.390.2902

www.theashleygroup.com • www.homebook.com

Covering the Midwest's floors for over 14 years!
We specialize in Hardwood Flooring, Finishes, Abrasives,
Sanding Machines, Cleaners, Ornamental Floors & More.

Pictured is our showroom floor which contains Red Oak, White Oak, Maple, Ash
Brazilian Cherry, American Walnut, and Purpleheart Flooring. Also shown is a
Nevada Sunburst medallion and an Aztec border from Dynamic Laser Applications.

Buy your flooring supplies where the contractors shop and
get the product and application information that you have
been looking for! Our showroom is stocked with samples
of floors, medallions, borders, machines and finishes,
and most of our products are available in our online store!

Visit our website at:
www.onlinefloorstore.com

Erickson Decorating Products, Inc.
www.onlinefloorstore.com
6040 North Pulaski Road
Chicago, IL 60646
773.539.7555
773.539.9698 Fax
info@onlinefloorstore.com

PMI

333 Washington Avenue
LaGrange, IL 60525
Phone: (630) 842-4540
Fax: (708) 352-5597

Protective Maintenance, Inc.
Residential and Commercial Floor Coatings

Easy to Clean/Maintain

Protects Concrete

Durable

Looks Great

Ceramic
Tile

FRANK ZANOTTI TILE & STONE CO., INC....**(847) 433-3636**
6 Walker, Highwood
Fax: (847) 433-8950
See Ad on Page: 588, 589
800 Extension: 1100
Principal/Owner: Frank Zanotti
Additional Information: "Old World Charm can be evoked with materials such as limestone, slate or tumbled marble, while stainless steel or glass bends perfectly in a high tech home."

**"Style is not something applied.
It is something that permeates."**

— *Wallace Stevens*

FRANK ZANOTTI TILE & STONE CO., IN

6 WALKER HIGHWOOD, IL 60040

847-433-3636   FAX 847-433-8950

Marble, Tile &
Granite

CHICAGO GRANITE DESIGN, INC. ....**(847) 806-7000**
415 Busse Road, Elk Grove Village   Fax: (847) 806-7002
See Ad on Page: 560, 595   *800 Extension: 1050*

CIRCA B.C. INC. NATURAL STONE & DESIGN STUDIO ....**(312) 432-0303**
939 W. Randolph Street, Chicago   Fax: (312) 432-1918
See Ad on Page: 591   *800 Extension: 1054*
<u>Principal/Owner:</u> Spiro Tsiranois
<u>e-mail:</u> CircaBC@aol.com
<u>Additional Information:</u> Natural Stone, Glass, Mosaic Supply, Fabricator, Installer and
Distributor of Bath and Kitchen Fixtures & Hardware. Space Planner, Interior Design,
Construction.

EXOTIC MARBLE & TILE ....**(847) 763-1863**
8055 Monticello Avenue, Skokie   Fax: (847) 763-1865
See Ad on Page: 594   *800 Extension: 1091*
<u>Website:</u> www.exoticmarble.com   <u>e-mail:</u> sales@exoticmarble.com

GRANITE PRO ....**(312) 432-1122**
1826 South Clinton, Chicago   Fax: (312) 432-9842
See Ad on Page: 592   *800 Extension: 1114*
<u>Principal/Owner:</u> Greg Siwek

STONECRAFTERS, INC. ....**(847) 526-9594**
430 Wegner Road, Lakemoor   Fax: (847) 526-9507
See Ad on Page: 602, 603   *800 Extension: 1287*
<u>Principal/Owner:</u> David Hammerl
<u>Website:</u> www.stonecrafters.com
<u>Additional Information:</u> In business over 15 years, new location with new showroom,
25 employees, over 25 different colors in stock.

TERRAZZO & MARBLE SUPPLY CO. ....**(847) 353-8000**
77 South Wheeling Road, Wheeling   Fax: (847) 353-8001
See Ad on Page: 596, 597, 724   *800 Extension: 1308*
<u>Principal/Owner:</u> Jeff Dahlberg, Manager
<u>Website:</u> www.tmsupply.com   <u>e-mail:</u> tmsupply@aol.com
<u>Additional Information:</u> One of the largest Midwest distributors of natural stone.
Designer showroom - stocking thousands of square feel of stone.

UNIQUE MARBLE & GRANITE CORP. ....**(847) 263-6900**
4006 Grove Ave., Gurnee   Fax: (847) 263-6904
See Ad on Page: 593   *800 Extension: 1335*
<u>Principal/Owner:</u> Daniel Hahn, President
<u>Website:</u> www.uniquemarbleandgranite.com   <u>e-mail:</u> uniqueg@ameritech.net

G R A N I T E   P R O

CUSTOM GRANITE & MARBLE FABRICATORS

1826 SOUTH CLINTON • CHICAGO, IL 60616
PHONE 312-432-1122
FAX 312-432-9842
WWW.GRANITEPRO.COM

North Shore's Premiér Provider

* DESIGNS
* SERVICE
* SATISFACTION

UNIQUE

MARBLE & GRANITE
CORP

4006 Grove Ave.
Gurnee, IL 60031
847.263.6900 Fax 847.263.6904
uniquemarbleandgranite.com

EXOTIC MARBLE & TILE, INC
IMPORTERS - DISTRIBUTORS - MANUFACTURERS

MARBLE • GRANITE • LIMESTONE • TUMBLED STONE
BORDERS AND ACCENTS • COUNTERTOPS • FIREPLACES
PEDESTALS • COLUMNS • FLOORS • WALLS • DESIGN

8055 N. Monticello Ave.
Skokie, IL 60076
ph 847.763.1863   fax 847.763.1865
www.exoticmarble.com

More home owners trust us to do their kitchen counter tops everyday.

More professionals trust us with their client's home than ever before

It might be something in the air. But we think it is because we deliver better value, better quality all the time. And everyone knows it.

Nothing Adds Value to Your Home like Natural Stone

Finally... Chicago's Own Home & Design Sourcebook

The **Chicago Home Book** is your final destination when searching for home remodeling, building and decorating resources. This comprehensive, hands-on sourcebook to building, remodeling, decorating, furnishing, and landscaping a luxury home is required reading for the serious and discriminating homeowner. With more than 700 full-color, beautiful pages, the **Chicago Home Book** is the most complete and well-organized reference to the home industry. This hardcover volume covers all aspects of the process, includes listings of hundreds of industry professionals, and is accompanied by informative and valuable editorial discussing the most recent trends. Ordering your copy of the **Chicago Home Book** now can ensure that you have the blueprints to your dream home, in your hand, today.

Order your copy now!

Published by
The Ashley Group
1350 E. Touhy Ave. Des Plaines, IL 60018
847-390-2882 fax 847-390-2902
www.chicagohomebook.com

Solid
Surfaces

AVONITE, INC. (NORTH STAR SURFACES, LLC)............................**(800) 383-9784**
23 Empire Drive, St. Paul   Fax: (800) 378-9110
See Ad on Page: 600, 601   *800 Extension: 1019*
<u>Website:</u> www.avonite.com   <u>e-mail:</u> chas@nssurfaces.com
<u>Additional Information:</u> Avonite, Inc. is the leading innovator of solid surface products with over 60 color choices. North Star Surfaces, LLC is the Avonite distributor for this region.

CHICAGO GRANITE DESIGN, INC. ....**(847) 806-7000**
415 Busse Road, Elk Grove Village   Fax: (847) 806-7002
See Ad on Page: 560, 595   *800 Extension: 1051*

EXOTIC MARBLE & TILE ....**(847) 763-1863**
8055 Monticello Avenue, Skokie   Fax: (847) 763-1865
See Ad on Page: 594   *800 Extension: 1093*
<u>Website:</u> www.exoticmarble.com   <u>e-mail:</u> sales@exoticmarble.com

PARKSITE SURFACES ....**(630) 761-9490**
1563 Hubbard Avenue, Batavia   Fax: (630) 761-6820
See Ad on Page: 492, 558, 559   *800 Extension: 1232*
<u>Website:</u> parksite.com
<u>Additional Information:</u> Parksite Surfaces is an authorized distributor and marketer of DuPont Corian and DuPont Zodiaq. Through our efforts, we are able to obtain insights on current needs which we share with DuPont to create better solutions for our customers.

SILESTONE BY COSENTINO (NORTH STAR SURFACES, LLC) ....**(800) 383-9784**
23 Empire Drive, St. Paul   Fax: (800) 378-9110
See Ad on Page: 600, 601   *800 Extension: 1276*
<u>Website:</u> www.silestoneUSA.com   <u>e-mail:</u> chas@nssurfaces.com
<u>Additional Information:</u> Silestone is the leading brand of quartz surfacing and is ideal for counters, wall cladding and floors.

STONECRAFTERS, INC. ....**(847) 526-9594**
430 Wegner Road, Lakemoor   Fax: (847) 526-9507
See Ad on Page: 602, 603   *800 Extension: 1286*
<u>Principal/Owner:</u> David Hammerl
<u>Website:</u> www.stonecrafters.com
<u>Additional Information:</u> In business over 15 years, new location with new showroom, 25 employees, over 25 different colors in stock.

599

HE'S YOUR LITTLE PICASSO.

SILESTONE®
by Cosentino
QUARTZ SURFACING

www.silestoneusa.com

For more information,
call North Star Surfaces at
1-800-383-9784

THIS TECHNOLOGY BRINGS CREATIVITY THAT LASTS A LIFETIME.
Quartz Surfacing combines the beauty of nature and the strength of technology
to form "The Most Practical Countertop" on the market today. Also excellent
for wall cladding and flooring this 93% natural quartz with polymers results in
a beautiful nonporous low maintenance material that is stronger than granite.

*S*tonecrafters

FINE HANDCRAFTED GRANITE & MARBLE

Stone, Slate
& Concrete

**❝Vision without action
is a daydream;
action without vision
is a nightmare.❞**

— *Japanese Proverb*

HOME
FURNISHINGS
&
DECORATING

Prairie in the Round

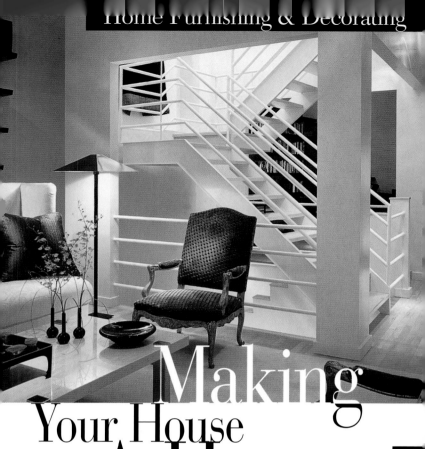

Making
Your House
A Home

A beautiful designed, meticulously planned house becomes a home when the furnishings are set in place. Comfortably upholstered sofas and chairs in the family room, a unique faux-finished foyer, richly appointed windows in the dining room, all give a home its individual flair and welcoming livability.

Today's homeowners, whether they're in their first or final home, have the elevated taste that comes from exposure to good design. They know what quality furniture looks and feels like and they want it in their homes.

In the home furnishing industry, one item is more outrageously gorgeous than the next, and anything you can imagine can be yours. This freedom can be overwhelming, even intimidating, if you don't keep a sharp focus.

By visiting the finest stores, specialty shops, and artisans, like those presented in the following pages, you'll find your quest for fine quality is already understood, and knowledgeable professionals are ready to guide you. Enjoy.

Photo courtesy of **Gregory Maire Architects**

TAKE TIME TO CHOOSE FURNITURE

Your interior designer, or qualified store personnel, can direct your search and keep you within the scale of your floor plan. Their firsthand knowledge of pricing, products and features will help you find the best quality for your money.

To save time, take along your blueprint or a detailed drawing with measurements, door and window placements, and special architectural features. If your spouse or anyone else will be involved in the final decision, try to shop together to eliminate return trips. Most stores can deliver most furniture within eight weeks, but special custom pieces may take up to 16 weeks.

When furnishing a new room, concentrate on selecting one important piece to create a focus, like a Chinese Chippendale-style daybed or an original Arts & Crafts spindle table. Select around whatever special pieces you already own.

Ruthlessly assess your current interior. Clear out pieces that need to be replaced or no longer work with your lifestyle, even if you have no clear idea of what you'll be replacing them with. Sometimes empty space makes visualizing something new much easier.

Be open-minded and accept direction. Salespeople at top stores can help you find exactly what you're seeking, and, if you ask them, can guide you away from inappropriate decisions, towards more suitable alternatives. Keep these thoughts in mind:

• What are your priorities? Develop a list of "must have," "want to have," and "dreaming about."

• Do you want your furnishings to follow the architecture? This always proves a good starting point.

• What colors or styles are already established through the flooring, walls, windows, or cabinetry?

• Can you get the furnishings through the doorway, up the elevator, or down the stairs?

• Does the price reflect your tastes? Don't be influenced too strongly by what looks great in a showroom or designer house.

• What major pieces will be with you for a long time? Allow a lion's share of your budget for these.

• Does the piece fit the overall decorating scheme? Although the days of strict adherence to one style per room are over, it's still necessary to use coordinated styles.

• Do you have something (a lamp, antique candlesticks, a framed picture) you can put on the table you're considering? If not, choose accessories when you choose the table.

• Will a piece work for your family's lifestyle? Choose

MODERN IDEAS

With an evolutionary array of styles, contemporary furnishings add excitement, elegance and personality to a home. From Bauhaus, Retro, and Deco, to pure modern, these artful furnishings satisfy the desire for unique, individual expression.

KEEP IT ALIVE!

Regardless of your budget, you needn't sacrifice quality or style. Set your priorities and let your home take on a dynamic, ever-changing feel as you add or replace furnishings over a period of time.

upholstery fabrics, colors and fixtures that will
enhance, not hinder, your everyday life.

• Is the piece comfortable? Before you buy, sit on the
chair, recline on the sofa, pull a chair up to the table.

CONSIDERING CUSTOM FURNITURE

Our area is home to many talented, accessible
furniture designers who can create whatever
you need to fill a special space in your home, and to
satisfy your desire for owning a unique, one-of-a-kind
object.

Contacting a furniture designer is the first step
toward attaining a fabulous piece of individualized art
for your home. Some of the best known designers
working here today are listed in the following pages
of the Home Book. You can contact them directly, or
through your interior designer.

The second step is an initial meeting, during
which you'll see examples of the designer's work and
answer questions like:

• What kind of piece do you want? Freestanding
entertainment system, dining table, armoire?

• What functions must it serve? It is a piece of art,
but the furniture still must function in ways that make
it practical and usable. Explain your needs clearly.

• Do you have favorite woods, materials or colors?
As with ordering custom woodwork, the possibilities
are almost unlimited. Different woods can be painted
or finished differently for all kinds of looks. It's best to
have some ideas in mind.

• Are you open to new ideas and approaches?
If you'd like the designer to suggest new ways of
reaching your goal, let him or her know.

If the designer's portfolio excites you, the
communication is good, and you trust him or her
to deliver your project in a top quality, professional
manner, then you're ready to begin. Ask the designer
to create a couple of design options. Make sure you
and the designer are in agreement regarding finishes,
materials, stain or paint samples you want to see, and
a completion date. Most charge a 50 percent deposit
at the beginning with the balance due upon
completion. If you decide not to go ahead with
construction of a piece, expect to be billed a
designer's fee. A commissioned piece of furniture
requires a reasonable amount of time to get from
start to finish. If you want an entertainment system
for Super Bowl Sunday, make your final design
decisions when you take down the Halloween
decorations. Keep in mind that the process cannot be
rushed.

THREE IS THE MAGIC NUMBER

In accessorizing a home, thinking in "threes" is a good rule of thumb: Three candlesticks with candles of three different heights. Three colors of pottery grouped together, one less vibrant to highlight the others. Three patterns in a room.

611

One Person's Project Estimate:

Custom Designing a Cherry Wood Table

It's fun to imagine, but what might it actually cost to undertake a project described in this chapter? The example below describes a typical project and gives a general estimate of the costs involved.

Project Description

Custom design and construction of a 48" x 96" dining room table.

A couple moving to a new home in another region had trees from their old home site harvested, sawed into lumber, dried, and built it into a Cherry table for their dining room.

Trees harvested (felled) ($30/hr x 2 hours)...$60

Trees sawn and dried..$175

Design (included in the project cost)
    Clients were first asked about their desires for the table, then books and catalog research was done for examples. Once a basic concept is formulated, a full-scale drawing is done. Generally, clients may or may not see it these drawings. In this case, the clients only saw rough sketches before it was delivered to them.

Labor Cost $5,000
    Fine sanding, construction, varnishing

Special materials (included in cost)...$0
    Varnish, etc.

*Delivery (local) $0

Total:.. $5,235

*If more than 100 miles away, delivery is $250

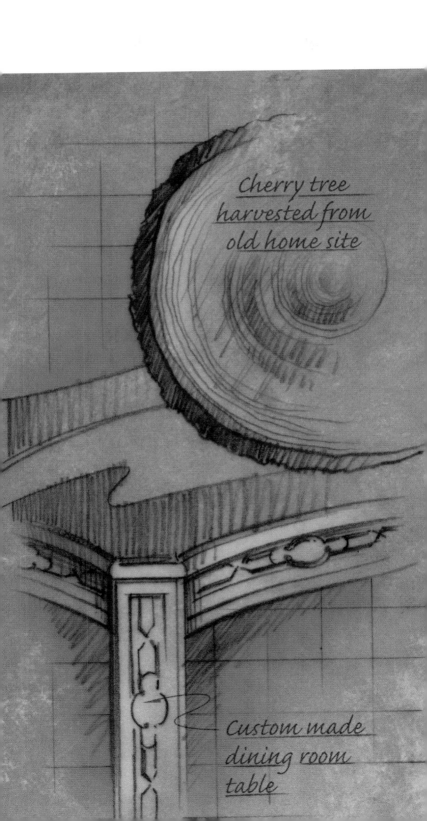

cherry tree harvested from old home site

Custom made dining room table

LOFT LIGHTING

Lofts do have large windows, but they're usually on one wall. That presents a lighting challenge that is often met with new low-voltage systems. The transformer is hidden in a closet or soffit; decorative transformers are mounted on a wall. The halogen bulbs last thousands of hours - very important given the height of loft ceilings.

A BRIGHT IDEA

Buy a few clip-on lights with 50-watt bulbs and take them home with you to pinpoint your needs and favorite lighting looks. Experiment with them to create different effects. See if you like up- or downlights to highlight an architectural feature. Get an idea of how much light it takes to illuminate a room.

SPOTLIGHT ON LIGHTING

Lighting can be the focal point of a room, or it can be so subtle that it's almost invisible. The trick is knowing what you want to accomplish. Indeed, when we remember a place as cozy, elegant, or dramatic; or cold and uncomfortable, we're feeling the emotional power of illumination.

The industry is filled with options and combinations, from fixtures and bulbs to dimmers and integrated systems. Top lighting retailers in the area employ in-house design consultants to guide you, or you can employ a residential lighting designer.

To deliver a superior lighting scheme, a designer must know:

• What is your budget? One of the biggest mistakes custom homeowners make is under-budgeting their lighting program.

• What are your needs? Lighting falls into three categories - general, task, and atmospheric. A study/work area, a cozy nook or a kitchen each require different lighting.

• What feeling are you trying to create?

• What "givens" are you working with? Where are your windows or skylights? The use of artificial, indoor light depends to a great degree on the natural light coming in.

• What materials are on the floor and what colors are on the walls and ceiling? This affects reflectance.

• Where is your furniture placed, and how big are individual pieces? This is especially important when you're choosing a dining room chandelier.

• If you're replacing something, why are you replacing it? Know the wattage, for instance, if a current light source is no longer bright enough.

• Are there energy/environmental concerns? Lighting consumes 12 to 15 percent of the electricity used in the home. An expert can develop a plan that maximizes energy efficiency.

• Who lives in the house? Will footballs and frisbees be flying through the kitchen? Pass on the hanging fixture and choose recessed lighting instead.

"DECKED OUT" FOR OUTDOOR LIVING

As homeowners strive to expand comfortable living space into their yards, top quality outdoor furniture responds with new and innovative styles. Before you go looking at outdoor furniture, think about:

• What look do you like? The intricate patterns of

wrought iron? The smooth and timeless beauty of silvery teak wood? The sleek design of sturdy aluminum?

• What pieces do you need? Furnishing larger decks and terraces requires careful planning. Area homeowners are buying more seating and end tables and phasing out umbrellas.

• Will you store the furniture in the winter or will it stay outdoors under cover?

• Can you see the furniture from inside? Make sure the outdoor furnishings won't distract from established design inside or outside.

THE SPECIAL QUALITY OF PIANOS

A new or professionally reconditioned piano makes an excellent contribution to the elegance and lifestyle of a growing number of area homes. Pianos add a dimension of personality that no ordinary piece of furniture can match. They are recognized for the beauty they add, visually and acoustically.

First time piano buyers may be astonished at the range of choices they have and the variables that will influence their eventual decision. Go to those showrooms that carry the best brand name pianos. Not only will you be offered superior quality instruments, but you'll also get the value of the sales staff's professional knowledge and experience. Questions that you need to answer will include:

• Who are the primary players of the instrument?

• What level of players are they (serious, beginners)?

• Who are their teachers?

• What is the size of the room the piano will be placed in?

• What are your preferences in wood color or leg shape?

• Are you interested in software packages that convert your instrument into a player piano?

Pianos represent a significant financial investment, one that will not depreciate, and may actually appreciate over time. If a new piano is out of your financial range, ask about the store's selection of reconditioned instruments that they've acquired through trades. The best stores recondition these pieces to a uniformly high standard of excellence and are good options for you to consider. These stores also hold occasional promotions, when special pricing will be in effect for a period of time.

THE GLOBAL MARKETPLACE

There are so many exciting lighting designs available from all over the world, a lighting retailer can't possibly show you even half of them in the showroom. Allow yourself enough time to pour over the catalogs of beautiful chandeliers, luminaries (lamps) and other lighting fixtures available to you. A special order may take up to eight weeks, but it may net you the most beautiful piece of art in your room!

615

LIGHTING YOUR ENTERTAINMENT ROOM

One suggestion for properly lighting a 20 ft. x 20 ft. room to be used for watching television, listening to music and entertaining friends:
• General lighting provided by recessed fixtures
• A wall-mounted dimming package, with remote control
• A decorative ceiling fixture for more lighting when entertaining.

THE PRICE OF GETTING ORGANIZED

• An 8 ft. closet, round steel chrome plated rods, double and single hang, with a five-drawer unit: $800 to $1,000

• His-and-Hers walk-in closet, full length and double hang rods, two five-drawer units, foldable storage space, mirrored back wall, shoe rack: $1,000 to $4,000

• Conversion of a full-size bedroom into closet area with islands, custom designed cabinets with full extension drawers and decorative hardware, mirrors, jewelry drawers, and many other luxury appointments: $15,000

• Customized desk area, with file drawers, computer stand and slide shelves for printer, keyboard and mouse pad, high pressure surface on melamine with shelves above desk: $1,000

• Average garage remodel, with open and closed storage, sports racks for bikes and fishing poles, a small workbench, and a 4 ft. x 8 ft. pegboard, installed horizontally: $2,500

ART-OUT OF THE FRAME

Through their travels, reading and exposure to art and design, sophisticated homeowners are aware of the beauty that can be added to their homes with specialty decorative painting. They see in walls, furniture and fabrics the perfect canvases for unique works of art. The demand for beautiful art applied directly to walls, stairs or furniture has created a renaissance in decorative painting. Faux finishes, trompe l'oeil and murals have joined the traditional finishes of paint, wallpaper and stain for consideration in outstanding residential interiors.

Specialty painters of the highest caliber, such as those on these pages, can help you fine-tune your idea, or develop a concept from scratch. At your initial meeting, discuss your ideas, whether they're crystal clear or barely there. Don't be apprehensive if you don't have a clear idea. Artists are by profession visually creative, and by asking you questions and showing you ideas, you can develop a concept together.

Ask to see samples of his or her other work, and if possible, visit homes or buildings where the work is installed. Ask for, and call, references. Find out if the work was completed on time and on budget. Based on your initial conversations, a painter can give you a rough estimate based on the size of the room and the finish you've discussed.

A deposit is generally required, with balance due at completion. Discuss payment plans in the initial meeting. Surface preparation, such as stripping and patching, is not usually done by the specialty painter. Ask for references to do this work if you don't have a painter you already use.

Before painting is begun in your home, the artist should provide you with a custom sample large enough to provide a good visual sense of what the technique will look like in your home, with your fabrics and cabinets.

One artist averages two meetings with clients before painting begins. If all decision-makers can attend these meetings, the process will move along more quickly. You can expect the artist to get back to you with sample drawings, showing color and technique, usually within a week.

THE HOME OFFICE ARRIVES

At the beginning of the 21st century, the home office is a "must have" room for many homeowners. More businesses are being operated from home, and increasing numbers of companies are allowing, even encouraging, telecommuting. Spreading out on the dining room table or kitchen table is no longer anywhere near efficient.

Because the home office requires specific wiring

and lighting, be sure your architect, designer and builder are involved in the planning process. If you're simply outfitting an existing room to be your home office, designers on staff at fine furniture stores can guide you. However, it's still most practical to get some architectural input for optimum comfort and functionality of the space.

Unless you're designing a home office that will be architecturally separated from the rest of your home (such as a 'loft' office over the garage) it's a challenge to effectively separate work and home. As you plan a home office, ask yourself these questions:

• How do I work best? Close to the action or tucked away where it's quiet?

• How much space do I need? More than one desk, space for computer equipment and other technology, or reference books and files? Space for seeing clients?

• How many phone lines will I need? Do I like a window view? Consider natural light as well as artificial light.

• How will I furnish the office? Will the space also serve as a library or guest room? ■

'FAUX' FINISH TROMPE L'OEIL?

Any painting technique replicating another look is called a 'faux' (fake) finish. There are many methods to achieve wonderful individual effects. Trompe l'oeil (fool the eye) is a mural painting that creates illusion through perspective. A wall becomes an arched entry to a garden.

617

Home
Furnishings

FIREPLACE PRODUCTS US INC. ....**(773) 992-2501**
9742 W. Foster Ave., Chicago
See Ad on Page: 623
Principal/Owner: Robert Little
Website: www.regency-fire.com/
Additional Information: Toll free phone number: (888) 355-2501 ; Toll free fax number: (888) 388-0125
Fax: (773) 992-2505
800 Extension: 1096

JAYSON HOME & GARDEN...**(773) 525-3100**
1885 & 1911 N. Clybourn Ave., Chicago
See Ad on Page: 620
Principal/Owner: Jay Goltz
Website: jaysonhome-garden.com e-mail: home@jaysonhome-garden.com
Additional Information: Beautiful antiques, reproductions and upholstered furniture are displayed in an inspiring setting filled with exquisite lighting and home & garden accessories.
Fax: (773) 525-3151
800 Extension: 1143

KARLSON KITCHENS...**(847) 491-1300**
1815 Central Street, Evanston
See Ad on Page: 460, 461, 608, 654
Principal/Owner: David Karlson
Website: www.karlsonkitchens.com
Fax: (847) 491-0100
800 Extension: 1147

KREISS COLLECTION ....**(312) 527-0907**
415 North LaSalle Street, Chicago
See Ad on Page: 619
Website: www.kreiss.com e-mail: chicago@kreissshowrooms.com
Fax: (312) 527-5347
800 Extension: 1166

LEMONT KITCHEN & BATH, INC.....................................**(630) 257-8144**
106 Stephen St., Lemont
See Ad on Page: 483
Principal/Owner: Gary A. Lichlyter
Fax: (630) 257-8142
800 Extension: 1180

LIGNE ROSET ....**(312) 867-1207**
56 East Walton Street, Chicago
See Ad on Page: 624
800 Extension: 1189

continued on page **629**

KREISS

COLLECTION

OFF THE BOLT

MILL DIRECT

1333 N. KINGSBURY
CHICAGO, IL 60622
312.587.0046

FENG SHUI FUNDAMENTALS

Briskey Photograp

Alter or enhance
the energy in your
home or office with:

FOUNTAINS*
in slate, copper and ceramic

CHIMES
in glass, wood and metal

CRYSTALS
hanging, all shapes & sizes

CANDLES
scented and unscented

**OIL LAMPS &
DIFFUSERS**

Items of beauty
in all the elements

S·E·N·S·E·S ®

GIFT GALLERY

GIFTS & TREASURES TO DELIGHT EVERY SENSE

Corner of Wilmette & Central Aves in downtown Wilmette
(847)256-1302 • M-F 10-6 (Thurs until 8), Sat 930-530, Sun 12-4
Special orders are welcome (4 different manufacturers, including huge wall fountains)

TOP 5 REASONS THAT PEOPLE CHOOSE

ADD TO THE ENJOYMENT AND VALUE OF YOUR HOME

THEY LOOK GOOD IN ANY ROOM

CUT HEATING COSTS...EVEN WORKS DURING POWER OUTAGES

THEY KEEP ON WORKING – BACKED BY A LIMITED LIFETIME WARRANTY

REGENCY & WATERFORD DEALERS ARE COMMITTED TO YOU!

The P42 Bay Gas Fireplace

- 35,000 BTU
- 82% Optimum Efficiency
- Up to 50% Turn Down
- Large Viewing Area
- Flush Front Available
- Optional Remote Control or Thermostat

The Ashling Wood Stove

- 45,000 BTU
- Up to 8 Hours Burn Time
- Maximum Log Size 18"
- Heats up to 2,000 Sq.Ft.
- Can be Hearth Mounted
- Top or Rear Venting

The U35 DV Gas Insert

- 35,000 BTU
- 79% Optimum Efficiency
- Direct Vent
- Bay Front Also Available
- Panoramic Viewing Area
- Optional Remote Control or Thermostat

The Emerald DV Insert

- 38,000 BTU
- 80% Optimum Efficiency
- Direct Vent
- True Bay Styling
- Beautiful Cast Iron Design
- Optional New Fireplace Kit

The P36 Flush Gas Fireplace

- 30,000 BTU
- 82% Optimum Efficiency
- Up to 50% Turn Down
- Double Screen Door Option
- Bay Front Also Available
- Optional Remote Control or Thermostat

The Emerald Gas Stove

- 38,000 BTU
- 79% Optimum Efficiency
- Top or Rear Venting
- B Vent or Direct Vent
- Decorative Front Grill and Side Shelves Option

TELEPHONE: 888-355-2501
www.regency-fire.com

FAX: 888-388-0125
www.waterfordstoves.com

LE STYLE

ligne roset

DE VIE.

Distinctive, understated furniture, lighting, and
home accessories crafted in France.

(800) BY-ROSET
www.ligne-roset-usa.com

KARLSON KITCHENS

Studio Becker Wardrobe System:

An established luxury in Europe, the wardrobe system is making a big impact in the United States. Residential storage has grown rapidly, but few have captured the elegance and accessibility seen in the Studio Becker wardrobe system. Luxurious details include wooden inlays, hand-stitched leather handles and carousels that light up corner spaces.

ARTEMIDE

Tolomeo Luminaires:

In three sizes for the desk, these table standing luminaires are available for orientable direct task incandescent and fluorescent lighting. The luminaires feature fully adjustable, articulated arm body structures in extruded aluminum; joints and tension control knobs in polished die-cast aluminum; tension cables in stainless steel; and a diffuser in stamped, anodized matte aluminum. Rotatable 360 degrees on lampholder with incorporated on/off switch.

Showroom

NO PLACE LIKE
*Hand Cast
Acrylic Tables:*
Conceived for the complexities of urban living, Studiolo by Robert Kirkbride is a new line of hand-cast, acrylic 'table-ettes' — coffee tables, and café tables that are without hardware and self-leveling. The tables assemble and disassemble quickly and store flat. Pieces can be used interchangeably for tables, landing pads for laptops or stools. They are perfect bedside and armchair companions.

TOWER LIGHTING
Wrought Iron Wall Sconce:
Wrought iron collections are notable for their distinctive designs and for a craftsmanship that is still carried out by hand. This wall sconce is a unique and timeless fixture suited to today's interiors. The handcrafted fixture combined with the proper lighting achieves dramatic effects.

oto by **Michael A. Marcotte**

MIDWEST SOLAR CONTROL CORP.
Soleil:
Soleil, a new window-film product by 3M, cuts fading from ultraviolet rays. Homeowners and interior designers like the fact that the product doesn't change the tint of the room. And, being clear, the film doesn't look dark from the outside. Soleil provides protection from the sun, yet allows for natural sunlight, a natural appearance a natural view.

Only
If You
Want the Very
Best...

The
Ashley
Group

1350 E. Touhy Avenue, Des Plaines, Illinois 60018
888.458.1750   Fax 847.390.2902

www.theashleygroup.com • www.homebook.com

Home Furnishings & Decorating

continued from page **618**

NO PLACE LIKE ....**(312) 822-0550**
300 W. Grand Avenue, Chicago
See Ad on Page: 625
Fax: (312) 822-0577
800 Extension: 1211
Principal/Owner: Lee Pomerance
Website: www.noplacelike.net e-mail: lee@noplacelike.net

OLAFSEN DESIGN GROUP ....**(312) 664-4738**
233 East Erie, Suite 305, Chicago
See Ad on Page: 329
800 Extension: 1219

PINE & DESIGN IMPORTS ....**(312) 640-0100**
511 W. North Avenue, Chicago
See Ad on Page: 630
Fax: (312) 640-0019
800 Extension: 1237
Principal/Owner: Bill Kowalski, General Manager
Additional Information: Old world reproduction furniture, restored european antiques, personalized and custom made pine furniture- eclectic

RITA RUGS ....**(773) 880-0031**
3040 N. Lincoln, Chicago
See Ad on Page: 573
Fax: (773) 880-0155
800 Extension: 1250
Principal/Owner: Sudershan Goel
Website: www.ritarugs.com
Additional Information: Rita Rugs has been offering customers the finest selection of oriental rugs at the best possible dollar value since 1977.

SENSES GIFT GALLERY ....**(847) 256-1302**
1138 Central Ave., Wilmette
See Ad on Page: 622
Fax: (847) 256-1326
800 Extension: 1273
Principal/Owner: Laurie Carver
e-mail: lcarverlee@earthlink.net
Additional Information: Senses Gift Gallery is a relaxing haven for gifts and home décor. This unique store in a 100 year old pharmacy is organized by the six senses: sight, sound, scent, touch, taste and thought.

629

SWARTZENDRUBER HARDWOOD CREATIONS ....**(800) 531-2502**
1100 Chicago Ave., Goshen
See Ad on Page: 606, 607, 631
Fax: (219) 534-2504
800 Extension: 1303
Principal/Owner: Larion Swartzendruber
Website: www.swartzendruber.com e-mail: info@swartzendruber.com
Additional Information: Specialists in custom hardwood furniture.

VISBEEN ASSOCIATES INC. ....**(616) 285-9901**
4139 Embassy Dr. S.E., Grand Rapids
See Ad on Page: 203
Fax: (616) 285-9963
800 Extension: 1338
Principal/Owner: Wayne E. Visbeen, AIA, IIDA
e-mail: visbeenaia@aol.com
Additional Information: Visbeen Associates Inc. specializes in architecture, offering full design services from concept to finished project, including interior design.

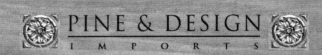

Lighting

ACTIVE ELECTRICAL SUPPLY ....**(773) 282-6300**
4240 W. Lawrence Avenue, Chicago · Fax: (773) 282-5206
See Ad on Page: 435, 634, 635 · *800 Extension: 1002*
<u>Principal/Owner:</u> Skip Leigh

ARTEMIDE ....**(312) 475-0100**
223 W. Erie Street, Chicago · Fax: (312) 475-0112
See Ad on Page: 640 · *800 Extension: 1016*
<u>Principal/Owner:</u> Elizabeth Bockelman
<u>Website:</u> www.artemide.com/www.tizio.com <u>e-mail:</u> artemide_US@artemide.com

BRASS LIGHT GALLERY ....**(800) 351-4911**
131 S. 1st Street, Milwaukee · Fax: (414) 271-2180
See Ad on Page: 636, 637 · *800 Extension: 1028*
<u>Website:</u> www.brasslight.com <u>e-mail:</u> showroom@brasslight.com

LIGHTOLOGY ....**(312) 642-1586**
215 West Chicago Avenue, Chicago · Fax: (312) 642-6605
See Ad on Page: 638, 639 · *800 Extension: 1187*
<u>Principal/Owner:</u> Peter Pechianu

TOWER LIGHTING ....**(708) 246-9429**
1100 Hillgrove Avenue, Western Springs · Fax: (708) 246-9352
See Ad on Page: 633 · *800 Extension: 1330*
<u>Principal/Owner:</u> Stuart Smiley
<u>e-mail:</u> TowerLighting@aol.com

632

"Lighted shelving can highlight treasured art objects.**"**

— *Karlson Kitchens*

FINE ~ IMPORTED ~ LIGHTING
ΤΟWER LIGHTING

ᴿESIDENTIAL AND COMMERCIAL LIGHTING GALLERY

00 Hillgrove Avenue
estern Springs, IL 60558

Phone: (708) 246-9429
Mon-Fri 10-5, Sat 10-3

From Contemporary

Active Electrical Supply

4240 West Lawrence Avenue
Chicago, Illinois 60630
Phone 773-282-6300
Fax 773-282-5206
Hours: Mon. - Fri. 7:30AM - 5PM
Thurs. till 8PM Sat. till 2PM

To Traditional

SCHONBEK
BEYOND LIGHTING™

At *Fox Lighting Galleries*, we don't just improve atmosphere, we create it. Since 1953, value, selection and personal service have made us Chicagoland's leading single supplier of lighting. Stop in or call and see why.

Better lighting for your

home and garden

Lightology

Formerly **Tech Lighting Galleries**, now the largest distributor of Tech Lighting products in the U.S.

RESIDENTIAL AND COMMERCIAL CONSULTATIONS

215 West Chicago Ave. • Chicago, IL 60610
Tel 312.944.1000 • Fax 312.642.6605 • www.lightology.com

FEATURING

MONORAIL

KABLE LITE

RADIUSWIRE

TWINRAIL

BY

TECH LIGHTING

ALSO

Come See Our Spectacular New Showroom!

Featuring the Largest
Collection of Contemporary
Lighting in the USA!

ARTEMIDE

CASABLANCA

ERCO

ESTILUZ

FLOS

FORTUNI

ITALIANA LUCE

ITRE

LEUCOS

LUCEPLAN

TECH LIGHTING

TERZANI

TOBIAS GRAU

and others from
around the world
including an
incredible selection
of Murano glass!

Showroom Hours:
Mon-Fri 10-6
Sat 10-5

Pianos

HENDRICKS PIANOS ....**(630) 969-5082**
421 Maple Avenue, Downers Grove
See Ad on Page: 642, 643   *800 Extension: 1125*

KARNES MUSIC CO. ....**(312) 663-4111**
333 South State Street, Chicago
See Ad on Page: 642, 643   *800 Extension: 1149*

MAR-COLE MUSIC ....**(630) 980-3200**
400 West Army Trail Road, Bloomingdale
See Ad on Page: 642, 643   *800 Extension: 1199*

ORTIGARA'S MUSICVILLE ....**(708) 423-7910**
10830 South Central Avenue, Chicago Ridge
See Ad on Page: 642, 643   *800 Extension: 1224*

**❝There is music
wherever there is
harmony, order
and proportion.❞**

— *Sir Thomas Browne*

641

The Secret to Great Entertaining is Gr

*Disklavier
DGT2*

There's nothing like live music to turn an ordinary party into a major social event. And the Yamaha Disklavier® piano brings famous musicians, like George Gershwin and Chick Corea, into your home to play exclusive concerts for you and your friends. The Disklavier is not limited to piano music, though; it can perform the entire orchestral score of a Broadway hit, Mozart concerto or pop song – complete with vocals! With the Disklavier's unique system, every nuance of the artists' original performance are recreated precisely – and down to the smallest detail.

Hendricks Pianos, 421 Maple Avenue, Downers Grove, 630.969.5082
Karnes Music Co., 333 South State Street, Chicago, 312.663.4111

ertainment.

rtKey
eature

If *you've* always wanted to play but never had the chance to learn, Yamaha's exclusive SmartKey® feature will help you sound incredible the very moment you sit down.

When you have a Yamaha Disklavier, the best entertainment in town is right in your living room. To find out how to get this remarkable piano there, visit one of the authorized Yamaha dealers below.

*Disklavier
DC2A*

Window Coverings
Fabric & Upholstery

CHARDONNAY DESIGNS, INC...**(847) 808-7272**
15 E. Palatine #118, Prospect Heights   Fax: (847) 808-7373
See Ad on Page: 542, 543, 647   *800 Extension: 1044*
<u>Principal/Owner:</u> Charmaine D. Nilles
<u>Website:</u> www.chardonnaydesigns.com
<u>Additional Information:</u> As well as custom art glass, we are a full service design
source for home or office.

H & R CUSTOM DESIGNS...**(847) 562-0487**
300 Skokie Blvd., Northbrook   Fax: (847) 562-9487
See Ad on Page: 364   *800 Extension: 1121*
<u>Principal/Owner:</u> Helene Weiner

MIDWEST SOLAR CONTROL CORPORATION.............................**(847) 438-8080**
888 E. Belvidere Rd., Ste. 205, Grayslake   Fax: (847) 438-8040
See Ad on Page: 645   *800 Extension: 1201*
<u>Principal/Owner:</u> Daniel Wubs

SHUTTER HUT, INC...**(847) 740-6790**
31632 N. Ellis Drive, Ste. 101, Volo   Fax: (847) 740-1369
See Ad on Page: 646   *800 Extension: 1275*
<u>Principal/Owner:</u> Michael Ready
<u>Additional Information:</u> Owned and Operated by The Ready Family since 1974.

SUNBURST SHUTTERS...**(847) 640-6622**
1315 Howard Street, Elk Grove Village   Fax: (847) 640-6742
See Ad on Page: 648   *800 Extension: 1294*

644

"Wisely improve the present. It is thine."

— *Henry Wadsworth Longfellow*

Sunlight can make a timeless Design look old fast.

Shutter Hut INC.

CUSTOM SHUTTER SPECIALISTS

PLANTATION SHUTTERS

Beautify your windows with custom shutters from Shutter Hut. Manufactured in the finest quality cedar or basswood, shutters are made in $1\frac{1}{4}$, $1\frac{7}{8}$, $2\frac{1}{2}$, 3, $3\frac{1}{2}$, 4, $4\frac{1}{2}$ or $5\frac{1}{2}$-inch width louvers. Custom stained or painted to match your decor. Come see full size displays in our well appointed showroom. Vinyl clad shutters, wood blinds, Silhouette® and $1\frac{1}{4}$ unfinished stock shutter panels now available..

Owned and operated by the Ready family since 1974.

Located at the Volo Commerce Center, Route 120 just east of Route 12 in Volo, IL
Daily 8:30 to 5:00 • Saturday 10:00 to 4:00 • Closed Sunday

847-740-6790

Shown below 8' sliding door

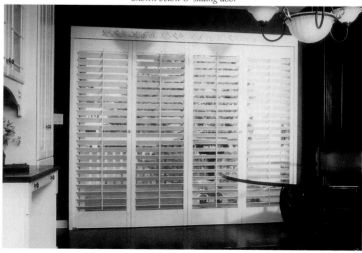

Chardonnay Designs

SGO of the North Shore
Specialty Art Glass

windows
entryways
cabinets
mirrors
ceiling panels
shower doors

Complete Design Service
Commercial and Residential

15 East Palatine Road Suite 118
Prospect Heights, IL 60070
Tel. 847.808.7272

Specialty Painters
& Wall Finishes

HESTER DECORATING CO., INC...**(847) 677-5130**
7340 N. Monticello Ave., Skokie
See Ad on Page: 650
<u>Principal/Owner:</u> Thomas J. Hester
<u>Website:</u> www.hesterdecorating.com <u>e-mail:</u> info@hesterdecorating.com
<u>Additional Information:</u> With over 33 years of experience, Hester Decorating provides fine residential painting, paper hanging, faux and specialty finishes throughout Chicagoland.

Fax: (847) 677-5139
800 Extension: 1126

"Subtle nuances in color
and texture can dramatically
impact the feeling in a room.**"**

— *Hester Decorating*

649

Office & Closets
Furnishings

CALIFORNIA CLOSETS ....**(847) 541-8666**
275 12th Street, #B, Wheeling
Fax: (847) 541-8974
See Ad on Page: 652
800 Extension: 1038
<u>Principal/Owner:</u> Ray Reddi
<u>Website:</u> www.calclosets.com <u>e-mail:</u> www.calclosets-chicago.com

CALIFORNIA CLOSETS ....**(630) 916-7393**
123 Einsenhower Lane S, Lombard
Fax: (630) 916-7420
See Ad on Page: 652
800 Extension: 1039
<u>Principal/Owner:</u> Charles Alstrin/Walter Burrell
<u>Website:</u> www.calclosets.com <u>e-mail:</u> www.calclosets-chicago.com

CLOSET WORKS ....**(630) 832-3322**
953 N. Larch, Elmhurst
Fax: (630) 832-6878
See Ad on Page: 653
800 Extension: 1056
<u>Website:</u> www.closetworks.com

CLOSETS UNLIMITED (A DIV. OF SCE UNLIMITED, INC.) ....**(847) 228-1000**
1901 Landmeier Road, Elk Grove Village
Fax: (847) 228-5562
See Ad on Page: 656
800 Extension: 1057
<u>Website:</u> www.closetsunlimited.com

HOME OFFICE SOLUTIONS ....**(847) 724-1498**
1498 Waukegan, Glenview
See Ad on Page: 655
800 Extension: 1132
<u>Principal/Owner:</u> Marc Levin
<u>Website:</u> www.officedesigns.com

651

OLAFSEN DESIGN GROUP ....**(312) 664-4738**
233 East Erie, Suite 305, Chicago
See Ad on Page: 329

"If you refuse to accept
anything but the best,
you very often get it."

— *W. Somerset Maugham*

life, stuff, storage **- The Bedroom Closet.**

The home is the heart of life. An ever chang
story of ourselves, our family, our friends.
welcome retreat where we protect, nurture a
sustain all that is needed and loved.

Let California Closets share 25 years experier
with you to create the finest custom stora
solutions for all the areas of your home. Live t
way you dream. Call today for a compliment
consultation in your home.

800.2SIMPLIFY (274-6754) www.calclosets.co

Showrooms:
2071 N. Clybourn, Chicago
Studio 41, Highland Park
Downtown Hinsdale
Downtown Naperville

CALIFORNIA CLOSET

Relax - You're in Control

Your home is your sanctuary, and it's time to take control.
Frustration is eliminated and peace of mind prevails.

With systems by Closet Works you can organize every part of your home. From Closets, to Pantries, to Offices and Garage. Take back your house - simplify - and make it the home you and your family have always dreamed of.

Call for showroom locations or to
schedule a free in home consultation

1-800-273-6511

www.closetworks.com

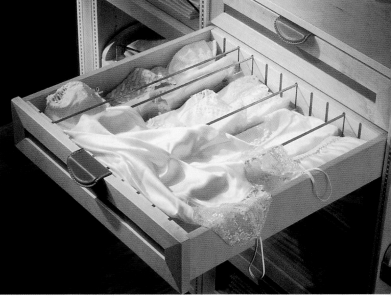

a division of SCE Unlimited, Inc.

Shutters, Closets and Exteriors Unlimited

Limited Space…Unlimited Solutions.

Garage * Pantry* Laundry Room* Basement
Home Office * Utility Room

Our experienced designers will work directly with you assuring a custom design to meet your storage needs.

The custom designed system will maximize the use of all available space. The flexibility & adjustability of our products will allow for changes in the future as your needs change.

The knowledge and commitment of our designers, quality of products and craftsmanship of our fabricators & installers are second to none in the industry.

(847) 228-1000 www.closetsunlimited.com

CLOSETS Unlimited™

1901 Landmeier Road
Elk Grove Village, IL 60007

Is your once beautiful leather dull and used?

Is wear and tear eroding your leather investment?

What can be done about a stain or hole?

What are your options?

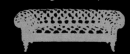

THE LEATHER SOLUTION®

"PROFESSIONALS IN LEATHER RESTORATION AND REPAIR"

6612 W. Irving Park Road • Chicago, IL 60634 • (773) 685-2162
www.leathersolutions.com

Restoration

THE LEATHER SOLUTION .... **(773) 685-2162**
6612 West Irving Park Road, Chicago — Fax: (773) 685-2268
See Ad on Page: 657 — *800 Extension: 1321*
Principal/Owner: Rob Loncarevic
Website: www.leathersolutions.com e-mail: tlschgo@speedsite.com
Additional Information: We restore and refurbish all leather furniture. In addition, we reupholster and make some custom furniture.

"Truth is the secret of
eloquence and of virtue,
the basis of moral authority,
it is the highest summit
of art and of life."

— Henry Frederic Amiel

ART &
ANTIQUES

HILI
520

IMPROVING YOUR QUALITY
OF LIFE WITH FINE ART

Renoir - Etude de Femme
Nue, Assise

Miro - Series
Personnages1974

Kreutz - Sunburst: Pontavon

Buffet - Flower Bottle Brigade

Wolton - Lush Pond

Pan - Untitled

360 Historical Lane Grove, IL
Gallery in the Historical Shopping Village 847.634.4242

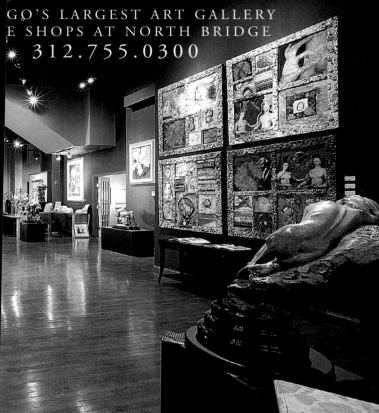

*G*allery Northwest is a truly unique destination for anyone looking for a broad selection of traditional to contemporary art. Add to this an impressive selection of over 2,000 frame choices and a wide array of mats, fillets and liners and you begin to get a feel for the unlimited possibilities of acquiring great pieces of art and making them everything they can be through custom framing. All of this can be done at Gallery Northwest – a wonderful taste of Chicago in the suburbs. Particular attention is paid to quality materials with an emphasis on conservation framing. No detail is too small to make your art look its best throughout the millennium. This even includes wonderful visions of custom mirrors. So come surprise your artful senses at Gallery Northwest. You'll be glad you made the trip.

Gallery Northwest

Fine Art & Custom Framing

234 North Northwest Highway • Palatine, IL 60067
(847) 991-0014 Fax (847) 358-1538 Web www.artNframing.com

Something Old
Something New

663

T he fine art and antiques scene is as dynamic as ever. From cutting-edge modern galleries to showrooms of stately antiques, few places in the world offer more choice for bringing truly unique works of art into the home.

Beloved one-of-a-kind items give a home personality in a way that other furnishings can't match. Fine art speaks to the soul of the owner. Antique furnishings tell their stories through the generations.

Art and antiques, unlike so many other pieces purchased for the home, have the potential to become a family's heirlooms. Even an inexpensive "find" may someday become a most treasured item because of the warm memories it calls to mind. Truly, these choices are best made with the care and guidance of an experienced professional who understands the significance of these items in your home.

Photo courtesy of **Rouzati Rugs**

LEARN ABOUT ART & ANTIQUES

Part of the pleasure of collecting art or antiques is learning about them. Many homeowners buy a particular painting or sculpture they love, and find that following the art form or the artists becomes a lifetime passion.
  The best place to start to familiarize yourself with art is at one of the many wonderful museums in the Chicago area. Wander through historic homes in the different historic neighborhoods of the city and get an idea of what the art feels like in a home environment.
Go to auctions. Buy the catalog and attend the viewing. At the sale, you'll begin to get an idea of the values of different types of items. Finally, get to know a dealer. Most are pleased to help you learn and want to see more people develop a lifetime love affair with art, similar to their own.
Haunt the local bookstores and newsstands. There are many publications dedicated to these fields.

THE WORLD OF ANTIQUES

Homeowners find their way to antiques by many different paths. Some are adding to an inherited collection that connects them with past generations of family or with the location of their birth. Some are passionate about pottery or porcelain, clocks or dolls, and want to expand their knowledge while building a life-time collection.

Antique furniture, artwork and collectibles also can be used to make a singular statement in an interior. Through a 19th Century English chest, or an American Arts & Crafts table, homeowners put a personal signature stamp on their interior design.

Making the right selection is as much a matter of taste and personal aesthetic as it is knowledge and experience. An interior designer or gallery owner will be a good guide to making a choice.

As top quality antique paintings, photographs and other desirable items become more and more difficult to find, getting expert guidance in identifying good and worthwhile investments is crucial. Top galleries in the area are operated and staffed by knowledgeable professionals who will do just that.

When you enter a store or gallery, be prepared to seriously consider what type of investment you wish to make and how it will work in a given interior. If someone besides yourself will be involved in the final decision-making process, try to have them with you.

If you're pursuing pieces to add to an existing collection, do your research to determine which galleries in town cater to your interests. Or, check with a favorite gallery for information.

Be open to ideas and suggestions, especially when you're just beginning a collection, or a search for a special antique. The best galleries are gold mines of information and ideas. There is so much to know about so many different objects, time periods, and design, that it truly does take a lifetime to develop an expertise. The owners of these establishments are first and foremost interested in finding you an antique that will impress and delight today, and in the future, and usually prefer to have you invest in one or two good pieces, than in a handful of items that won't bring you as much pleasure in the long run.

VISITING ART GALLERIES

More than anything else, choosing to make beautiful, distinctive art objects a part of your home brings the joy of living with beautiful things into the daily life of yourself, your family and your guests.

The most important rule to know as your begin or continue to add art to your home is that there truly are no "rights or wrongs." Find what reaches you on an emotional level, and then begin to learn about it.

Use your eyes and react with your heart. Look at art magazines and books. There are many, many beautiful periodicals, and just as many books published on artists and art genres. Visit the museums in town, and those in other cities as you travel. Go to the galleries. Visit many of them for the widest exposure to different possibilities. Let only your sense of beauty and aesthetics guide you at this point. Consider other constraints after you've identified the objects of your desire.

When you've found what really speaks to you on a personal level, start learning more about who creates art in that style, where it's available locally, and if it's within your budget. The more information you can take with you when you begin your shopping, the more help a gallery can be to you in your search.

EXPERT ADVICE

The most reputable art gallery owners and dealers have earned their reputation by establishing an expertise in their field, and serving their clients well.

Buying from these established and respected professionals offers many benefits. Their considerable knowledge of and exposure to art translates into opinions that mean a great deal. You can put stock in the advice and education they offer you. They've done considerable research and evaluation before any item gets placed in their gallery, and determined that it's a good quality item, both in terms of artistic merit and market value. You'll also enjoy a sense of security when you patronize these businesses. They will stand behind the authenticity of what they present in their galleries. Most offer free consultations, trade-back arrangements, and installation, and will help you with selling your art at some point in the future as your collection grows, you change residences, or your tastes change.

Don't expect a gallery to be an expert in categories outside of those they specialize in.

VALUE JUDGMENTS

Buy for love, not money. This is the advice we heard time and again from the best art galleries. Not all art appreciates financially - often it fluctuates over the years according to the artist's career, consumer tastes, and the state of the overall economy. If you love what you own and have been advised well by a knowledgeable professional, you'll be happiest with your investment.

THE FALL SEASON

Fall signals the beginning of the art season. Galleries will open exhibits and the excitement is contagious. Ask to get on gallery mailing lists to stay informed of fall openings.

VISIT OUR MUSEUMS

As you develop your passion for art and items of antiquity, take advantage of the collections and public education opportunities at some of Chicago's distinguished art museums, like:

**The Art Institute of Chicago
111 S. Michigan Ave.
Chicago, IL 60603
312.443.3600
www.artic.edu**

**Museum of Contemporary Art
220 E. Chicago Ave.
Chicago, IL 60611
312.280.2660
www.mcachicago. org**

**Terra Museum of American Art
664 N. Michigan Ave.
Chicago, IL 60611
Phone:
312.664.3939
www.terramuseu m.org**

665

The Finesse of Fine Art

It's fun to imagine, but what might it actually cost to undertake a project described in this chapter? The example below describes a typical project and gives a general estimate of the costs involved.

Project Description

Analysis, research and procurement of six art pieces for a Mediterranean-style home.

Before the project began, the client established a budget based on the type of art desired (sculpture, drawings, paintings, tapestry), the quality of the art, scale (size of objects), and provenance (history and notoriety of the artist).

The art

A print for the hallway	$ 8,000
A classical bronze sculpture, 4 ft tall	$ 3,000
A still-life painting	$ 8,000
Two tapestries ($2,000 ea.)	$ 4,000
A Dufy painting	$32,000

Art total: **$55,000**

Additional expenses

Appraisal expenses	$750
Framing of pictures	$2,500
Installation and handling	$2,500
Insurance	$1,250/yr
Security system (motion detector)	$1,250
Consultation fees	
(Ten percent of art)	$5,500
(Hourly fee: $150/hr x 40 hrs)	$6,000

Includes analysis of art needs based on scale and style of house and artist preferences, research done on availability of art pieces and procurement of those pieces.

Additional expenses: **$19,750**

Total: **$74,750**

Note: a project such as this one usually lasts 12 to 18 months.

8' x 6'
Tapestry

Frame for
Dufy painting

SEE THE SHOWS

The Chicago area abounds with arts, antiques, and collectibles shows and festivals. These are great places to browse for and learn about thousands of items - from jewelry to pop culture collectibles. Local newspapers and magazines run announcements for these kinds of events, or ask your favorite gallery owner for information.

There is no upper limit on what you can spend on an art collection, or a single artwork, and there are no set standards for pricing. Gallery owners set prices according to their own standards, evaluations and experience, to represent a fair market value. Set a working budget (possibly a per-piece budget) and let the gallery know upfront what the guidelines are. This saves both you and the gallery time and energy. You'll be able to focus on items that are comfortably within the range of your budget. Buy the best quality possible in whatever category you like. You will appreciate the quality for years. Don't hesitate to do some comparison shopping. Although each art object is unique in itself, you may find another piece in the same style that you enjoy equally as well.

The best dealers understand budgets, and respect your desire to get good quality at a fair price. They are happy to work with enthusiastic clients who want to incorporate beautiful art into their lives. Ask if the dealer offers terms, if you're interested in making your purchases on a payment plan. Also inquire about return or exchange policies, consignment plans, consultations and trade-up policies.

Only deal with dealers who are helpful and present their art fairly. If you feel intimidated in a gallery, or feel the dealer isn't giving you the time and information you deserve to make intelligent choices, visit another gallery. Never buy art under pressure from a dealer, or to meet an imposed deadline in your home interior timetable.

GO TO AN AUCTION HOUSE

Attending an auction is an excellent way to learn about decorative arts, develop and add to a collection, and simply have a good time. Whether you attend as a buyer, seller, or observer, an auction is an experience that will enrich your understanding and enjoyment of the art and antiques world.

If you're a novice, it's important to choose a well-established auction house with a reputation for reliability. Try to be a patient observer and learn about the process as well as the value of items you may be interested in later on.

Buy a copy of the catalog and attend the viewing prior to the beginning of the auction itself. Each item, or "lot," that will be available for sale at the auction will be listed, and a professional estimate of selling price will be included. Professionals will be available during the viewing to answer questions and help you become familiar with the art objects as well as the process. Once bidding starts, it is done by "paddle," small numbered placards used to signal a bid, which are obtained before or during the auction.

CHOOSING AN AUCTION

Find out about interesting auctions from the proprietors of galleries you like, or ask to be added to the mailing list of a reputable auction house. With these sources of information, you'll be informed of events that will feature quality items of interest to you. Local newspapers and magazines also print upcoming auction dates and locations. The established auction houses that have earned a reputation for reliability and expertise generally have a single location where they hold their auctions. Sometimes an auction will be held at an estate site, or a seller's location.

Before attending the auction, spend some time researching the art or antique you're interested in bidding on, so you'll be informed about its value and can make an informed decision. Talk to people at the galleries. There also are books available that publish recent auction sales to help you get an idea of price and availability. Check your library or bookseller for publications like Gordon's Price Annual.

There is an air of mystery and sophistication that surrounds the auction experience, but don't let that discourage you from discovering the auction experience. Auctions are enjoyable and educational for anyone who is interested in obtaining or learning about art and antiques.

BE REALISTIC

For many of us, an auction might seem an opportunity to pick up an item at a bargain price. Realize that there may be bargains to be found, but in general, auctioned items are sold for a fair price. There may be a "reserve price," which is a private agreement between the seller and the auctioneer on the amount of a minimum bid.

If you educate yourself about the category you're interested in, you'll be in better stead at an auction. It's equally important to research the market value of any lot you may be considering. Remember that there is an auctioneer's commission of 10 to 15 percent of the hammer price, to be paid on top of the purchase price, as well as applicable sales taxes.

Auctions are essentially competitive in nature, with potential buyers bidding against one another. Until you've attended enough auctions to feel confident in your own knowledge, as well as in your understanding of the auction process, don't become an active participant. It's easy to get swept up in the fast pace and excitement. While you won't end up making the top bid simply by tugging your ear, it's important to pay attention when you're bidding. Be aware of the way the auctioneer communicates with the bidders and always listen for the auctioneer's "fair warning" announcement just before the gavel falls. ■

MATCHING ART TO ARCHITECTURE

If you're renovating an historic or old home of distinction, ask your favorite gallery owner or renovation specialist for guidance in choosing art that will fit your home.

669

Antiques

DALE CAROL ANDERSON, LTD. **(773) 348-5200**
2030 N. Magnolia, Chicago
See Ad on Page: 340, 341
Fax: (773) 348-5271
800 Extension: 1066
Principal/Owner: Mrs. Dale Anderson

PAGE ONE INTERIORS INC. ....**(312) 587-8490**
707 N. Wells, Chicago
See Ad on Page: 362
800 Extension: 1225
Principal/Owner: Adele Lampert, ASID
Website: interiorspageone.com e-mail: pageoneinteriors@aol.com
Additional Information: Beautiful showroom with antiques, reproductions and accessories. Full design services including architectural & CAD, residential & commercial.

PAGE ONE INTERIORS INC. ....**(847) 382-1001**
320 E. Main, Barrington
See Ad on Page: 362
Fax: (847) 382-0484
800 Extension: 1230
Principal/Owner: Adele Lampert, ASID
Website: interiorspageone.com e-mail: pageoneinteriors@aol.com
Additional Information: Beautiful showroom with antiques, reproductions and accessories. Full design services including architectural & CAD, residential & commercial.

ROUZATI RUGS ....**(847) 328-0000**
1907 Central Street, Evanston
See Ad on Page: 572
Fax: (847) 328-2306
800 Extension: 1257
Principal/Owner: Jafar Rouzati

ARLENE SEMEL & ASSOCIATES, INC. ....**(312) 644-1480**
445 N. Franklin, Chicago
See Ad on Page: 326, 327
Fax: (312) 644-8157
800 Extension: 1013
Principal/Owner: Arlene Semel
e-mail: asemel@asachicago.com
Additional Information: We, at Arlene Semel & Associates, Inc., believe that good interior design solves the practical problems of function and comfort, while defining and enriching the art of every day living.

TROWBRIDGE GALLERY ....**(312) 587-9575**
703 N. Wells Street, Chicago
See Ad on Page: 671
Fax: (312) 587-9742
800 Extension: 1331
Principal/Owner: Cecily Brainard McAfee

Art Galleries

THE CRYSTAL CAVE ....**(847) 251-1160**
1141 Central Ave, Wilmette
See Ad on Page: 673
Principal/Owner: Josef Puehringer
Website: www.crystalcaveofchicago.com e-mail: allcrystal1141@aol.com
Additional Information: Custom crystal gifts, crystal engraving, glass & crystal repair.

Fax: (847) 251-1172
800 Extension: 1320

GALLERY NORTHWEST ....**(847) 991-0014**
234 N. Northwest Hwy., Palatine
See Ad on Page: 662, 674
Website: www.artNframing.com e-mail: GalleryNW@artNframing.com

Fax: (847) 358-1538
800 Extension: 1108

HILLIGOSS GALLERIES ....**(312) 755-0300**
520 N. Michigan Avenue, Chicago
See Ad on Page: 660, 661, 678
Principal/Owner: Thomas Hilligoss

800 Extension: 1128

PENNY & GENTLE FINE ART STUDIO ....**(312) 432-1452**
900 West Lake Street, Chicago
See Ad on Page: 672
Principal/Owner: Mary Jane Maher, Partner

Fax: (312) 432-1453
800 Extension: 1235

PRINTS UNLIMITED GALLERIES ....**(312) 372-8988**
28 N. Wabash, Chicago
See Ad on Page: 675
Principal/Owner: Daniel Bondi
e-mail: printsun@aol.com

Fax: (312) 372-8582
800 Extension: 1243

672

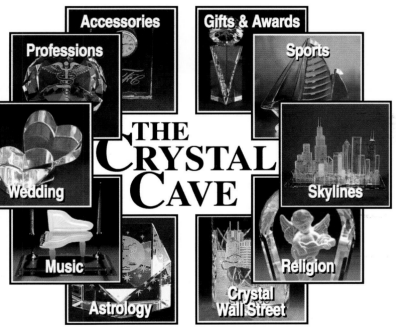

Photography: Rich Sistos Photography/Oak Brook

$\mathcal{G}$ allery Northwest is a truly unique destination for anyone looking for a broad selection of traditional to contemporary art. Add to this an impressive selection of over 2,000 frame choices and a wide array of mats, fillets and liners and you begin to get a feel for the unlimited possibilities of acquiring great pieces of art and making them everything they can be through custom framing. All of this can be done at Gallery Northwest – a wonderful taste of Chicago in the suburbs. Particular attention is paid to quality materials with an emphasis on conservation framing. No detail is too small to make your art look its best throughout the millennium. This even includes wonderful visions of custom mirrors. So come surprise your artful senses at Gallery Northwest. You'll be glad you made the trip.

Gallery Northwest
Fine Art & Custom Framing

234 North Northwest Highway • Palatine, IL 60067
(847) 991-0014 Fax (847) 358-1538 Web www.artNframing.com

Prints Unlimited Galleries

A COMPLETE CORPORATE ART SERVICE

WE SUPPLY THE PERFECT FINISHING TOUCH
TO CORPORATIONS,
HEALTH CARE,
FINANCIAL, AND
RESIDENTIAL CLIENTS

• FINE ART

• POSTERS

CUSTOM FRAMING

• LIMITED EDITION

PRINTS

• PHOTOGRAPHY

CHICAGO LOOP
28 N. WABASH

LINCOLN PARK
1461 W. FULLERTON

The A Grou

THE ASHLEY GROUP

The Ashley Group is the largest publisher of visual
quality designing, building and decorating information and
For more on the many products of **The Ashley**
Cahners Business Information (www.cahners.com),
U.S. provider of business information to 16
manufacturing and retail. Cahners' rich content portfolio
Publishers Weekly, Design News and 152 other

shley
p

RESOURCE COLLECTION

home resource images, and strives to provide the highest
resources available to upscale consumers and professionals.
Group, visit our website at <u>www.theashleygroup.com</u>.
a member of the Reed Elsevier plc group, is a leading
vertical markets, including entertainment,
encompasses more than 140 Web sites as well as *Variety*,
market-leading business-to-business magazines

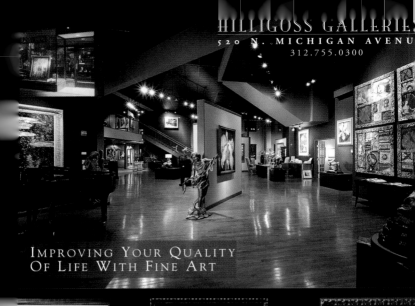

Miro-Series Personnages 1974

Chagall-Bateau-Mouche au Bouquet

Rembrandt-Clemente de Jongh

Buffet-Flower Bottle Brigade

Royo-Luz Suave

Shima-Road Through Wheatfield

Kreutz-Sunburst: Pontavon

Gorg-Couple

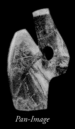

Pan-Image

Pan-Untitled 8A

The Chicago areas best resource for
fine prints by the masters and
original paintings by many of the world's top artists.
Chicago's largest galleries offer the largest selection with
professional service in our galleries... or in your home.
Please call or visit - we're open everyday

Auction
Houses

BUNTE AUCTION SERVICES, INC. ....**(847) 214-8423**
755 Church Road, Elgin   Fax: (847) 214-8802
See Ad on Page: 680   *800 Extension: 1035*
<u>Principal/Owner:</u> Kevin & Kerry Bunte
<u>Website:</u> www.bunteauction.com <u>e-mail:</u> bunteauction@aol.com

> **"**I don't want life
> to imitate art,
> I want life to be art.**"**
>
> — *Carrie Fisher*

679

The Ashley Group Luxury Home Resource Collection

The **Ashley Group (www.theashleygroup.com)** is pleased to offer as your final destination when searching for home improvement and luxury resources the following **Home Books** in your local market. Available Now: *Chicago, Washington D.C., South Florida, Los Angeles, Dallas/Fort Worth, Detroit, Colorado, New York, Atlanta, Arizona, Philadelphia, San Diego, North Carolina,* and *Las Vegas*. These comprehensive, hands-on guides to building, remodeling, decorating, furnishing, and landscaping a luxury home, are required reading for the serious and selective homeowner. With over 700 full-color, beautiful pages, the **Home Book** series in each market covers all aspects of the building and remodeling process, including listings of hundreds of local industry professionals, accompanied by informative and valuable editorial discussing the most recent trends.

Order your copies today and make your dream come true!

Finally...
Chicago's Own
Home & Design
Sourcebook

The **Chicago Home Book** is your final destination when searching for home remodeling, building and decorating resource. This comprehensive, hands-on sourcebook to building, remodeling, decorating, furnishing, and landscaping a luxury home is required reading for the serious and discriminating homeowner. With more than 700 full-color, beautiful pages, the **Chicago Home Book** is the most complete and well-organized reference to the home industry. This hardcover volume covers all aspects of the process, includes listings of hundreds of industry professionals, and is accompanied by informative and valuable editorial discussing the most recent trends. Ordering your copy of the **Chicago Home Book** now can ensure that you have the blueprints to your dream home, in your hand, today.

Order your copy now!

CHICAGO
HOME
BOOK

Published by
The Ashley Group
1350 E. Touhy Ave. Des Plaines, IL 60018
844-390-2882 fax 847-390-2902
www.chicagohomebook.com

HOME THEATER & TECHNOLOGY

KASS
ELECTRONICS

- Structured Wiring
- Kass Electronics designs and installs systems to meet a wide range of price levels
- Showroom with state of the art technology
- Complete documentation and simple instruction cards for all systems that we install

- Our installers and sales representatives are trained on all products that we use
- Work coordinated with other subcontractors
- Advanced engineering background
- Exhaustive attention to detail
- All systems designed to be easy to use

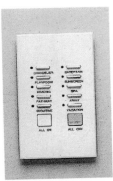

er
ght.

Sit back. Relax. Touch the button. The lights dim, the movie starts. Through a digital music and film system, you are transported to another world. From Hitchcock to Harrison Ford, you choose the destination. We provide the room. Any room, any time. We invite you to visit the world's most exciting audio and home theater store. Or call for an in-home consultation.

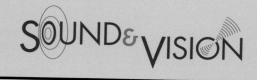

Living
the
Tech Life

Home theaters just keep getting better and better. Technology wizards continue to deliver bigger and better products less obtrusively, and more affordably, into our homes. What was once a rare home luxury has become a top priority item in new custom homes, and in home additions and renovations.

Sophisticated Chicago homeowners have had their level of appreciation for quality in sight and sound elevated through the years of experience in concert halls, movie theaters and sports arenas. As they gravitate toward making the home the focus of their lifestyle, and strive to incorporate that high level of performance into their leisure time at home, home theater becomes a more desirable and practical investment. Systems are used for viewing commercial movies, home videos, live concerts and sport events, playing games, and accessing interactive technology. Media or entertainment rooms, custom-sized and designed to deliver concert hall sound and a big, sharp picture, are frequently specified in new construction and remodeling projects. Interest in upscale prefabricated home theaters, which are far more luxurious than some of today's movie theaters, continues to increase. "Hey kids, let's go to the movies!"

Photo courtesy of **Quintessence Audio**

Your Personal Screening Room

It's fun to imagine, but what might it actually cost to undertake a project described in this chapter? The example below describes a typical project and gives a general estimate of the costs involved.

Project Description

Outfitting a room in the mid- to high-scale price range for a home theater

Initial consultation:	$0
Labor: $55/hour	$3,500
50-inch television	$4,000
DVD player	$900
VHS	$200
Amplifier with surround-sound decoder	$10,000
Six speakers with subwoofer	$10,000
Satellite dish (high definition)	$1,000
Delivery/installation	$2,500
Seating: Eight leather module seats	$15,000
Infrared sensors (Crestrom) to control lighting, motorized drapes, security system	$10,000
Total	**$57,000**

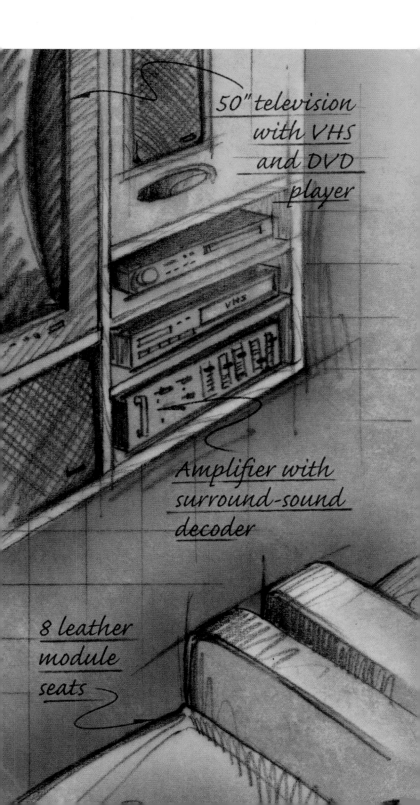

50" television
with VHS
and DVD
player

Amplifier with
surround-sound
decoder

8 leather
module
seats

THE IMPORTANCE OF A
HOME THEATER DESIGN SPECIALIST

Home theater is widely specified as a custom home feature today. The sophisticated homeowner with a well-developed eye (and ear) for quality demands the latest technology in a home entertainment system that will provide pleasure for many years. Because of the fluid marketplace, the vast possibilities of the future, and the complexity of the products, it's crucial to employ an established professional to design and install your home theater.

The experts presented on the following pages can advise you on the best system for your home. They can find an appropriate cabinet (or direct you to expert custom cabinet makers), expertly install your system, and teach you to use it. Their expertise will make the difference.

THE HOME THEATER DESIGN PROCESS

Tell your builder or remodeling specialist early if you want a home theater, especially if built-in speakers, a large screen or a ceiling-mounted video projection unit are part of the plan.

Inform the interior designer so proper design elements can be incorporated. Window treatments to block out light and help boost sound quality, furnishings or fabrics to hide or drape speakers, and comfortable seating to enhance the media experience should be considered. If you plan to control the window treatments by remote control, these decisions will have to be coordinated.

Visit one of the following showrooms. Be ready to answer these questions:

• What is your budget? There is no upper limit on what you can spend.

• Do you want a television tube or projection video system? A DVD player or hi-fi VCR? Built-in or free-standing speakers?

• Do you want Internet access?

• What style of cabinetry and lighting do you want? Do you want lighting or a built-in bar? How much storage is needed?

• What are the seating requirements? Seating should be at least seven feet from the screen.

• Do you want whole-house control capability so you can distribute and control the system from different rooms of the house?

• How will you incorporate the system with the rest of the room? Must the home theater room meet other needs?

• Do you want extra luxuries, like multiple screens, or a remote control system that allows you to dim the lights and close the draperies?

PLAN AHEAD

Even if you aren't installing a home theater system right away, have a room designed to serve that purpose later. Get the wiring done and build the room an appropriate shape and size. Get the right antenna. Ask for double drywall for noise control.

THE FUTURE'S HERE

**Smart homes, those with whole-house integrated control systems and computerized automation, automation, are a reality in the new century.
Many professionals believe it will one day be as standard as central air conditioning. It will be commonplace for a system to start your morning coffee, crank up the furnace, close drapes during a downpour or send a fax.**

Ask your salesperson for ideas.

• Will this room function in the future? As technology continues to change our lifestyle, plan for this room to grow and change as well. Ask your salesperson for advice.

Take your blueprints or pictures to a specialty store where an "experience room" is set up for firsthand testing of different components and knowledgeable consultants can answer your questions. Electronics is a complex subject, but a good consultant will educate, not mystify you.

An in-home consultation with the designer should take place early in the planning stages. You can discuss issues like speaker placement and location of wall control panels.

Before hiring a designer, make sure your service needs will be met in a timely and expert manner. Ask for the names of former and repeat clients for references.

Experienced audio-video or media consultants can astutely determine your needs. They can design and install an end product that is properly sized for your room, satisfies your desire for quality, and meets the terms of your budget. They respect cabinetry requirements and the decorating elements that must be addressed in the deliverance of a top quality home theater.

The media consultant should be willing to work with the architect, builder and interior designer to make sure your requirements will be met.

Home theaters are installed at the same time as the security and phone systems, before insulation and drywall. In new construction or remodeling, start making decisions at least two months before the drywall is hung. Allow four weeks for delivery and installation scheduling.

BEST TIP:

Have phone lines pulled to every TV outlet in the house for Internet access and satellite reception.

69

CREATING A HOME THEATER

For the best seat in the house, you'll need:

• A large screen television and/or projection video system (from 32-inch direct view up to 200-inches, depending on the size of the room). New, compact products are available now.

• A surround-sound receiver to direct sound to the appropriate speaker with proper channel separation

• A surround-sound speaker system, with front, rear, and center channel speakers and a sub-woofer for powerful bass response

• A hi-fi stereo VCR or DVD (digital video) player for ultimate audio and video quality

• Appropriate cabinetry, properly vented

• A comfortable environment, ideally a rectangular room with extra drywall to block out distractions. ■

Home Theater
Design

AUDIO CONSULTANTS ....**(847) 864-9565**
1014 Davis Street, Evanston
See Ad on Page: 702
Principal/Owner: Simon Zreczny
Fax: (847) 864-9570
800 Extension: 1018

BANG & OLUFSEN OAK STREET ....**(312) 787-6006**
15 East Oak Street, Chicago
See Ad on Page: 693
Fax: (312) 787-9532
800 Extension: 1021

BANG & OLUFSEN THE LOOP ....**(312) 920-0639**
10 South LaSalle Street, Chicago
See Ad on Page: 693
Fax: (312) 920-0883
800 Extension: 1022

BANG & OLUFSEN WOODFIELD ....**(847) 995-8605**
K315 Woodfield Mall, Schaumburg
See Ad on Page: 693
Fax: (847) 995-8607
800 Extension: 1023

COLUMBIA AUDIO/VIDEO ....**(847) 433-6010**
1741 Second Street, Highland Park
See Ad on Page: 696
Principal/Owner: Gary Rozak, President
Fax: (847) 433-9332
800 Extension: 1058
Website: www.columbiaaudiovideo.com e-mail: info@columbiaaudiovideo.com
Additional Information: For over 50 years, Columbia Audio/Video has provided the
best in audio/video equipment.

692

KASS ELECTRONICS ....**(630) 221-8480**
26 W 515 St. Charles Road, Carol Stream
See Ad on Page: 684, 685, 703
Principal/Owner: Bill Dwyer
Fax: (630) 221-8430
800 Extension: 1150
Website: www.kasselectronics.com

QUINTESSENCE AUDIO ....**(847) 966-4434**
5701 W. Dempster, Morton Grove
See Ad on Page: 698, 699
Fax: (847) 966-0932
800 Extension: 1245

REESE CLASSIC RESIDENCE, INC....**(847) 913-1680**
350 Old McHenry Road, Long Grove
See Ad on Page: 218
Principal/Owner: Mark Farrahar
Fax: (847) 913-1684
800 Extension: 1248
Website: www.rclassicres.com e-mail: mark@rclassicres.com
Additional Information: Reese Classic has completed over 80 homes since being
established in 1992 and is known for exceptional commitment to customers' needs.

continued on page **702**

Go on, spoil yourself...
...with the ultimate in Home Theater entertainment

Pictures so sharp you feel you can reach in and touch the world beyond. Perfect sound from every direction wraps you in a total audio/video sensation.

The real world is put on hold as B&O puts you right in the center of the action.

We specialize in custom installations, light control and superb customer service wherever and whenever our customers need it.

To set up a free consultation in your home with one of our product specialists just call the store closest to you or better yet, stop by our store and experience Home Theater the way it was meant to be.

The BeoTheater Components
Available in 5 matching colors to coordinate with a wide range of decors.

BeoVision Avant 30"	BeoSound 9000	Beo4

| 30" State of the Art wide screen TV. | Integrated 6 CD music system. | Simple remote for easy operation. |

Surround Sound speaker system with front, rear and center channel speakers.

BeoLab 1   BeoLab 6000   BeoLab 4000

| Top of the line amplified loudspeaker. | High performance amplified loudspeaker. | Book shelf/wall mount amplified loudspeaker. |

BANG & OLUFSEN

Bang & Olufsen Woodfield
5 Woodfield Mall
Schaumburg, Illinois 60173
Phone: 847.995.8605
847.995.8607

Bang & Olufsen The Loop
10 South LaSalle Street
Chicago, Illinois 60603
Phone: 312.920.0639
Fax: 312.920.0883

Bang & Olufsen Oak Street
15 East Oak Street
Chicago, Illinois 60611
Phone: 312.787.6006
Fax: 312.787.9532

Products

- Home Theater Interiors
- Lobby & Concession Treatments
- Custom Cinema Seating
- Acoustical Products
- Audio/Video Systems
- Lighting & Control Systems

Showroom available by appointment.

the multiplex experience...

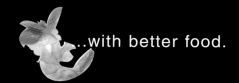

...with better food.

25 Years of

Experience in

Design and

Installation

Zenith Electronics Corporation

- Home Theatre

- House-wide Music

- High Performance Audio

- Home Automation

- Lighting Control

- New Construction Pre-wiring

- Satellite Systems

- HDTV-High Definition Television

Quintessence Audio Ltd.
"Audio/Video Systems for Discriminating Individuals"

5701 W. Dempster
Morton Grove, IL 60053
(847) 966-4434
(847) 966-0932 Fax

EXPERTS IN

- Big Screens

- Satellite Systems

- Plasma TV

- Home Theatre

- Whole House Audio

- HDTV

- Projection Systems

• AUDIO •

- Structured Wire

• VIDEO •

- Whole House Video

- Inwall Speakers

- Theatre Seating

- Motorized Screens

- Custom Cabinetry

Sound & Video
C O N S U L T A N T S

8 4 7 - 7 7 6 - 1 6 1 1

Fine Audio and Video Systems

- Custom Design Consultation
- Meticulous Installation
- Thorough Documentation
- Continuing Service

SIMPLY STEREO

1280 West Higgins Road
Hoffman Estates, IL 60195
847.882.2885

continued from page **692**

SIMPLY STEREO ....**(847) 882-2885**
1280 W. Higgins Road, Hoffman Estates
See Ad on Page: 701
Principal/Owner: Rod Swanson
Fax: (847) 882-8795
800 Extension: 1277

SOUND & VIDEO CONSULTANTS ....**(847) 776-1611**
96 W. Northwest Hwy., Palatine
See Ad on Page: 700
Fax: (847) 358-8230
800 Extension: 1280

SOUND & VISION ....**(708) 403-2500**
14474 S. LaGrange Road, Orland Park
See Ad on Page: 686, 697
Website: www.soundandvisionusa.com e-mail: info@soundandvision.net
Fax: (708) 403-2428
800 Extension: 1281

THEATRE DESIGN ASSOCIATES..**(800) 786-6832**
2224 W. Fulton, Chicago
See Ad on Page: 694, 695
Principal/Owner: Scott T. Carlson
Website: www.theatredesign.com e-mail: sales@theatredesign.com
Fax: (312) 829-1308
800 Extension: 1325

702

Location,
Location,
Location!

What better LOCATION for
your advertisement than the
CHICAGO HOME BOOK!

Just as our readers realize how important
location is when choosing a home,
we realize that it's just as important to you
when allocating your advertising dollars.
That's why we have successfully positioned
the CHICAGO HOME BOOK to reach
the high-end consumers you want as clients.

**Call 847-390-2882 to find out about our
unique marketing programs and
advertising opportunities.**

Published by
The Ashley Group
1350 E. Touhy Ave. Des Plaines, IL 60018
847-390-2882 fax 847-390-2902
www.chicagohomebook.com

Home
Security

KEYTH TECHNOLOGIES ....**(847) 433-0000**
1575 Oakwood Avenue, Highland Park   Fax: (847) 998-0000
See Ad on Page: 706, 707   *800 Extension: 1163*
Principal/Owner: Keith Fisher
Website: www.keyth.com e-mail: keith@keyth.com

"Common sense is
the knack for seeing
things as they are, and
doing things as they
ought to be done.**"**

— *Harriet Beecher Stowe*

KEYTH® TECHNOLOGIES
Voice: 847.433.0000

To Service

Alarms/Siren Sounder

Telephone Voicemail Systems

FutureProof Tech/LAN Wiring

Locksmithing Services

CCTV/Video Surveillance

Smart House Controls

Advanced Smart Security
Starting at
$479

SECURITY
PRO

Security Is A Family Matter.™

Visit us on line...
Keyth.com

d Protect ™

Security/Fire Systems

Card Access

**Biometrics
Fingerprint Access**

**Safes in Stock and
Installed**

Residential/Commercial

KEYTH®
TECHNOLOGIES

1575 Oakwood Ave., Highland Park, IL 60035

Phone: **847.433.0000**	*Office/Showroom:* **Highland Park**
Fax: **847.998.0000**	*Interactive Showroom:* **Studio 41, Highland Park**
E-Mail: **keith@keyth®.com**	*Science Research Center:* **Chicago**

State License:
127-000121

Automatic
backup power
within seconds!

Emergency **Power**

STEINER ELECTRIC/POWERTRON ....**(847) 956-3098**
1250 Touhy Avenue, Elk Grove Village   Fax: (847) 956-5013
See Ad on Page: 708, 709   *800 Extension: 1285*
<u>Principal/Owner:</u> Brian Mygatt
<u>Website:</u> www.stnr.com   <u>e-mail:</u> bmygatt@stnr.com
<u>Additional Information:</u> Distributor of generators, UPS systems, power protection, home automation and electrical supplies.

"Homeowners want high-tech gizmos they can 'hide' in their home offices.**"**

— *Gray & Walter Associates*

courtesy of **Skiffington Architects**

LOCATION

Located in Batavia

Phone 630-357-3300

Directions: Take I-88 west to the Orchard Road exit. Turn north (right) on Orchard Road to Oak Street. Turn west (left) on Oak to Deerpath Road. Turn north (right) on Deerpath 1-1/2 miles to Deerpath turnoff. Continue on Deerpath 1-1/2 miles to the Tanglewood Hills entrance.

Kings Court Builders • 630-406-6139

Oak Hill Builders • 630-482-3100

Kozlowski Development • 630-406-7978

Located in Batavia

Tanglewood Hills

Homes from the $500,000's

Directions: Take I-88 west to the Orchard Road exit. Turn north (right) on Orchard Road to Oak Street. Turn west (left) on Oak to Deerpath Road. Turn north (right) on Deerpath 1-1/2 miles to Deerpath turnoff. Continue on Deerpath 1-1/2 miles to the Tanglewood Hills entrance.

NATURALLY DEVELOPED BY OLIVER-HOFFMANN.

Home Sweet Home

One of the most endearing charms of this area is the wide diversity and individuality of its neighborhoods. Whether your fantasy is to live in a stately, traditional home surrounded by lush sweeping lawns, or an ultra-modern custom-built home overlooking a golf course, you are sure to find a neighborhood to call you home. To savvy homeowners, location is the most valuable of assets, and has long been their mantra.

Today's state-of-the-art homebuilders have given life to new communities in masterfully planned environments. Visually delightful and diverse, yet cohesive in architectural style and landscape, these communities address with impeccable taste the needs of their residents: proximity to excellent schools, shops, restaurants, favored leisure pursuits, the workplace. Safe havens, often in country or golf course settings, these developments cater to the homeowners' active lifestyles. Artistically designed for ease, these gracious homes welcome family and guests; they are sanctuaries in which to entertain, relax and nourish the spirit.

THE ULTIMATE IN LUXURY LIVING

The builders and developers of custom homes in upscale locations throughout the area realize the value of simplicity and strive to deliver it.

Simplicity is one of the qualities we most desire in our lives. By offering a community designed and built on the philosophy that homeowners deserve a beautiful environment, peaceful surroundings and luxurious amenities to enhance their lives, locations like those featured in the following pages deliver simplicity on a luxury scale.

Homeowners who live in these kinds of communities and locations know what they want. They want an environment where architecture and nature exist in harmony. Where builders have proven dedication to protecting the natural surroundings. They want recreation, like golf, swimming, lakes, walk and biking paths, or tennis courts. They want to live where there is a sense of community, and the convenience of close-by shopping and transportation. Finally, they want the conveniences of a well-planned community - guidelines on buildings and landscaping, strong community identity, and commitment to quality.

FINDING THE PERFECT LOCATION

Think about what kind of location would enhance the lifestyle of yourself and your family:

• Do you need to be near transportation?

• Do you want the security of a gated community?

• What kind of recreational amenities do you want? Golf, tennis or pool? Paths, fishing lakes, or horse trails? Party facilities, restaurants?

• What kind of natural environment do you prefer? Wildlife sanctuary, urban elegance, club luxury?

• What kind of home do you want to build? Determine if your dream house fits the overall essence of a particular community. Some planned communities allow only certain builders at their locations. Find out if these builders create homes that would satisfy your desires.

THE VALUE OF A LUXURY LOCATION

The availability of building sites diminishes with every passing year, and the builders and developers of our finest residential locations know that quality must be established to attract custom home owners. Their commitment to building top quality homes is apparent in the designs and materials used in their projects and in the reputations their locations enjoy.

The demand for homes built in these locations is growing. Their benefits, plus the unique opportunity to build a new custom home in a totally fresh, and new environment, are very enticing. ■

THE COMMUNITY SPIRIT

Enclave neighborhoods built in luxury locations have the benefit of being part of two communities. The neighborhood identity is strong and so is the larger community spirit. It's the best of both worlds.

THE MASTER PLAN

Homes and landscapes in "master plan" locations are as unique and customized as anywhere in the Chicago area. However, they are established according to a well-defined overall plan, which gives the homeowners the security of knowing that the high-quality look of their neighborhood will be rigorously upheld.

16

Location

HACKLEY/LANG & ASSOCIATES, INC. ....**(847) 853-8258**
440 Green Bay Road, Kenilworth   Fax: (847) 853-8351
See Ad on Page: 187   *800 Extension: 1124*
<u>Principal/Owner:</u> Chip Hackley & Bill Lang
<u>Website:</u> www.hackley-lang-architects.com   <u>e-mail:</u> hackley_lang@hotmail.com

TANGLEWOOD HILLS ....**(630) 357-3300**
Batavia   Fax: (630) 357-1742
See Ad on Page: 712, 713, 714   *800 Extension: 1305*

WYNSTONE REALTY ....**(847) 381-7100**
101 S. Wynstone Drive, North Barrington   Fax: (847) 304-2880
See Ad on Page: 717, 718, 719   *800 Extension: 1353*
<u>Principal/Owner:</u> Ron Sever
<u>Website:</u> www.wynstone.com   <u>e-mail:</u> contact@wynstone.com

"We cannot do great things on this earth. We can only do little things with great love.**"**

— *Mother Theresa*

717

Dream it – Play it – Liv

Good friends and good times await you

ɔme and enjoy the ultimate Wynstone lifestyle

101 S. Wynstone Drive ● North Barrington, Illinois 60010
Phone 847.381.7100 ● FAX 847.304.2880
www.wynstone.com   email: broker@wynstone.com

Reach for the best that life has to offer.

Experience your own private paradise.

Your dreams become reality at Wynstone.

101 S. Wynstone Drive • North Barrington, Illinois 60010
Phone 847.381.7100 • FAX 847.304.2880
www.wynstone.com   email: broker@wynstone.com

INDEXES

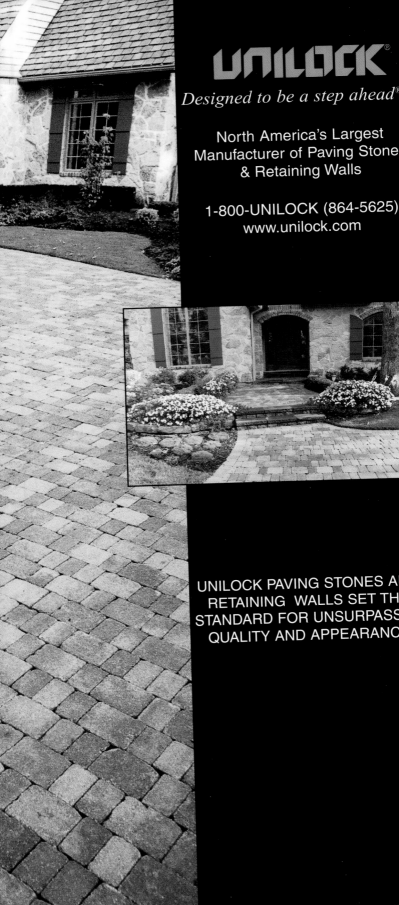

Alphabetical Index

Alphabetical Index

Architects

Professional Index

Roberts Architects Ltd. 202
Rovituso Strange Architects Inc. 197
Rugo/Raff Ltd. Architects 148, 149
David A. Schaefer Architects PC 212
Skiffington Architects, Ltd. 185
Swanson + Donahue Architects 154-157
Visbeen Associates Inc. 203

Vacation
Balsamo, Olson & Lewis Ltd. 190, 191
Paul Berger & Associates 192, 193
Bryan Associates, Inc. – Architects 206
Nicholas Clark Architects 211
Stuart Cohen & Julie Hacker Architects 130-135
Cordogan, Clark & Associates, Inc. 165
Culligan Abraham Architects 152, 153
FWC Architects, Inc. 205
Geudtner & Melichar Architects 150, 151
Kemper Cazzetta, Ltd. 168, 169
Frank J. Klepitsch, AIA 160, 161
Konstant . Architecture . Planning . . .138, 139
LA Design 208, 209
Morgante Wilson Architects 140-143
Rovituso Strange Architects Inc. 197
Rugo/Raff Ltd. Architects 148, 149
David A. Schaefer Architects PC 212
A. William Seegers Architects 199
Stuart D. Shayman Architects 196
Skiffington Architects, Ltd. 185
Styczynski Walker & Associates 116, 163
Swanson + Donahue Architects 154-157
Visbeen Associates Inc. 203

Victorian
Alberts Associates, Inc. 186
Balsamo, Olson & Lewis Ltd. 190, 191
Becker Architects, Ltd. 136, 137
Bryan Associates, Inc. – Architects 206
Cordogan, Clark & Associates, Inc. 165
Culligan Abraham Architects 152, 153
FWC Architects, Inc. 205
Geudtner & Melichar Architects 150, 151
Gibson/Darr Architecture & Consulting 166
Erik Johnson & Associates 126
Kemper Cazzetta, Ltd. 168, 169
Konstant . Architecture . Planning 138, 139
LA Design 208, 209
Rugo/Raff Ltd. Architects 148, 149
David A. Schaefer Architects PC 212
Skiffington Architects, Ltd. 185
Styczynski Walker & Associates 116, 163
Swanson + Donahue Architects 154-157
Visbeen Associates Inc. 203

Art & Antiques

Antiques
Dale Carol Anderson, Ltd. 340, 341
Page One Interiors Inc. 362
Rouzati Rugs 572
Sandra Saltzman Interiors 320, 321
Arlene Semel & Associates, Inc. 326, 327
Trowbridge Gallery 671

Art Galleries
The Crystal Cave 673
Gallery Northwest 662, 674
Hilligoss Galleries 660, 661, 677
Penny & Gentle Fine Art Studio 672
Prints Unlimited Galleries 675
The Studio of Long Grove 660, 661, 678
Trowbridge Gallery 671

Auctions Houses
Bunte Auction Services, Inc. 680
Framing
Gallery Northwest 662, 674
Prints Unlimited Galleries 675
Stonegate Builders, Inc. 230, 231
Repair & Restoration
Lange Custom Woodworking Inc. 524, 525

Contractors

Design/Build
Alberts Associates, Inc. 186
Apex Wood Floors 580, 581
Burack & Company 278, 279
Circa B.C. Inc.
  Natural Stone & Design Studio 591
JMD Builders, Inc. 216, 217, 260, 261
Keystone Builders, Inc. 292, 293
Lucas – Andre Builders 254, 255
Orren Pickell Designers
  & Builders 263–270, 294, 295, 487
The Poulton Group 194, 229
Reese Classic Residence, Inc. 218
Roberts Architects Ltd. 202
Sebern Homes, Inc. 287
Sevvonco Inc. 232, 233
Skiffington Architects, Ltd. 185
Stonegate Builders, Inc. 230, 231
Swanson + Donahue Architects 154–157
Thomas Homes, Inc. 284
Historic Renovation & Preservation
Alberts Associates, Inc. 186
Apex Wood Floors 580, 581
Burack & Company 278, 279
Keystone Builders, Inc. 292, 293
Lucas – Andre Builders 254, 255
Orren Pickell Designers
  & Builders 263–270, 294, 295, 487
The Poulton Group 194, 229
Leslie Reilly Studio 482
Roberts Architects Ltd. 202
Swanson + Donahue Architects 154–157
Windsor Builders, Inc. 281
Wujcik Contruction Group, Inc. 271
Home Builders, Custom
Alberts Associates, Inc. 186
Apex Wood Floors 580, 581
Bryan Associates, Inc. – Architects 206
Burack & Company 278, 279
Cedar Roofing Company, Inc. 297
Distinctive Custom Homes, Inc. 274, 275
Glen Ellyn Homes 256, 257
Group A Architects Builders 164, 258, 259
J & B Builders, Inc. 276, 277
JMD Builders, Inc. 216, 217, 260, 261
Kerkstra Precast/Spancrete Great Lakes . . .285
Keystone Builders, Inc. 292, 293
Lichtenberger Homes 252, 253
Lucas – Andre Builders 254, 255
Mihovilovich Builders, Inc. 273
Charles L. Page Architect . . .114, 115, 288, 289
Orren Pickell Designers
  & Builders 263–270, 294, 295, 487
The Poulton Group 194, 229
Reese Classic Residence, Inc. 218
Roberts Architects Ltd. 202
Sebern Homes, Inc. 287
Skiffington Architects, Ltd. 185

731

Professional Index

736

Professional Index

Notes

740

741

742

743

744